The Palaces of
Leningrad

Text by AUDREY KENNETT

The Palaces

with 205 plates, 31 in colour, and 35 text illustrations

Photographs by VICTOR KENNETT

# of Leningrad

Introduction by JOHN RUSSELL

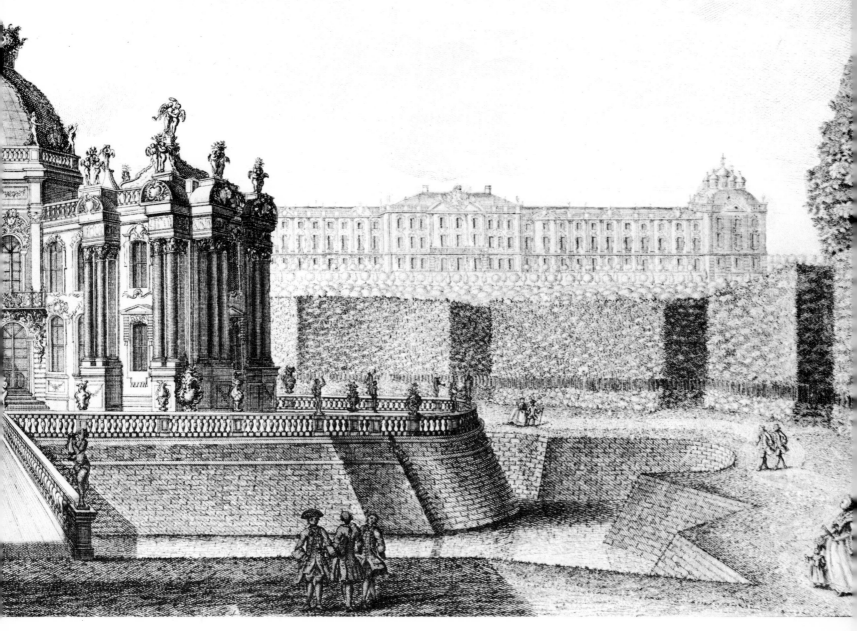

THAMES AND HUDSON

On the endpapers:
A view after Makhayev, of 1753, looking down the Neva along the
south bank of Vasilyevsky Ostrov. The bridge of boats that linked the
island to the mainland appears in the foreground. At the far right is
the Menshikov Palace, begun in 1710, the earliest important building
in St Petersburg; it had already been altered, but was not yet in its
present state (see pages 26–27, and plate 2).

On the title page:
The Hermitage at Tsarskoye Selo, designed by Rastrelli (see page 163,
figure 23).

© 1973 Victor and Audrey Kennett
Introduction © 1973 Thames and Hudson Ltd, London

Reprinted 1984

Filmset by Keyspools Ltd, Golborne, Lancashire, England
Printed and bound in Spain

Contents

TO OUR BROTHER
MIKHAIL ASAREVICH KRAMINSKY
ARCHITECT, AND RESTORER OF HIS CITY'S MONUMENTS

AND TO HIS, AND OUR, FRIEND AND COLLEAGUE
THE LATE ALEKSANDR SERGEYEVICH TITOV

Foreword

THE MATERIAL for this book has been gathered during nine visits to Leningrad since 1958. The majority of the photographs have been taken in the last six years, when we have spent many months in Leningrad. We have been able to watch the processes of restoration in the palaces, and on every visit have seen new rooms finished and opened to the public.

From 1945, the year the war ended – and in spite of the desperate need for new homes, factories, offices and shops – the Soviet government has spent many millions of rubles in reconstructing and redecorating the eighteenth- and nineteenth-century buildings which were damaged or destroyed in Leningrad and its neighbourhood. This work of restoration has been not only on an unprecedented scale, but of unprecedented quality. The original architects were apt to design every item of decoration and furnishing, so it has often been possible for their Russian successors to hand these drawings out anew to artists and craftsmen gathered from all over the Soviet Union. The resources of the state have enabled the finest materials to be used – stone, marble, rare woods, gold leaf – and not twentieth-century substitutes. Often a restoration reflects the intention of its first designer, with later changes swept away. The clutter of styles introduced by later owners has been discarded, and one now sees the rooms in something approaching their original state. As far as possible, the furniture, pictures and ornaments are those that originally belonged to the palace; though it has often been necessary to supplement these with items of the same period. It is only as a result of nearly thirty years of dedicated expert work that we are able to enjoy the greater part of the buildings and decoration shown here. Indeed a full understanding of this 150-year period of architectural history must be incomplete without some knowledge of this incomparable city and its environs; since the work of many of the greatest architects and decorators can be seen nowhere but in Leningrad.

Restoration is still continuing. All the time, more rooms are being completed in palaces already shown to the public. Small changes are constantly being made, so that visitors may find furniture and *objets d'art* in different situations from those in our photographs. We can only show and write of rooms as we saw them. Where important palaces are omitted altogether, it is because they are occupied by an organization which does not permit even exterior photography. Where no interiors are shown, it is either because photography is not at present permitted, or because the building is used for some purpose – office, hospital or club – which obscures the interior decoration, if indeed it has still been maintained. One must hope that in days to come it will be found possible to restore and open some palaces now occupied by government organizations.

continued on page 10

7

St Petersburg, based on an English map of 1834. Palaces discussed in this book are indicated by numbers, other buildings and landmarks by letters.

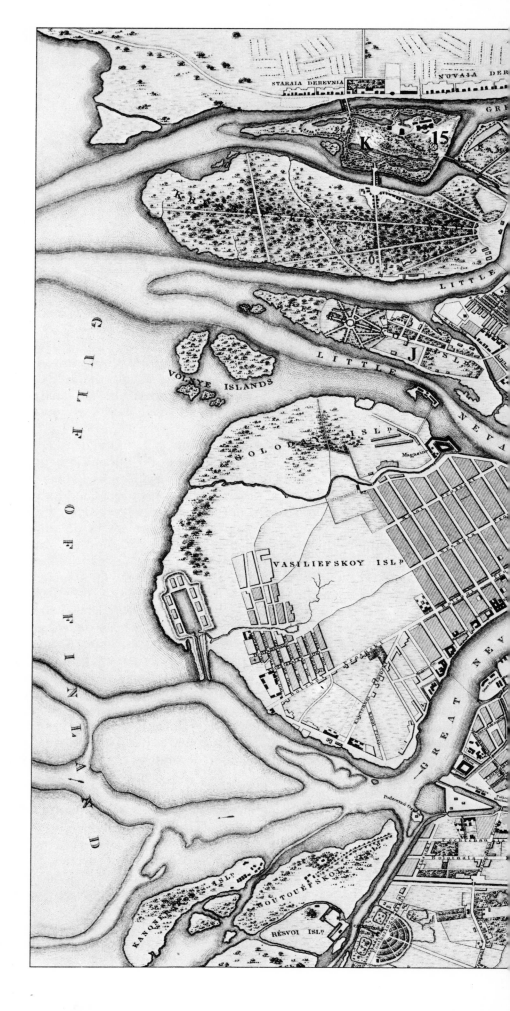

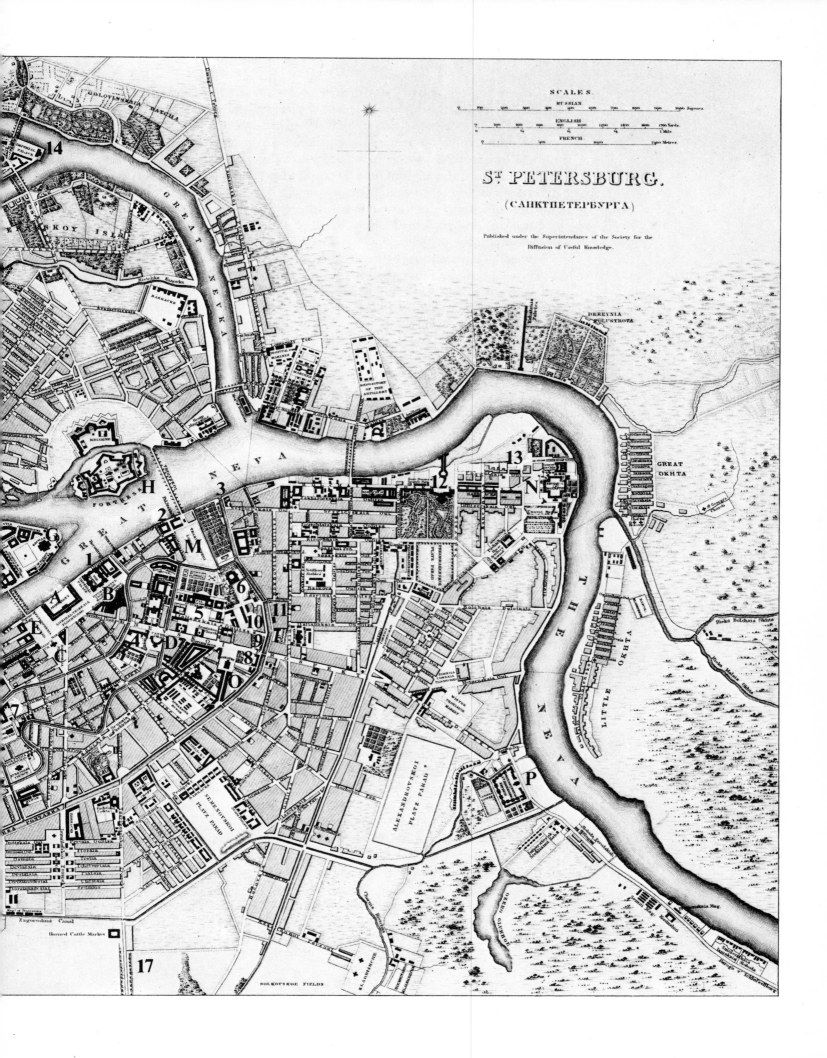

SCALES.
RUSSIAN
ENGLISH
FRENCH

St. PETERSBURG.

(САНКТПЕТЕРБУРГА)

Published under the Superintendance of the Society for the
Diffusion of Useful Knowledge.

On the matter of attributions to one architect or another, leading authorities frequently conflict. Sometimes recent research has thrown doubt on earlier attributions. In many cases written evidence has not been and may never be found, so attributions are based on circumstantial evidence and personal judgments, which are not free from chauvinism, according to the nationality of the writer. We have tried to balance the arguments and to mention some of the most important of the differing opinions. For our information we have drawn not only upon published sources, but upon the knowledge of those who have taken a leading part in the restorations and have had access to all the relevant material on the building and decorating of the palaces.

Houses of past centuries also possess something beyond their outward appearance. They were built and furnished for people to live in and to enjoy. The owners of the palaces shown here had tastes that were definite and informed. They were men and women of strong personality – many of them themselves making history – who took an intense interest in the creation of their homes. By including among our photographs some early views, and by quoting from contemporary travellers and observers of the Russian scene, we have attempted to bring the palaces to life, and to throw light on the characters of those for whom they were created. It is our hope that by presenting the palaces from an architectural, decorative and human standpoint, this book will be interesting to visitors before and after their travels, and also to those who enjoy such subjects, whether or not they are able to see them for themselves.

The transliteration of Russian names has long been a vexed subject. Our quotations from early travellers show a wonderfully varied range. A note on the system we have used will be found on page 281. We have adopted the Western form of the names of Russian rulers, as they are familiar and anything else would seem pedantic; but where a patronymic is used we have employed the Russian form of the first name as well, so as to avoid a Western-Russian hybrid. For example, Peter the Great's younger daughter is referred to as Yelizaveta Petrovna before she becomes empress, and as Elizabeth after her accession.

An even more difficult problem arises from the Russianization of foreign names. From Petersburg's earliest days many foreign architects, sculptors and artists worked there: Italians, Germans, Frenchmen, Englishmen and others. The Russians transliterated their names according to their – often inaccurate – idea of how they were pronounced, and the result gives no clue to the correct spelling of such names in their country of origin. This is recognized by the Russians themselves. In a lecture on the early days of Peterhof, given in 1924 to a Congress of Art Historians in Paris, M. Polovtsoff said, 'The names of foreigners employed are often so disfigured by Russian transcriptions of the eighteenth century that it is impossible to list accurately the men who contributed to its creation.' Transcriptions of more recent date continue to conceal the original spelling. The case of first names and initials is bewildering, because the Russian equivalent is frequently employed: so that Giovanni becomes Ivan; Bartolomeo, Varfolomey. It is easy to disentangle these puzzles in the case of well-known men, but not so easy when they are relatively obscure, and perhaps never worked in their own countries.

In the quotations from some of the early travellers we have preferred to give the date of the journey when they made their observations, rather than the year – sometimes considerably later – in which their book was published (see the bibliography, pages 279–81).

Finally we should like to thank our friend Mr G. R. Talbot for lending us his rare copy of the Pavlovsk Centenary Volume, 1777–1877; and Baron Dimsdale for permission to use an extract from the unpublished diary of his ancestress, Elizabeth Dimsdale.

A K
V K

Introduction

BY JOHN RUSSELL

ONE OF the most redoubtable of man-made objects is the wax effigy of Peter the Great which was completed by Carlo Rastrelli in 1725. There are other portraits of Peter the Great – above all, the famous equestrian statue by Falconet (1) – and even among Rastrelli's own likenesses of his master there are some which stand higher in art history. There is a bronze bust, for instance, which is very fine in a straightforward way; and there is the equestrian statue (55) which stands in front of that strange building, the Engineers' Castle, of which Mr and Mrs Kennett give us so lively an account. The equestrian statue can be related back, by way of Andreas Schlüter's statue of the Grand Elector in Berlin, to its prototype: Girardon's Louis XIV. That is the kind of pedigree that goes down well with historians, and Rastrelli did a more than competent job. But he did not do it until quite some while after Peter the Great was dead, and as a likeness the equestrian statue is distanced not only by the conventions of high art but by the respect and awe which were owed to Peter the Great by posterity.

The wax effigy is quite another matter. It had been a part of Rastrelli's original contract with Peter the Great that in addition to making sculptures in bronze and marble and working for the theatre, the opera, and the ballet he would make wax figures from the living model. When he came to make his effigy of Peter himself he had access, naturally enough, to the Tsar's wardrobe. He modelled not only the head but the entire body: most notably the impatient and tentacular hands, the skeletal unending shanks, and the quintessential posture in which were mingled authority and impatience, tenacity and forthrightness. Unspectacular in his dress, anonymous in his surroundings, Peter dominates by personality alone. We do not doubt for a moment that what we are looking at is will-power personified and made visible. The livid bulge of the eye would alone make that clear. The gigantic stature, the bunched muscles around the mouth, the look of green ivory about the skin – all these strike terror, even today. From the wax effigy we learn something that no state portrait could tell us: just what was the look, in private, of the man who cut off two hundred heads with his own hands when his palace guard in Moscow turned against him. We see, in particular, how the huge head sat on the terrible neck – that neck which was subject throughout Peter's life to violent and premonitory contortions.

An uncomfortable image, therefore, of a more than uncomfortable companion. 'It can't be done: therefore I shall do it' was the principle on which Peter the Great decided to build his capital on inhospitable marshlands not far from the Finnish border. Even in 1773, when St Petersburg was already one of the world's most beautiful cities, Prince Narishkin said to Diderot, a new arrival, that it simply made no sense to rule Russia from its north-western extremity. ('What would you think', he said, 'of an animal that had its heart in its fingernails and its stomach somewhere at the end of its big toe?') People grumbled well into the nineteenth century about the climate of St Petersburg, about the cheerless flatlands which surrounded it, and even about the oblique angle of the sun's rays, which to the Marquis de Custine in 1839 seemed to symbolize the 'disfavour in which the area was held by the Creator'. As to that, Peter the Great put the Creator in his place when he saw to it that the Tsar's throne in the Petropavlovsky (Peter and Paul) Cathedral was two steps above the floor to the altar's one. There was only one creator around when Peter the Great was alive; and it is to him, ultimately, that Russia owed the entirely civilized interiors which are the main subject of this book.

But Peter the Great died in 1725, and he did not even think of St Petersburg as his capital till 1712. The city which he founded has been in continuous evolution for the best part of three centuries, and there is hardly a decade during that period which has not, somewhere, its specific monument. It is a mistake, therefore, to think of St Petersburg as an eighteenth-century city islanded in time. Its over-riding characteristic is, on the contrary, that of a continuous motor energy: a power of adjustment and adaptation which is as active today as ever it was.

Much in this can be traced to the predispositions of Peter the Great. It was not from perversity that he fixed on the site of St Petersburg. It was because he knew about ships and the sea. He wanted Russia to have, somewhere and somehow, free access to the sea. He thought about the Black Sea, in this context; but the Black Sea ended in the narrows of the Bosphorus, and the narrows of the Bosphorus were held by the Turks. Peter enjoyed making model boats with his own hands and setting them afloat upon enclosed waters; but if he was going to found a great navy, enclosed waters like those of the Black Sea were not enough. For this reason he turned to the north. Having turned to the north, he acted with characteristic despatch. In 1702 he got control of a Swedish fortress at the seaward end of Lake Ladoga, and in 1703 he began work on the fortresses both of St Petersburg itself and of Kronstadt, a few miles to the west. The status of St Petersburg as a masterpiece of civilization was incidental, therefore, to its status as the first great centre of Russian sea-power; and it is as a shipbuilding and ship-holding centre that it is still best understood.

Initially Peter was much exercised as to the possibility of a raid by the Swedish navy which would put an end to his grand design. After the Swedes had been beaten at the battle of Poltava in 1709 this idea could be discounted. But St Petersburg had begun as a fortress, and it kept the style of one for many years. If the trumpets are floated aloft in low relief, white on yellow, above the great round arches of the Admiralty, it is because fame and the sea, security and the sea, riches and the sea are things that go together in the history of St Petersburg. The waterfront along the Neva is one of the wonders of the world, beyond all dispute; but what serves the whole city as a compass-needle, appearing and reappearing no matter how wayward our course, is the tower of the Admiralty, two hundred and thirty feet high and topped by a weathervane in the form of a crown and a ship. Ships are no longer cradled within the Admiralty itself, as once they were; and Petropavlovsky Fortress, across the river, is now largely ornamental, with sunbathers on the foreshore and only the noonday gun to remind us that it once had the fire-power to sink any enemy ship that came within range. The high-walled shipbuilding yards in what is called New Holland have gone picturesque, with age, and natives of the city talk of Piranesi when they get within sight of the majestic entrance gate by Vallin de la Mothe which leads off from the Moika towards a large internal harbour in the shape of an axe-head. But it doesn't do, even now, to discount the role of the sea in the fortunes of Leningrad. It was a warship, the light cruiser *Aurora*, which gave the signal for the assault on the Winter Palace in 1917; and anyone who walks along the Krukov canal at the end of the day-shift can see for himself that New Holland is still very much in business. The *tempo primo* of life on a summer evening along the

Nevsky Prospekt is set by the sailors, as much as by anyone; and if you chart the meridian of Leningrad you will find that it passes – where else? – through the court-yard of the Admiralty.

The sea brought security to St Petersburg; but in 1712 the city itself remained to be built. Where people were to live, and what they were to live in, were questions still wide open. Peter thought first of what is now called Vasilyevsky Ostrov (Basil Island); and this in time became the focus of the city's intellectual life, with the Academy of Sciences, the Academy of Arts, the University of Leningrad and many another reminder of the city's role in the development of the European intelligence. (In this context I recommend a visit to the apartment of the famous physiologist Pavlov, pioneer of the conditioned reflex. The apartment has been preserved intact, with the two plain single bedsteads which Pavlov bought with his first professional fees and the little toy dog, now kept under glass, which was lowered from the balcony of the Senate House by a group of undergraduates when Pavlov was given an honorary doctorate at Cambridge; the flat is not a thing of beauty, by the standards of its neighbour, the Menshikov Palace (2), but it evokes with a most persistent exactitude the way of life of a distinguished savant in the Leningrad of the 1920s and 30s.)

Peter the Great was not the man to put up with obstruction from any human source. If there was a shortage of builders and of building materials, he made it known by a decree dated October 1714 that the use of brick and stone was allowed in St Petersburg only; anyone who disobeyed would have his property confiscated and be sent into exile. But in one respect Nature got the better of him: there simply was no way, in the first quarter of the eighteenth century, to keep Vasilyevsky Ostrov open to traffic for the whole of the year. The Neva is the most authoritative of rivers, with a speed, a thrust, and a bulk that can never be disregarded. Much of the charm of Leningrad comes precisely from this: much of its amenity, also. Without the Neva and its auxiliaries the city's many changes of humour would never have found so free an expression; from the captain of heavy industry to the group of friends bent on a party of pleasure, people have at all times based a part of their calculations on the Neva. But there is also something ominous about the great river; Pushkin gave matchless expression to this in his 'Bronze Horseman', and if you go to Leningrad in late April, when the last plaques of ice come downstream at the pace of racing bicyclists, you will sense it at once. You may also infer it from the look of the great granite embankments which keep the river within bounds, and from the annotated high-water marks which record how once the river got out of hand and overflowed: ankle-high, knee-high, waist-high. Even Peter the Great could not rule from an island which for much of the year might be only precariously accessible. Initially he directed his building operations from the little single-storeyed blockhouse which still stands on the north bank of the Neva; but before long he made a tactical withdrawal in the face of Nature, and from that day onwards the centres of power in Leningrad have, with the exception of Petropavlovsky Fortress, been on the mainland – that is to say, on the south bank of the Neva – with uninterrupted access to the rest of Russia.

Location was the least of Peter the Great's problems. Others, more pressing, remained to be solved. Who was to build the new city? Who was to lay it out? And what was it to look like? He expressly did not want an Old Russian city. Since his sojourns in London and Amsterdam he had quite different ideas. From the naval dockyards of Deptford he derived the notion of a great navy, built, equipped and manned from the resources of a capital city close at hand; from Amsterdam, the notion of unbroken rows of town houses built on both banks of concentric canals. But the fundamental question was one of style: Peter himself was indifferent to luxury and cared nothing for dress, but he believed that a great nation must have a great cosmopolitan capital. He did not wish to fall back on the solutions which could be found near at hand in the once-great city of Novgorod. Still less did he want to get his ideas from Moscow, since Moscow was to be superseded. (It was also to be outshone: Peter saw to it that the steeple of Petropavlovsky Cathedral was higher than the bell-tower of Ivan Veliki in the Kremlin, just as the great monastery of Aleksandr Nevsky was meant to outdo the abbey of St Sergius which had been founded at Zagorsk, near Moscow, in 1340.)

As to the individual palaces which Peter the Great commissioned, Audrey Kennett has said what most needs to be said. My own concern is with the general character of the city which resulted. For although the development of Leningrad was in some respects erratic and polyvalent – one early visitor was 'surprised to find instead of a regular city, as I expected, a heap of villages linked together like some plantation in the West Indies' – there has survived even into our own generation the international instinct which was pioneered by Peter the Great. (To what else, after all, can we attribute the design of the new Leningrad Hotel on the north bank of the Neva?) That instinct is to be found as much in the grid-like layout of Vasilyevsky Ostrov as in the three long straight streets which radiate outwards, on the model of Versailles, from the Admiralty. We see it in the look of the island of Petrograd, where the moneyed middle-classes set themselves up at the turn of this century in apartment buildings that would not look out of place in Passy or Neuilly; we see it again in the post-revolutionary cinemas and the stepped-back housing projects which bear the mark of international constructivism in the 1920s. Peter the Great is somewhere at the back of all this.

Sometimes his importations turned out very well; sometimes they didn't. Just once, he got double value for money: the sixteen-year-old son of the sculptor Carlo Rastrelli grew up to be an architect, and to make what is perhaps the finest individual contribution to the evolution of the city. At the opposite extreme was the case of Andreas Schlüter, who was signed on in 1713 with the title of overall architectural director. The philosopher Leibnitz had recommended Schlüter for the post, and he had great things to his credit in Germany; yet the Schlüter who arrived in St Petersburg was not the young man of genius who had built the Royal Palace in Berlin but a decrepit wreck who turned out to be obsessed with the problem of perpetual motion and died in St Petersburg, in 1714, without ever having built anything.

Peter the Great may well have been irked, in this instance, just as he was irked when the grid of Dutch-style canals which had been planned for Vasilyevsky Ostrov turned out to be too narrow for its function and had to be filled in. But his was a pragmatic and an eclectic nature; and something of it survived as a permanent characteristic of Leningrad, where a certain buoyancy can always be relied upon in difficult times. When the Winter Palace was seriously damaged by fire in 1837, for instance, there were good men around, and in one or two spectacular cases they were given their heads. It is in this way that the city became what it is: not a one-style, one-period city but a sophisticated amalgam that never ceases to startle and astonish.

An aspect of this which does not form part of the Kennetts' brief is the extent to which, here and there in Leningrad, Old Russia takes its revenge. Sometimes that revenge is purely ironical, a by-product of Western taste: how many visitors from English-speaking countries gasp aloud with delight on first seeing the Church of the Resurrection which commemorates the assassination of Alexander II? Yet this church, which to an inexperienced eye looks the epitome of Old Russia, was not completed till 1907 and is pure pastiche, though pastiche of a particularly resourceful kind. More to the point, in this context, are the monasteries of Smolny and Aleksandr Nevsky and the Nikolsky Cathedral by the Krukov canal. These are distinctly of the eighteenth century in their origin; yet it is impossible not to feel in the two great monasteries, and in the two-storeyed cathedral with its separate bell-tower, the after-echo of an earlier Russia. In the design of the Aleksandr Nevsky, with its high walls, its two cemeteries, its ancient trees, its many churches, its archbishop's palace and its complex of related and hardly less beautiful auxiliary buildings, there is retained the concept of the abbey as a state within the state. Spiritual power is as impressive, here, as is temporal power a mile or two downstream; and while Catherine the Great was thinking about Voltaire and Diderot, in the last third of the eighteenth century, a new generation of Russian architects (Chevakinsky in the Nikolsky Cathedral, Starov in the Troitsky or Holy Trinity Cathedral in the Aleksandr Nevsky monastery) was adapting the idiom of European Baroque and Neo-classicism to patterns of worship evolved by the Russian Orthodox Church.

Those patterns were conversational in tone. In France or Germany or Italy a Baroque church was altar-oriented, but in Russia it was important that people should be able to move freely from image to image. There was also the tradition of the *iconostasis*, the screen on which images were piled one on top of the other. This did not fit in with the strict spatial divisions of Western Europe, and French art-historians who got down to work in Petersburg at the end of the nineteenth century were displeased to find that the most conspicuous of the city's monuments had often something freakish about them. Louis Réau found it ridiculous, for instance, that the inner space of Petropavlovsky Cathedral should be cut in half by what seemed to him a disproportionately large *iconostasis*; as for the gilded spire, he found it Germanic, or at best Danish, in its derivation, and altogether a most wilful and grotesque addition to a building which already offended him deeply.

Some of these buildings are admittedly very queer. The cross-breeding of European Baroque with the perambulatory conventions of Russian Orthodox church-going was bound to lead to genetic impurities; but the churches of Leningrad impose themselves when we least expect it. A key episode, in this context, is the one experienced by Dostoyevsky in 1849: led out, as he thought, to be executed, and with a rational expectation of not more than another minute or two of life on this earth, he found that his attention was fixed above all by 'a church with a gilded dome on which the sun sparkled. In a few moments, I felt, I should myself be in the place from which those sunbeams were shining down . . .'.

Still, that was Dostoyevsky. Leningrad in general has always, like its founder, been very much of this world. (Peter the Great was superstitious, but no one could call him devout.) Baedeker in 1914 listed the following, within a short walk of the Nevsky Prospekt: an Armenian church, a Dutch church, a Greek church, a Roman Catholic church, a Lutheran church, a Methodist Episcopal church, a Finnish church, a British and American Congregational chapel. But these were concessions to the foreign colonies which at that time played a substantial part in the life of the city; more to the point, in the general context of St Petersburg life, was the stylish exterior of the English church, designed by Quarenghi in 1815, which carries itself to this day like just one more palace. Quarenghi was seventy-one at the time. He had never been good-looking (see plate 170) – contemporaries remarked on his hideous and pustular nose – and the first syllable of his name reminded his patrons of the Russian word for a croaking frog. But in his art, if not in his person, he understood the meaning of *una bella figura*.

And *una bella figura* was what a great deal of St Petersburg was all about. Not the seats of learning, not the museums, not the libraries (though, even there, the acquisition of Voltaire's library had an undeniable element of panache): but just about everything else. It was in the name of *bella figura* that so many of the great houses and the fantasticated objects of art which Mr and Mrs Kennett set before us were first brought into being. It was in the name of *bella figura* that Pushkin got himself killed. Architects of Italianate origin had a great hand in the building of St Petersburg: Trezzini initially, Rastrelli not long after, Quarenghi, Rossi. There was nothing flimsy or theatrical about their concern. Nothing was done for immediate effect; but, even so, they knew how to make the very best of a difficult site. For a superlative example of this, the visitor has only to explore the complex of buildings by Rossi which includes the Pushkin (formerly the Aleksandrinsky) Theatre.

Rossi is represented in this book both by the Yelagin Palace which he built among centenarian oaks on an island to the north-west of the city and by the immense grandeurs of the Mikhaylovsky Palace, now the Russian Museum (57–59, VIII, 60–65); but his real genius was not for individual buildings. He was the last of the great co-ordinators: the men who gave Leningrad an appearance at once august and convivial. Other architects had endowed the city with great individual buildings; Rossi was the man who came along afterwards and pulled the whole thing together. When he returned from Moscow in 1816 and began his architectural career, there was nobody around to challenge him. Starov had died in 1808, Zakharov in 1811, Thomas de Thomon in 1813, Voronikhin in 1814, and Quarenghi had only a year to live. Thanks to these big men, the city had already acquired (or was shortly to see completed) many of the monuments for which it is famous: among them the Admiralty, the Kazan Cathedral (so dexterous in its evocation on a smaller scale of St Peter's in Rome), the Exchange, the Troitsky Cathedral in the Aleksandr Nevsky monastery. With the exception of Zakharov's Admiralty, none of these was an adventurous building; they carried on the tradition established by Quarenghi when he said quite frankly in 1785 that he had taken what he wanted from his contemporaries in Western Europe. But if there is a tradition of anthologizing in the architectural history of Leningrad there is also a tradition of all-out rivalry which manifested itself in patronage of an exceptionally lavish and unheeding sort. As a result of this, the architect who wanted to do large-scale work in the city in the 1820s had to be something of a diplomatist; it was no longer a matter of giving the city character, but of fitting in with the character that it already had.

That character was not simply a matter of palaces run up regardless of expense and of public buildings which had been begun at a time when much of the city had a look of open country still only half-reclaimed. It was a matter of detail. It had to do with grilles and gates and iron railings (most of them still unchanged); with trees and statues and chevroned lamp-posts; and with bridges over the canals which were as elegant as they were practical. St Petersburg had ceased to be a city built *a priori*; in barely more than a hundred years it had acquired a specific and most powerful personality, and that personality was as evident in small things as in great ones. It is still very much there; and it seems natural to natives of the city that dominoes should be played on most summer afternoons in the garden beside the Nikolsky Cathedral, just as you can exchange your apartment by pinning a notice on one of the trees beside the little bridge, with its four lions *couchant*, that spans the Griboyedov canal not far from the Conservatoire. Cities develop a flavour, and a rhythm, and a set of habits which cannot be planned in advance.

So there was no question of Rossi just staking out a good position and going ahead. He had to accommodate himself to what was already there. Rastrelli had built the Winter Palace at a time when it was still possible to catch a hare in the adjoining field of oats; but when Rossi began to design the buildings which were to face the Winter Palace across Palace Square he had to reckon with Rastrelli's densely and richly articulated façade (IV). (This did not always, by the way, have its present metropolitan aspect. When the Victorian traveller Augustus Hare went to Russia he was told how not long before 'there had nestled many a one in this palace not included in the regular inhabitants. The watchers on the roof – placed there for different purposes – among others to keep the water in the tanks from freezing during the winter by casting in red-hot cannon-balls – built themselves huts between the chimneys, took their wives and children there, and even kept poultry and goats who fed on the grass of the roof; it is said that at last some cows were introduced . . .'.)

Rossi had to deal, therefore, with a building across the way which was long, straight, flat and heavily ornamented. He made his own buildings as different as possible, and spread them out in a hemicycle which seems to give way at every point to the Winter Palace. So far from trying to outdo Rastrelli, he devised a majestic triumphal arch which in effect holds in reserve the first sight of Rastrelli's façade as a key moment in the visitor's experience. Approach the Winter Palace from the curved street which leads towards it from Nevsky Prospekt and you will see how delicately, but with what a superb assurance, Rossi hands you over to his great predecessor (18). I know of no finer compliment from one professional to another.

Rossi also dealt very skilfully with the problem of what to build as a background to the famous profile view of Falconet's equestrian statue of Peter the Great. His solution – the linked buildings which formerly housed the Senate and the Synod – is a model of tact; but for discretion of a kind not often met with in Leningrad, first place in his career should go to the quarter known (not least from Tamara Karsavina's memoirs) as Theatre Street. Rossi had the theatre in his blood – his mother had been an Italian ballet-dancer – and it was predictable that he would produce a façade which was both dignified and inspiriting, with an elaborate use of the Corinthian order which best corresponded to his own nature. But the sides of theatres, and even more so their backs, incline to be dull; blind walls, most often, on which no love has been lavished. This was not at all Rossi's idea: he wanted his theatre to be as beguiling at the back as it was at the front, and he gave it, in the end, two façades of equal splendour. The rearward one looks out on to Theatre Street, now most justly renamed Rossi Street. At its farther end were other buildings by Rossi; but the peculiarity of Theatre Street is the musical precision with which Rossi organized the space between the flat back of the Aleksandrinsky Theatre and the curving half-circle of the little *place* which Theatre Street enters, at an acute angle. Theatre Street is twenty-two metres (seventy-two feet two inches) wide; its uniform buildings are twenty-two metres high; its length is exactly ten times twenty-two metres. This is eye-music of a particularly deft and discreet sort: we learn all over again that the best architecture, like the best behaviour, disdains to call attention to itself.

It was clear to Rossi that the city had a configuration and a personality which should be respected. The industrial age had not yet begun, the structure of society still seemed secure, and the patterns of life in St Petersburg were very pleasant indeed for those who were privileged to make the most of them. The great palaces which appear in this book had virtually all been built, and the supreme opportunities were not likely to come again. Rossi had come to manhood in the eighteenth century, and his was the last drawing-board from which nothing but good was certain to come to the city. There were to be later buildings of quality in the historic centre of Leningrad; there were to be apartment houses of a personable and cosmopolitan sort on the other side of the Neva; and there were to be country houses, some of them most winningly eccentric, on the more distant islands. After the Winter Palace had been partly burnt out in 1837 there were extensive and unexpected opportunities of a redecorative sort. Between 1839 and 1844 a Bavarian architect, A. I. Stakenschneider, built the former Mariinsky Palace, now the headquarters of the Leningrad Soviet; and it is with him that the tradition of the palace as fundamental to the city may be said to have ended. Stakenschneider had a metallic brilliance which can be mistaken for the real thing – his Pavilion Hall in the Hermitage is an example of this (30, 31) – and he never forgot that every city of a certain age has a scale that is natural to it and should not be exceeded.

In that context, I myself regard St Isaac's Cathedral as a betrayal of what Leningrad should stand for. Much of this introduction is being written, as it happens, in the Astoria Hotel and within sight of St Isaac's. The great gilded dome is the first thing that I see in the morning and the last thing that I see at night, and I must concede to it a certain mysterious variety of humour. In the very early morning it seems to hover in the air, pale pink and all but incorporeal. At mid-day, if the weather is good, it has a note of brassy self-assurance. As evening draws on, it often turns livid and streaky, as if with an access of uncontrollable bad temper. St Isaac's took forty years to build, and every day of it shows in its grotesquely inflated proportions and its uneasy commingling of local materials – red Finnish granite, many-coloured marbles, hollow iron columns veneered with lapis lazuli and malachite – with a design lifted in part from St Paul's Cathedral in London and in part from the Panthéon in Paris. *Materia superat opus* was Louis Réau's lapidary epitaph on an adventure which violated the proportions of the city once and for all. Réau was a fine and a severe scholar, but he was also a patriot; a man who liked to think of the St Petersburg he knew as permeated above all by the achievement of the French eighteenth century. It irked him that, in the century that followed, the sumptuous but wrong-headed experiment of St Isaac's Cathedral should also have been owed to a Frenchman, Ricard de Montferrand. (Montferrand did, of course, get his brief from Tsar Alexander I; Alexander told him to make a church that would stand comparison, inside and out, with the best that Italy had to show.) All this is the more ironical in that Alexander I, who reigned from 1801 to 1825, was one of the first great preservationists. The last thing that he wanted to do was to break the continuity of design in St Petersburg. He even appointed a committee whose duty it was to bring about, wherever possible, a 'uniform exterior beauty' throughout the city. He loved the past of St Petersburg, and it was genuinely his desire that visitors should wish to begin their letters, as Peter the Great had begun his, with the words 'From Paradise, otherwise known as St Petersburg'.

In architectural terms I think we may say that he succeeded. The post-Napoleonic era in St Petersburg had an extensive and particular brilliance: to the extent that Leningrad can still be regarded as one huge museum of Neo-classical inspirations, much credit is owed to Alexander I. It is true that in all this he did no more than continue an autocratic tradition that had begun with Peter the Great and was further extended through the reign of Nicholas I, Alexander's successor. It was not difficult to keep the city harmonious when only three or four types of building were authorized in any case; but, even so, those three or four types had to be chosen. There had to be good sense, as well as continuity; and I doubt if there has ever been a capital city more homogeneous in its beauty than the one through which Pushkin walked on the afternoon of 27 January 1837, to keep the appointment with Baron d'Anthès which led to his death.

Not everyone thought so well of St Petersburg. There were foreigners who thought they knew better and said even of the Palais Tauride (Tavrichesky Palace: VII, 50–53) that 'The marble is all false, the silver is plated copper, the pillars and statues are of brick, and the paintings are copies.' The Marquis de Custine in 1839 thought St Petersburg 'a city without character: pompous rather than impressive, extensive rather than beautiful. As for its architecture, it has neither style, nor taste, nor historical significance'; but then Custine had a bad time there. A city is not, after all, primarily something to look at: it is something to live in, and it is as 'a machine for living in' that it should finally be judged.

There is no shortage of foreigners' accounts of life in St Petersburg, and some of them make amusing and pertinent reading. Théophile Gautier enjoyed every minute of his stay. He was a champion describer, with a vocabulary that could never be faulted and the contagious energy of the very fat man whose fat serves rather to buoy him up than to weigh him down. Much of what he says is still relevant today, even if we can no longer count on getting bear-steaks in even the best restaurants of the town. So much of the history of Leningrad is involved with foreigners that we soon claim for ourselves the status of honorary citizens and feel at one with Diderot, with Berlioz, with Charles Cameron, with Euler the Swiss mathematician, with George Dawe the English portrait-painter, with Yuri Veldten, the German who designed the wrought-iron grille of the Summer Garden (figure 4), and with Gustave Mahler, whose concerts in 1907 were prized at their true worth. A perfected cosmopolitanism was always the mark of this city, and we can even identify with the Emir of Boukhara, who built for himself before 1914 a really very peculiar building not far from Petropavlovsky Fortress. The cosmopolitanism in question was not concerned only with people of individual genius: nor was it a matter exclusively of those persons whom La Bruyère categorized as *les grands*.

An admirable guide, in this context, is Miss E. M. Almedingen, a native of the city and a gifted writer whose childhood before 1914 is recorded for us in her *I Remember St Petersburg*. Here she is on cosmopolitanism of a kind not often examined by foreign visitors:

the city's numerous cotton and paper mills, her shipyards and steel works had Englishmen, Germans and Dutchmen for their owners and managers. Her dressmakers, tailors and glovers were mostly French, and her finest shoemakers German or English. The best restaurants were French again – with the exception of *Medvied* ('The Bear'), though I heard it said that the Russian name screened an Italian proprietorship. The best private schools were German. There was not a shop of importance but displayed boldly lettered notices: 'English Spoken', 'Ici On Parle Français', 'Man Spricht Deutsch'. It was difficult for a man or woman to find employment in such shops unless they knew at least two foreign languages.

Miss Almedingen is very good also about the smells of the waterfront – 'a mingled fragrance of unfamiliar spices, oranges, lemons, vanilla and tar'; and about the Circassians in cinnamon-coloured coats and caps trimmed with silver braid whose duty it was to sweep the quays beside the Winter Palace; and about the Pussy Willow Fair which began on Palm Sunday and offered, among other Easter presents, 'gaily coloured wooden eggs, beautifully carved boxes of rare Caucasian wood, hand-made lace from Valdai, richly spiced gingerbread from Viazma, and copper samovars from Tula.' There can have been no better place in which to grow up as the child of enlightened parents.

Of course there had been times when the great city went ahead too fast for its inhabitants. Pushkin's 'The Negro of Peter the Great' has not a good reputation with historians of literature, but I for one very much enjoy Pushkin's account of an evening at the Winter Palace in the time of Peter the Great. Not only is this the prototype of the great historical reconstructions in *War and Peace*, but it ideally suggests the uneasy and often hilarious alliance of habits old and new, imported and home-grown, which marked the first years of St Petersburg. 'In the great room', Pushkin tells us,

tallow candles burned dimly amid clouds of tobacco smoke. Wind instruments made continual music as grandees with blue ribbons across their shoulders strolled up and down with ambassadors, merchants from overseas, green-uniformed officers of the Guards, and shipbuilders in jackets and striped trousers. Of the ladies who sat round the walls, the younger ones had decked themselves out in the height of fashion. Their gowns were ablaze with gold and silver; their slender forms rose like the stalks of flowers from outsize farthingales; in their ears, in their perfectly-set hair, and around their necks diamonds were seen to sparkle. The older ladies had done their best, on the other hand, to blend the new fashions with the now-outlawed styles of the past. Their caps were remarkably close to the sable head-dress of Peter the Great's mother, while their gowns and mantillas were reminiscent of the national dress of Old Russia. They seemed astonished, rather than delighted, to be present at these new-fangled amusements; and they looked down on the wives and daughters of the Dutch sea-captains, who had come in dimity skirts and red bodices and sat knitting their stockings and laughing among themselves as if they were back at home in Holland.

When Peter the Great's daughter Elizabeth got on to the throne in 1741 there was a marked shift of emphasis in such matters. Elizabeth would have married Louis XV of France, if her father had had his way, and she had grown up in the belief that a great nation needed a great literature, a great theatre, and a predominant position in the arts and the sciences. She had also acquired a French taste for complex and uninhibited amusements. As often happens, destiny put the right people in her way: in the year of her accession, for instance, the many-gifted Lomonosov, then just thirty years old, arrived back in Russia after some years in Marburg and Freiburg. He had studied philosophy, physics, chemistry and practical mining, while working at the same time on the transformation of the Russian language into something which might one day rank with French, German and English as one of the finest and most flexible instruments of human expression. That Russia should eventually have a science and a literature equal to those of the West was the ambition of Lomonosov's life: where better to realize it than in St Petersburg, and under a monarch who had something of her father's universal curiosity?

It is to Lomonosov, above all, that Leningrad owes the tradition of tireless and impartial enquiry which is commemorated in the plaques which record one great name after another on the outer walls of the Academy of Sciences. And it is to another pioneer from the reign of Elizabeth that Leningrad owes its theatrical tradition: for in 1752 she heard of the existence of a good theatre-troupe in Yaroslavl, invited them forthwith to St Petersburg, and set in hand the long sequence of theatrical activity which is recorded in the Leningrad Theatre Museum. Like her father, Elizabeth did not care to be baulked; and those same senior citizens who had turned up their noses at the Dutch ladies in their dimity skirts were even more disconcerted to find that when the Empress Elizabeth invited them to a ball they were obliged to go dressed as men. Their husbands had to swallow their scruples, meanwhile, and get themselves up as women, complete with hoop-skirted ball-dresses: no exceptions were permitted.

If I bring up these matters it is not by way of a picturesque distraction. It is because despotic amusements and a highly-developed sense of play were fundamental to St Petersburg life for two centuries. There began at the very top of this pyramidal society and spread slowly and steadily downwards a determination to get the best, from all over and in every department of life, and to find it none too good. The supreme example of this in literature is *Eugene Onegin*; and I cannot too strongly recommend, in this context, the four-volume edition by Vladimir Nabokov of Pushkin's novel-in-verse. This is beyond question our best guide to what St Petersburg was like, as a machine for living in, in the 1820s and 30s. Pushkin's own methods were exact, succinct and incomparably ferocious, with never a syllable wasted or a detail left vague. Never was a writer more laconic; the visitor to Leningrad may well be reminded of him by the famous three-word epitaph – 'Here lies Suvorov' – which was all that the great eighteenth-century general would allow to be put on his tombstone and, equally, by the firm round brass full stop which gives a further finality to that inscription as we can see it, still today, in the Aleksandr Nevsky monastery.

There are natives of Leningrad, now in their seventies, who can remember just where were the bookshops and the tailors and the boot-makers and the garden-restaurants and the *maisons de passe* in which Pushkin and his friends chased the time away between 1817 and 1820. The buildings still stand, and the courtyards, and here and there a shop-front; but we come closest to Pushkin himself in the apartment on the Moika which he lived in during the last years of his life. This is not at all grand, by the standards of his day; but the two corner windows that look on to the canal are like a stage-box from which nothing could pass unnoticed. And as we stand there, sampling the sharp green of the house on the other side of the water, we realize how great was the role of propinquity in the life of the city. We see, for instance, how the little house was just across the way from the Winter Palace. We understand afresh why Nicholas I was annoyed when Pushkin turned up at a ball in the wrong clothes and could not be bothered to go home and change and come back again. We also remember how Nicholas I would ride past those same corner windows, day after day, and later told Pushkin's wife that it was really too bad of her never to raise her blinds. In our imaginations we can leave the house, as Pushkin left it on 27 January 1837, walking along the Moika, turning right at Nevsky Prospekt and stopping at No. 18, which was then Wolf's confectionery shop and the place at which Pushkin was to meet his second for the duel. We can also leave the house in the opposite direction and walk to the Equerries' Church in the former Imperial Stables, where Pushkin's body was taken at midnight on 31 January. Wolf's no longer exists, and the church has been cut into slices, horizontally, and filled with office-workers; but about the house itself, No. 12 Moika, there is something almost uncomfortably vivid. Simply to see the double-breasted jacket which Pushkin wore to the duel brings us very near to the tiny, irascible, overborne man of genius. This was tailoring trimmed to the last centimetre, with buttons no thicker than a worn farthing; but tailoring for a miniature man – one who could walk under the lectern of Peter the Great, in the Hermitage, without having to bend his head.

So dense is the crowd, most days, in the study where Pushkin died that it is difficult for a visitor to glimpse the volumes of Crabbe and Wordsworth and Southey that Pushkin ordered for himself from Belizard's bookshop on Nevsky Prospekt. His was an up-to-date library, in which nearly all the books had been published in the 1820s and 30s; and the room has still, against all the odds, a startling actuality. If sometimes we wish that we could be there for a moment alone, free of the shuffling crowds in their loosely-tied overshoes, we should remember that when Pushkin's body lay in state on that same worn leather sofa the mourners who filed by were not persons of fashion. The people who lived in the beautiful rooms shown in this book stayed home, during those two days, or went about their normal amusements. One of the few exceptions was Princess Meshchersky, who wrote later that

The people who came to pay him homage were of all ages and professions: women, old men, children, students, ordinary people in sheepskins, some of them even in rags. . . One could not but be deeply moved by these plebeian honours, while in our gilded drawing rooms and scented boudoirs there was hardly anyone who paused to think how brief had been his brilliant career. No one expressed regret: for the great poet, or for the unhappy husband. Insults and accusations came his way, all over the town, while everyone had a good word for the gentlemanly behaviour of the despicable rogue and seducer who had three separate homelands and went under two different names.

It is well to think of these lines when visitors fantasize, as they so often do, about the vanished life of St Petersburg. The stranger who walks along the quays in the very early morning, when no one else is about, will see a world in aquatint: palaces drawn with impeccable penmanship and stained with the lightest possible wash of colour, wide roads as yet uncorrupted by the motor-car, Marsovo Pole, the Champ de Mars, freshly raked for the parade of the Household Cavalry (black horses for the Horse Guards, chestnuts for the Chevaliers, dapple-grey for the Gatchina Hussars). Naturally it would be very pleasant to have been master of one of the great houses of St Petersburg at a time when (to quote from J. G. Kohl, a German traveller who lived for several years in Russia in the 1830s) a great town house included the following establishment:

a superintendent of accounts, a secretary, a *dvorezki* or maître d'hôtel, the valets of the lord, the valets of the lady, the *dyatka* or overseer of the children, the footmen, the *buffetshek* or butler and his assistants, the table-decker, the head groom, the coachman and postilions of the lord, the coachman and postilions of the lady, the educational staff, the German, French and Russian masters, the porters, the head cook and his assistant, the baker and the confectioner, the stove-heater, the brewer of *kvass*, the waiting-maids and wardrobe-keepers, the nurses in service, the retired nurses and, where a private orchestra is maintained, the Russian *Kapellmeister* and his musicians . . .

This life went on into our own century. It is a remarkable experience to explore the Yusupov Palace on the Moika (42, 43). This is not so much a unified town house, in the English sense, as an oriental-type labyrinth on which one generation after another of Yusupovs left their mark. There was no fancy so extravagant, in this house, that it could not be indulged; nor any practice so bizarre that it could not be concealed from the rest of the family by a secret door hidden behind a book-shelf, or beneath an English billiard table, or in the intestinal area below where Rasputin was lured to his death. Somewhere in all this was the private theatre which was built for Zenaide Yusupov and completed at the turn of the century: not the least extraordinary, this, of the feats of restoration which have lately been completed by the Soviet authorities. The theatre is, of course, 'late'; and the idea of shrinking the Residenztheater in Munich, fitting it into a Neo-classical mansion in Russia and equipping it with what passed in the 1890s for ceiling-paintings in the style of Tiepolo would not please a severe taste. But it relates back, even so, to the barbaric appetites of Peter the Great, who wanted the best from everywhere and didn't mind how he got it.

Not much is said in the guide books about certain aspects of Leningrad which none the less are fundamental to its history over the last hundred and fifty years. Those who prize Russian literature as one of the supreme forms of human expression will know, for instance, that there is a great deal more to the city than its palaces. Ever since the Decembrist rising of 1825 Leningrad has been super-sensitive, in political terms. Political power has been transferred to Moscow; but a very important part of the history of the human race has been acted out in Leningrad and it would most certainly be a mistake to assume that a firm round brass full stop, like the one on Suvorov's tomb, has now brought it to an end.

Leningrad has had, from its beginnings, a complex and phantasmagorical character: this comes out very strongly in Pushkin's 'Bronze Horseman', and it also found luxuriant expression in *Petersburg*, a Symbolist novel published by Andrey Biely in 1913. 'The Bronze Horseman' draws in part upon a specific historical event: the great storm of November 1824, when the Neva overflowed its banks and caused widespread and spectacular destruction in the city. But its force comes above all from the notion of Peter the Great as the man who mastered Destiny, and from the idea that one day Falconet's equestrian statue (1) would come to life and gallop through the moonlit streets. To be pursued by the Bronze Horseman was the worst of nightmares for a native of St Petersburg. And when Biely came to write his novel he too brought the runaway horse and its rider before his readers: 'the neighing of the horse could be heard across the city like the whistle of a locomotive and the steam from its nostrils splashed luminous spray into the street.' Leningrad is and has always been an unnatural city, and its history has a more than normal abundance of strange and terrible episodes: who can forget the scene in Eisenstein's film *October* when the two halves of the bridge swing up, to prevent any further traffic across the Neva, and a dead horse slides slowly down from top to bottom?

Extreme social inequality of the kind that was so flagrant in Leningrad in the second half of the nineteenth century should not be forgotten: we owe it to those who endured those conditions to take a walk in the area, once called the Moskovskaya quarter, which Dostoyevsky describes in *Crime and Punishment*; in this same area the poet Nekrassov saw a young peasant girl being flogged in public. There is a lot to be learned about Leningrad in that quarter, just as there is a lot to be learned from the high-faced apartment houses in which Tchaikovsky and Gogol lived, and from the hotels – not all of them still in use – where Berlioz and Alexandre Dumas put up on their visits to the city and where the poet Yesenin, husband of Isadora Duncan, hanged himself in 1925. Leningrad is not one of those places which, like Bath or Nancy, has fine architecture but went quiet a long time ago, in human terms. Nor is it a place which, like Dijon or Aachen, had its great moment in history and thereafter subsided. Leningrad had its yesterday, but it also has its today. We do not have to pick and choose among its buildings, any more than we have to pick and choose among its people; everything and everyone counts. Had it not had this strong, coherent and enduring corporate personality it would never have survived the nine-hundred-day siege in 1941–44, any more than it would have survived those other and more gratuitous tribulations to which Anna Akhmatova gave definitive expression in her poems. The palaces of Leningrad are all that they are said to be; but it is in the total context of a very great and still completely alive city that we should look at them.

The united magnificence of all the cities of Europe could but equal Petersburg. There is nothing little or mean to offend the eye: all is grand, extensive, large, and open. The streets, which are wide and straight, seem to consist entirely of palaces.

DR EDWARD DANIEL CLARKE 1799

Such grandeur and symmetry in building, I never before beheld in any of the different capitals to which my fondness for travel has conducted me. Every house seems a palace, and every palace a city.

SIR ROBERT KER PORTER 1805

overleaf

Inhabitants of St Petersburg, from aristocrats and merchants to porters and beggars, on the Neva Quay in 1778. In this engraving after Le Prince we are on the south bank, looking west; in the distance on the right is the spire of Petropavlovsky Cathedral in the Fortress; in the centre, the tip of Vasilyevsky Ostrov, linked to the south bank by a bridge of boats, far left (see the endpaper illustration)

References in roman numerals indicate colour plates; in arabic numerals, black and white plates. These numbers are printed in **bold** type unless they refer to an illustration in another section.

I Palaces in Leningrad

Menshikov Palace

MENSHIKOV PALACE was the earliest important building of Petersburg. It was begun in 1710 by the Italian architect Giovanni Maria Fontana, and continued by the German, Gottfried Schädel. These two – with Domenico Trezzini, whom Peter the Great put in control of the design of his whole city (see page 30) – typify the foreign architects he brought in. He wanted not only a new capital but a new outlook; and he knew that if he used Russian architects he would simply find himself with a second Moscow. So through his own journeys, and his emissaries abroad, he sought talent everywhere. He flew high, writing personally to invite Sir Christopher Wren. Naturally, the most eminent architects, successful in their own countries, were unlikely to respond to such invitations. It is indeed remarkable that so many were enterprising enough to set off for such a distant and inhospitable site, and to stay and work for years – sometimes for the rest of their lives.

The original Menshikov Palace consisted of a rectangular building with its façade on the bank of Vasilyevsky Ostrov (Basil Island) in the Neva. It had a landing stage which enabled medium-sized ships to berth outside the main entrance. Two wings at right angles formed a court at the back. A large amount of land was laid out in formal gardens, with sculptures, fountains, grottoes and orangeries. The façade was broken up with pilasters with stone capitals on each storey. The form of the façade was altered in the late 1730s and early 1740s: the Dutch-style roof seen in Zubov's engraving (figure 2), with princely crowns on the front projections, gave place to the

The present façade

present form, with pediments on the wings and a curved central pediment decorated with a relief. The simple surrounds of the windows at the sides remain typical of the early eighteenth century, but in the centre their square shapes became rounded on the first and second floors, and at the same time the two tiers of pilasters were replaced by a giant order. This occurred during the second half of the eighteenth century, when an assembly hall was converted into a church for the cadets who then occupied the palace. Finally, Yuri Veldten's great embankment raised the ground by six feet, altering the proportions of the building. In spite of all, certain features of the exterior, and still more of the interior, basically preserve the original aspect of Menshikov Palace and make it one of the few remaining buildings which reflect the Petrine style of domestic architecture. It is painted the deep brilliant red which was popular at the time.

Peter the Great had known Menshikov from boyhood, when he was a stable lad, and later a street-seller of hot pies. He is often referred to as Peter's 'favourite' – generally a euphemism for 'lover'; and doubtless both were bi-sexual. Peter had a shrewd eye for talent and no conventional inhibitions about where he found it. So the pie-seller rose to be Prime Minister and Prince, and exercised great power.

26

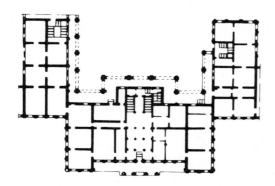

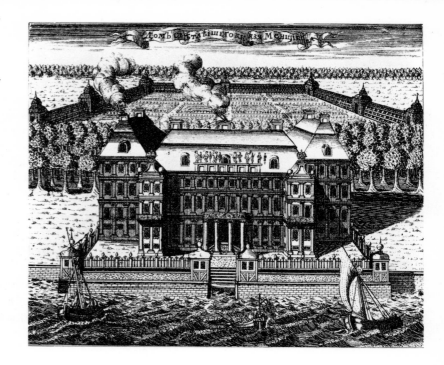

1, 2 Menshikov Palace. The plan is typical of the early palaces, with projecting bays at the front and wings at the rear. Right, an engraving by Zubov shows the palace's original appearance, with a Dutch roof, superimposed pilasters on the façades, and a row of statues above the entrance portico

There is a well-known story of Peter going off to the wars and leaving Menshikov in charge of the work at Petersburg. Peter had indicated a stretch of the bank of Vasilyevsky Ostrov as the site for a university, and told Menshikov that he could also take land for a house for himself. On his return he found that his Prime Minister was building the Twelve Colleges (the city's first university) at right angles to the river instead of along it – and had taken an unduly large slice of river front for himself. Characteristically, Peter boxed his ears when he discovered the situation. Recent expert opinion casts a different light on this episode. It says that Peter wanted, for political reasons, to play down the importance of his new city; that the Menshikov Palace was planned with Peter's authority, not merely as a private house but as the first public building of the capital, in which all manner of administrative and official business was to be conducted; and that his much-publicized buffeting of his Prime Minister was to mislead foreign opinion. This more subtle explanation appears to fit the facts, since the palace was undoubtedly planned to be far more than a private house. Not that the charge of misappropriating State property would have been out of order, if brought against Menshikov: a few years later he was to build an inordinately large palace at Oranienbaum (138). After enjoying a period of increased power in the reign of Peter's widow, Catherine I, his ex-mistress (see page 32), he was to fall at the hands of Catherine's successor, Peter II, a boy of eleven to whom Menshikov wished to betroth his daughter. Before the young Emperor died of smallpox at the age of fourteen, he had sent Menshikov and his daughters packing to Siberia – a reversal of fate which they, like so many others in Russian history, bore with dignity. After his fall, the palace became entirely a government establishment, and then a military school for cadets, Kadetsky Korpus.

An English visitor, Andrew Swinton, describes it in 1789:

The Cadet Corps, an Academy of War, formerly the Palace of Prince Menzikoff . . . is the nursery of young warriors, the sons of the Nobility and Gentry; and from this Seminary of Mars are taken the officers of the Army. The Palace . . . was applied to the present use by Count Munnich . . . the history of Menzikoff romantic: raised from the humblest station to the rank of Prince, then racked upon the wheel of Fortune; yet, in every situation, the art military continued his favourite study. During his banishment in Siberia, the table of his cottage was always crowded with maps and plans of the countries, the seats of former wars, and of battles in which he had been engaged . . . It must appease his *manes*, that his house is still the nursery of war!

The two French aristocrats (Fortia de Piles and Boisgelin de Kerdu) who, under the name of *Deux Français*, gave a detailed account of their northern journeys in 1790–92, write more practically that there were, in the palace,

27

five hundred cadets of Russian nobility, one hundred Livonian [Lithuanian] or Finnish nobility, eighty bourgeois. Every third year, 120 cadets are passed out, and the same number taken. They enter at five or six years old, stay fifteen years, pass out at twenty or twenty-one. The parents have to sign a paper renouncing the right to see them, except at public assemblies, or to take them away before fifteen years is passed. The site it occupies is immense; one would judge that it could accommodate 2200 people. It is a world in which one gets lost, if one is not familiar with the quantity of courts, galleries, corridors. At the foot of a tree there is a plaque saying that the prince, leaving for exile in 1727, drank his coffee under the tree.

Finally the palace was left to fall into disuse. Lenin visited it in 1917 and pronounced it to be a historic building which should be preserved. It is greatly to the honour of Lenin and the Russian people that so little of artistic value – at least in the secular field – was lost in the Revolution. Not only did Lenin lay down from the first that all art treasures and historic buildings must be preserved, but the Russian people, with their deep sense of pride in their cultural past, responded to this call. The palaces and their contents, which had once belonged to imperial and noble families, became the property of the nation, and are probably more widely appreciated and cherished than such things are anywhere else in the world.

Lenin's comment on Menshikov Palace was remembered, though not acted upon for nearly fifty years. Since about 1967, however, the work of interior restoration has been proceeding. It is a difficult task, as the ground floor has had to be excavated. In the process a remarkable sequence of vaulted rooms has been revealed: first the vestibule, the earliest example in Russia of the European Renaissance style; then the contrast of chambers at each side, handed over to master masons from Yaroslavl who constructed their vaults in the Byzantine style of the fifteenth and sixteenth centuries. Upstairs, whole rooms are lined with Dutch tiles, ordered by Peter for his own palace, but taken over by Menshikov. Even in those days the Dutch thought it too expensive to tile whole walls, and Peter's passion for tiles soon proved so costly that Menshikov called two masters from Holland, and set them to establish works in Russia. There is something endearing about the primitive folk-art designs of these first Russian tiles, used in the Menshikov Palace next to the accomplished product of Delft.

Altogether the bank of Vasilyevsky Ostrov – Universitetskaya Naberezhnaya – has an unbroken line of some of the finest eighteenth-century buildings in Leningrad: the Kunstkamera, beautiful in pale blue and white, with lantern dome, the city's first purpose-built museum, constructed by Zemtsov, Mattarnovi and others; the Academy of Sciences, by Quarenghi; the Twelve Colleges, by Trezzini; the University Library; the Menshikov Palace; and the Academy of Arts by Vallin de la Mothe. Over the water lie the Winter Palace, the Admiralty, St Isaac's – a marvellous panorama from either bank of the Neva, 'noblest of city rivers' (see the endpapers).

Kikina Palata

The origins of Kikina Palata are obscure, partly because its date is so early in the history of Petersburg, but mainly because its owner was executed within a few years, and the building was then put to various uses. The word *palata* indicates neither a palace nor a house; the nearest translation is 'chambers'. It is possible that it acquired this name because it so soon ceased to be a private home. It is a typical house of a wealthy man in the second decade of the eighteenth century. It is even partly in stone, whereas Peter I's own Summer Palace (4, 5) is in stucco, and its double stone stairway entrance is much handsomer than his. An interesting point is that the planning of the central section has a certain affinity with that of Peterhof, built in the same year, 1714. The painted areas are in the deep red colour which was an early favourite.

Kikina Palata's first owner, A. V. Kikin, was one of the able men who rose quickly from obscure backgrounds under Peter the Great. Military association was often the basis of such relationships: Kikin was Peter's military servant on the Azov campaign. Peter sent many young men abroad for their education, by which he meant that they were to learn valuable skills. In 1697 Kikin was sent to Holland to learn shipbuilding. On his return he worked in the dockyards; and in 1707 Peter appointed him to the governing body of the Admiralty. Seven years later (just at the time that this house was being built) he was arrested for misuse of power, and dismissed; but somehow he returned to his post, and entered on a much more dangerous, and ultimately fatal, course. He became friendly with Peter's only son, Aleksey Petrovich, who dreaded his father, and was hated and despised by him. Kikin first advised the young man to run away to France; then, in 1716, he persuaded him to hide in Austria and not to return to Russia. Unfortunately Aleksey was lured back by his father's false promises. Kikin was denounced, and beheaded; and the wretched Tsarevich died under torture, in which his father actually took part.

All this was in 1718. Kikin's property was confiscated and, for the next ten years, the 'chambers' were used to house the collection of curiosities which Peter had picked up in his travels: stuffed animals and birds, human deformities preserved in spirit (he was passionately interested in medicine, and would set about pulling teeth if anyone was rash enough to complain of toothache), and all kinds of instruments and gadgets. This was the first museum collection in Russia: later it was moved to the Kunstkamera. Here also was lodged Peter's personal library, which served as a foundation for the library of the Academy of Sciences.

By 1733 the 'chambers' were extended for use as barracks for the cavalry guards: there was a regimental hospital, and the great hall became the guards' chapel. Even Rastrelli took a hand, in 1744, building a belfry with cupola and cross. Kikina Palata underwent all kinds of alterations and disfigurement during the next century and a half; and ironically it has only come back to life through the damage which it suffered in the last war. The original structure was revealed: it was realized that an early Petrine building still lay concealed under the excrescences, and that the exterior at least should be carefully restored. Now it has emerged in much its original form. At present it is the headquarters of the Young Pioneers of the Smolny District.

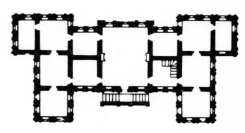

3   Kikina Palata. The plan is similar to that of the contemporary Menshikov Palace (figure *1*), with projecting bays flanking the entrance. The internal arrangement resembles that in the early, central part of Peterhof (see page 203, figure 27)

Summer Palace

Statue of Peter the Great

The character of Peter I – creator of St Petersburg in a sense that cannot be used of any one man in regard to any other great city – may be gauged from the many statues, busts and portraits which can be seen in Leningrad (see, for instance, plate 55). The one which best symbolizes the electrifying effect he had on his country is Falconet's equestrian statue (**I**), commissioned, more than half a century after his death, by Catherine the Great. Falconet himself, when questioned as to the way in which he had dressed his subject – at a time when armour, uniform or ceremonial robes would have seemed the only choice – said, 'The habit I have given the statue of Peter the Great, is the habit of all nations – of all men – of every age; in a word, it is an heroic habit.' Catherine, in one of her vivid letters to Baron Grimm, her artistic advisor in Paris, wrote after the unveiling of the statue in December 1782,

Peter I, when he found himself in the open air, gave us the impression of being as animated as he was noble; one might have said that he was pleased with his image . . . I felt a wave of emotion, and when I looked around, I saw tears in every eye. . . . He was too far away to speak to me, but he seemed to me to have an air of satisfaction, and I caught some of this from him, and it has encouraged me to endeavour to do better in the future, if I can.

Falconet had implored her to give him the shortest possible inscription for the plinth, and she responded with the phrase '*Petro Primo Catherina Secunda*' (and its equally brief Russian equivalent on the other side). She said with disarming candour that she had put the word *Secunda* because she wanted to be sure that people would always know that it was *she* who had erected the statue, and not Peter's wife, Catherine I.

A Scottish traveller, Leitch Ritchie, after visiting Peter's city in 1836, wrote, 'This man, rude in his manners, fierce in his passions ... was, in the finer parts of his nature, one of those intellectual giants who appear at long intervals among meaner men, like a comet among the stars.' Among his 'finer parts' was a dislike of ostentation. The tiny Summer Palace, that most unpalatial of palaces, was the home of a man who wanted somewhere to work and somewhere to house his wife and children (out of his way). His passion for boats of all kinds dictated the site: at the junction of the small river Fontanka with the Neva (**4, 5**). His love of simplicity and of all things Dutch dictated the design, though it was built by an Italian architect, Domenico Trezzini. Trezzini was born in Lugano in 1679 and died in Petersburg in 1734, after over thirty years of work there. Peter brought him in from the very beginning. His greatest work was the fortress and cathedral of Petropavlovsky, or Peter and Paul, which remains Leningrad's symbol and chief landmark (it appears in the distance beyond the Summer Palace in plate **4**).

This little two-storeyed house occupied the corner of what was then a country estate, with its Summer Garden stretching far along the banks of both rivers. Zemtsov and Leblond laid it out with the formality of a Dutch garden, embellished with statues, fountains and pavilions. It served as a setting for all kinds of festivities. There was a gallery for dances, an aviary, and a particularly fine grotto, which occupied the spot on the Moika river where Rossi's pavilion now stands, on the edge of Mikhaylovsky Palace park. But as time went on the pavilions crumbled, and the neat parterres became a pleasant park of grass and trees, along whose alleys the statues still stand, gleaming white from spring to autumn, but enclosed in sentry-box crates through the long winters to protect them from the frost.

The palace is built of stucco on brick, and painted primrose yellow. The steep roof is of sheet steel sections, clamped together. The entrance is utterly unpretentious. The only exterior decoration is a series of terracotta bas reliefs on mythological subjects, thought to be the work of the distinguished German architect Andreas Schlüter, who was called to Russia in 1713, but died the following year. It is said that he himself carved the staircase balustrade, for he excelled at all kinds of decoration. Some fifty years later Yuri Veldten surrounded the Neva side of the Summer Garden with a tall, delicate, wrought-iron railing which is one of the ornaments of Leningrad, and contrasts wonderfully with his own massive Neva embankments.

The ground floor was the domain of Peter I. In his reception room (**15**) the panelling, doors, window frames, shutters and fireplace (the first of many that we shall see placed in a corner) are original, though Peter's marble-tiled floor was replaced by inlaid wood during the restoration of 1820–40. The heavy carved oak furniture is of Peter's time. Between the windows stands the Admiralty Chair (**9**), in which Peter presided over meetings of the Admiralty Collegiate. Its arms are literally that – human arms and hands, carved to the measure of his own huge six-foot nine-inches frame. In his study, with a frieze of his favourite Dutch tiles round the walls, a tiled stove, and his models and pictures of ships, Peter prepared his shipbuilding projects, edited Russia's first newspaper, *The St Petersburg News*, studied mathematics and medicine, and approved or corrected every detail of the buildings springing up in his newly created city.

Best of all he loved his workshop, where he laboured constantly at his lathes and presses, and where he received statesmen, ambassadors, shipmasters and architects, in his working clothes. This clean, quiet room is only the ghost of the workshop which a contemporary described as 'filled with intruments, metal tools, presses large and small'. The Danish ambassador of the time wrote,

With the help of an orderly I penetrated to the Emperor's workshop, where I found him dressed in a leather jerkin like a workman, operating a lathe. He adored this work. In his mastery he could compete with the best turners, and he could also carve portraits and figures. During my visit, he from time to time left the lathe, walked to and fro, and discussed the most important affairs.

4 Gates of the Summer Garden, by Veldten

Peter the Great's reception room

The Admiralty Chair

This lathe was no doubt the one shown (**12**), which he insisted on taking with him on his travels. Here, too, is his famous instrument for determining the direction and velocity of the wind (**14**). It was carried out to his orders in Dresden, by the court jeweller and a mechanic called Andreas Gertner, at the court of the Saxon Duke Johannes Dinglinger. Of its three dials, the top one is a clock, for recording the times of taking readings, the left-hand dial shows the velocity of the wind, and the right-hand dial its direction. The dial hands are still connected with a weathervane of St George and the Dragon, and as this revolves, the hands are activated. *Peter's lathe and wind-measuring instrument*

Peter's dining room (**10**) was intended for meals with family or friends. He detested official entertaining, and gave Menshikov a fine large set of table and chairs, saying that he could take that over. The mahogany table could scarcely seat more than eight. The glass bottles and jar are among the earliest examples of Russian decorative manufacture. The heavily carved sideboard, with the gryphon supporting a double-eagle shield, is of the seventeenth century. In the corner there is a hatch into the kitchen. In an age when, in all countries, kitchens were at the end of long passages, or even in separate buildings, to keep cooking smells at a distance, Peter showed himself ahead of his time, in small matters as in great. He liked his food hot, so he had it served straight off the stove on to plates which were passed through the hatch to the table. And his kitchen (**11**) is modern, too: compactly planned, half Dutch-tiled, with a hood over the stove to carry the smoke up the chimney. The floor is stone-paved, the cooking pots of copper and iron, the store jars of earthenware. The water comes in to a black marble sink, through the pipes of the garden fountains' system – the first indoor water supply in Petersburg. Incidentally, the little river Fontanka, on which the Summer Palace stands, gained its name by supplying water for the fountains of the Summer Garden. *The family dining-room* *The kitchen*

In Peter's bedroom (**13**), the great four-poster bed has crimson velvet hangings. The ceiling painting, decoratively framed in plaster, shows the god of sleep, Morpheus, scattering poppies; its artist is unknown. The moulded figure of a boy on a dolphin, on the white plaster chimney-breast, is the work of Schlüter. *Peter's bedroom*

These six rooms form the whole ground floor. One often wonders, in regard to all the palaces, where the servants lived. The answer here is that a separate house was built for them, connected with the palace by a gallery: this separation, and consequent privacy, is another modern idea, now much favoured by the wealthy in Europe and America.

The first floor of the Summer Palace contains the apartments of Peter's second wife, Catherine. In the Empress's ante-room, a pair of small Russian tables in seventeenth-century style support branching candlesticks with a double-eagle motif. Above one hangs a copy of Nattier's portrait of the Emperor in ceremonial armour (**6**); above the other is a portrait of the Empress. The furniture in the nursery is contemporary with the palace, and the enchanting cradle shaped like a boat (**8**), lined with padded leather and bordered with a pattern in inlaid wood, is the one actually used for the little son of Peter I and Catherine – Pyotr Petrovich, nicknamed Shishenka, who died at the age of three. *The ante-room of Catherine I* *The nursery*

In the ballroom (**V**), with its handsome Delft-tiled stove, part blue and white, part brown and white, much of the furniture is original. There are portraits of Peter's favourite sister, Natalia, and of the Empress Catherine, by Nattier. The floor, inlaid in a striking star pattern, was restored in the nineteenth century. The elaborate walnut mirror-stand, with symbols of the chase, was at least partly carved by Peter himself (**7**). Tall, slender mirrors made in England at the beginning of the eighteenth century represent the first use in Russia of plate glass in decoration. In 1718 Peter had introduced 'assemblies', at which women had to be present. This was a first step towards civilizing a society which, in entirely male gatherings, generally became drunken and rowdy. When Catherine I became Empress, she went one better by laying down rules for these assemblies, one of which was that under no circumstances was any lady to get drunk – nor any gentleman before nine o'clock. *The ballroom* *The carved mirror-stand*

31

Catherine is sometimes described as a Lithuanian servant girl, but she was really a camp follower. She was first the mistress of the Prime Minister, Menshikov; then the mistress, and wife, of his Tsar. She bore Peter two sons (both died in infancy) and two daughters – Anna Petrovna, mother of Peter III, and the future Empress Elizabeth. In 1724, after twenty years of marriage, Peter crowned Catherine his Empress Consort. Nine months later he died, and she succeeded him. Peter had died leaving no will, and it was still the sovereign's prerogative to name his successor. Catherine I's accession was due to Menshikov, who understood very well that with her as empress he would be virtually emperor. C. F. P. Masson, writing about 1800, quotes a joke going round – that a journeyman pastrycook had proclaimed a servant girl Empress of all the Russias. Archdeacon William Coxe reports in 1784:

The reign of Catherine may be considered as the reign of Menshikov; that empress having neither the inclination nor abilities to direct the helm of government; and she placed the most implicit confidence in a man who had been the original author of her good fortune, and the sole instrument of her elevation to the throne. During her short reign her life was very irregular: she was extremely averse to business; would frequently, when the weather was fine, pass whole nights in the open air; and was particularly intemperate in the use of tokay-wine ... She could neither read nor write ... Gordon, who had frequently seen her, seems ... to have represented her character with the greatest justice, when he says, 'She was a very pretty well-lookt woman, of good sense ... The great reason why the tzar was so fond of her, was her exceeding good temper; she never was seen peevish or out of humour; obliging and civil to all, and never forgetful of her former condition; withal, mighty grateful.'

Coxe says that Peter suffered from fits of extreme depression, which produced a temporary madness, and he quotes from Motraye's *Travels*:

She has in some sort the government of all [Peter's] passions; and even saved the lives of a great many ... persons: she inspired him with that humanity, which, in the opinion of his subjects, nature seemed to have denied him ... A word from her mouth in favour of a wretch, just going to be sacrificed to his anger, would disarm him; but if he was fully resolved to satisfy that passion, he would give orders for the execution when she was absent, for fear she should plead for the victim.

Peter is known to have paid her at least one characteristic compliment. To a general who had won a vital battle he offered anything he chose to ask for 'except Moscow and Catherine'. She died after only two years on the throne, aged thirty-nine.

In after years, the Summer Palace became the home of heirs to the throne. The future Catherine the Great lived there with her husband (later Peter III), when they were Grand Duke and Duchess; and her son (later Paul I) lived there with his wife when they were first married. By the late eighteenth century a series of noblemen and courtiers came to occupy it until, by 1870, it began to be used no longer as a home, but for exhibitions. Shortly before 1914 it was opened to the public as a historical monument, though little of the original furniture was left. After the Revolution the government decided to restore the palace as far as possible to its original state, removing everything that belonged to later periods, and replacing it with pieces either known to have been there, or at least of the same date.

Winter Palace

The history of the Winter Palace spans almost the whole history of St Petersburg. In 1703 Peter I determined to found his city on the marshes of the Neva delta, near the point where it runs into the Gulf of Finland. A few years later, in 1711, he gave orders for the first Winter Palace: a small two-storeyed building, scarcely larger than his Summer Palace (4, 5). Ten years later the German architect, Georg Johann Mattarnovi, built the Second Winter Palace near the Winter Canal, which now runs under the gallery leading to the Hermitage Theatre. It was of modest size, with a high sloping roof, in the Dutch style of which Peter was so fond. He died there in

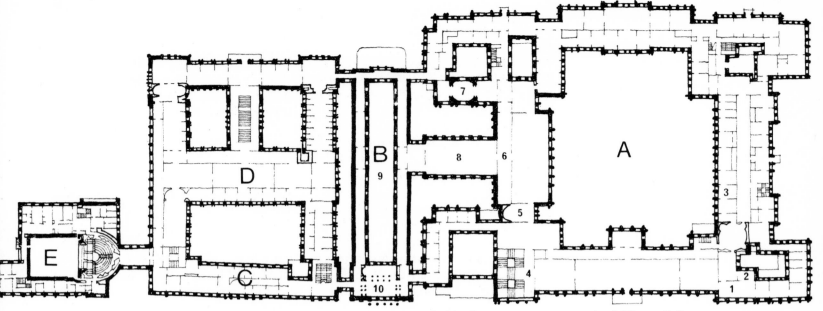

5	The Winter Palace complex at first floor level. The lower edge of the plan is the north façade, on the Neva	A	Winter Palace	1	Malachite Room	6	Military Gallery
		B	Little Hermitage	2	Small White Dining Room	7	Cathedral
		C	Old Hermitage	3	Room 159	8	Great Throne Room, or St George's Hall
		D	New Hermitage	4	Jordan Staircase		
		E	Hermitage Theatre	5	Small Throne Room, or Petrovsky Hall	9	Garden
						10	Pavilion Hall

1725, at the age of fifty-two. Domenico Trezzini, architect of the Summer Palace and director of all building work in the new capital, built the more imposing Third Winter Palace, which occupied the site of the present Hermitage Theatre. Still the new Empress, Anna Ioannovna, did not choose to live there. After her coronation in Moscow in 1731 she reluctantly returned to St Petersburg and moved into the house of Count Apraksin.

In the next year, 1732, the creator of the Winter Palace as we know it appeared on the scene, with the limited brief of 'making modifications'. This was Bartolomeo Francesco Rastrelli (1700–71). He had been brought to Russia at the age of sixteen by his father, the sculptor and Papal Count Carlo Rastrelli, whose equestrian statue of Peter the Great is shown in plate 55. Rastrelli *fils* was deeply versed in Western Baroque but, since he had spent his impressionable years in Russia, his designs were by no means alien importations. The churches and fortified monasteries of Moscow (many of them also by Russianized Italian builders) held a strong attraction for him, and he achieved an imaginative fusion of West and East in his characteristic style, known sometimes as Russian and sometimes as Elizabethan Baroque, after the Empress who used his genius to the full. During the next thirty years his name was to be associated with all the principal buildings of the period – not only in St Petersburg but in Moscow, Kiev and elsewhere. In addition to numerous palaces in and around Petersburg he built its most beautiful ecclesiastical complex, the cathedral and convent of Smolny.

Although Rastrelli was repeatedly ordered to alter and enlarge the palace (swallowing up noblemen's houses on the way), and although, in what is called the Fourth Winter Palace, he foreshadowed his design for the final version, it was not until well into the reign of Elizabeth that he was commissioned to prepare an entirely new project (**17**). It was approved in 1754, and a year later began the demolition of the jumble of buildings which had spread almost as far as the fortifications of the Admiralty. A Fifth Winter Palace, a temporary wooden structure, was built to house the court during the reconstruction.

By 1757 the scene of building activity almost resembled that of the earliest days of the city. Thousands of soldiers were used as labourers. Artisans and craftsmen were gathered from far and wide. Two thousand masons from Yaroslavl and Kostroma were at work. All were camped in the meadows. Rastrelli was acting under imperial

Rastrelli's project

33

orders, but they were not sufficient to release the money that was needed for such a vast enterprise. He himself had to appeal to the Senate – arguing that the palace was being built for the glory of all Russia.

The exterior The design was intended to be seen from all four sides. The south façade, on Palace Square, has in the centre of the main block three arched openings (**17**) leading to an inner courtyard. Two other entrances, one in each of the wings, are reached from ramps, with porticoes to shelter carriages (**IV**). The north façade, running parallel to the Neva (**16**), is more restrained in treatment and the approaches are not so strongly pronounced. The west façade, opposite the Admiralty, has two short jutting wings enclosing a garden. The east façade has long been hidden by the erection of a series of 'Hermitages'. The palace towered among the buildings of the time on account of its great size and height – three storeys, half-basement and imposing roof top – whereas the ordinary town house was no more than two storeys high.

Rastrelli's genius lay in the grand proportions of his buildings, and in his ability to diversify and lighten them by the use of architectural devices, ornamentation and colour. The façades of the Winter Palace have two great superimposed ranges of columns, Ionic and Doric, divided by a string course, but otherwise running from ground to roof, adding to the effect of height. The design of the windows varies from floor to floor and from façade to façade. Above each is one of Rastrelli's characteristic designs in moulded plaster, usually a mask, sometimes simply a shell, with surrounding fronds. The walls – of stucco, as in almost all the palaces – are painted water-green, the columns and window frames white, the plaster mouldings bronze-coloured. A balustrade runs all round the roof, and above it stand a host of figures, perhaps twice life-size, interspersed with classical urns, while other figures rest on the pediments which surmount the entrance sections. These statues, of bronze, are caught in a variety of attitudes, dignified yet aware – like spectators of great events in the square below. At all hours their impressive silhouettes give an extra dimension to the palace, but in moonlight, or during the 'White Nights' of midsummer, their presence dominates the scene unforgettably.

Meanwhile the Neva banks, so close to the palace, had been giving trouble. It was decided to enlarge them; and, by the time the Sixth and last Winter Palace was finished in 1760, the left bank was enclosed in its first granite quay. The Neva is a difficult, tumultuous river. Though short, it surges towards the sea from Lake Ladoga with tremendous force. When Leningrad has already been enjoying spring weather and the river runs free, the skies suddenly mist over and the temperature drops again, as Ladoga sends down its massive ice blocks to crash through to the waters of the Gulf of Finland. So it was not surprising that those first quays were unsuccessful. It was not until 1772–73 that Veldten, director of the newly created Academy of Arts, tamed the river with the splendid embankments which bring the life of the city flowing all along the waterfronts.

At the same time, too, the Hermitage was developing under the hands of architects who were deserting Baroque for Neo-classicism. Its first version, the 'Little Hermitage', was built by Veldten in 1764–65, to house Catherine II's growing collection of paintings and sculptures. There was a hanging garden (still in existence) connecting it with the palace. Later in the same decade the French architect J. B. M. Vallin de la Mothe added a north pavilion known as the 'Old Hermitage'. De la Mothe held the earliest chair of architecture at the Academy of Arts, and taught gifted Russians such as Bazhenov and Starov. In the early 1780s Giacomo Quarenghi built the theatre of the Hermitage (**36**), a remarkable achievement, edged into a confined space and attached to Rastrelli's overwhelming palace, yet holding its own with dignity and tact, its beautiful façade enriched by columns and niches with sculptures. Half a century later, in 1839–52, the German architect Leo von Klenze built the 'New Hermitage', conspicuous for its porch, supported by gigantic Atlas figures sculpted by A. I. Terebenev.

An English visitor in 1827, A. B. Granville, gives statistics on 'this continuous line

34

of Imperial palaces unequalled in extent in any part of Europe'. He says that the Winter Palace occupies an area of 400,000 square feet, and that it and its attendant Hermitages present a frontage along the Neva of about one-third of a mile. 'Upwards of two thousand persons habitually reside in this Palace, and even a larger number are lodged in it when the Emperor is in St Petersburg.'

Rastrelli's plan had great clarity and logic. Galleries, supported on powerful pillars, ran through the whole of the ground floor, which housed all the palace services – the administrative offices, stores, kitchens, areas for servants and for soldiers. On the first floor was the enfilade of state rooms. Above, again, were bedrooms, and rooms for the innumerable courtiers in attendance. The state rooms were all decorated in the height of Russian Baroque. Catherine II, who tore down so much of Rastrelli's interior decoration at Tsarskoye Selo, left it mainly intact in the Winter Palace, and none of her successors had her passion for building and rebuilding. But a terrible fire broke out in mid-December 1837. The poet Zhukovsky, who saw it, described it as 'a vast bonfire with flames reaching the sky'. Practically the whole interior was gutted; and the treasures of the Hermitage and other rooms were saved only by the heroic efforts of soldiers and firemen, many of whom were burnt to death. The news was taken to Nicholas I at the Mariinsky Theatre (now called Kirov). One account states that he rushed to the scene; another, that he said it was God's Will, and saw the performance to the end. However, he was a tireless and efficient organizer, and quickly set up an architectural commission, headed by V. P. Stasov.

Reconstruction started that same winter; and again there was the spectacle of some eight thousand building workers camped in the snow. They worked so hard that by the end of 1839 most of the important halls had been restored. J. G. Kohl commented at the time:

The rapidity with which buildings are run up in St Petersburg is truly astonishing. This is partly due to the shortness of the season, during which building operations can be carried on, but also to the characteristic impatience of the Russians to see the termination of a work they have once commenced. The new Winter Palace is one of the most striking examples of this. Within one year not less than twenty millions of rubles were expended upon the building. The operations were not even allowed to suffer interruption from the frosts of winter, but fires were kept burning every where to prevent materials from freezing and to dry the walls . . . Palaces, in short, are put together with a rapidity that can be compared only to that with which theatrical decorations are arranged.

Great honour is due to Stasov, perhaps the last distinguished representative of the school of Russian Neo-classicism. Though given an opportunity which a lesser man might have tried to turn into self-glorification, he resisted the temptation to design everything afresh, and faithfully reconstructed Rastrelli's Jordan Staircase (**I**) and cathedral (**26**), Rossi's Military Gallery (**28, 29**) and Montferrand's Petrovsky Hall, or Small Throne Room (**27**). The Great Throne Room underwent constant reconstruction before as well as after the fire. It was originally designed by Rastrelli (**19**), and then, in 1776, Catherine the Great commissioned Quarenghi to redesign it (**24**). The new Throne Room was also called the Marble Gallery, from the fact that it was decorated with vari-coloured Russian marble. After the fire Stasov and N. E. Yefimov restored it to a similar design, but using a white Carrara marble which makes it splendid but rather soulless (**25**). It then also became known as St George's Hall. It was last used with full court ceremony in 1906 and, in the same year, as the setting for the first session of the Duma (Parliament) before it was established for its brief life in Tavrichesky Palace.

Stasov was not only a fine architect but an expert technician. He abolished the charming but dangerous stoves which were such a feature of Russian homes, from the palace to the hut, and he introduced the first system of pipes carrying heated air. Instead of mere wooden partitions between rooms he used brick.

There was more great damage to be repaired after the last war, when the Winter

The Great Throne Room or St George's Hall (figure 5, no. 8)

Palace suffered from bombing and shell-fire, and from deterioration during bitter winters without heating. Now it stands, majestic and serene, closing one side of that vast Palace Square so miraculously created by Rossi in the 1820s. He threw out the great arms of his General Staff building to encircle the southern side of the square, and made that wonderful theatrical entrance from Nevsky Prospekt, through wide double arches which frame the palace façade and the Alexander Column (**18**). No greater ensemble has been created, or greater architectural sympathy shown, since Bernini built the approach to St Peter's in Rome.

Palace Square

The column, sometimes called the Peace Column, since it celebrates the end of the war against Napoleon, is something of a miracle in itself. It is a single block of polished red granite from the quarries of Pytterlax, 140 miles away in Finland. Its bronze pedestal and capital are made from cannon taken in the wars against the Turks. Its height, including the angel on top, is 154 feet, its diameter fifteen feet. It is thought to be the largest single stone ever cut, and it is to Palace Square what the obelisk is to the Place de la Concorde in Paris.

Of the fifteen hundred rooms of the Winter Palace we can only look at a few of those which have been preserved much as they were lived in by the tsars through the nineteenth century. The rest are given over to the Hermitage art collection, which is one of the greatest in the world. Everywhere, in what were the first-floor state rooms, the palace setting is evident.

The rooms along the whole of the north façade look across the Neva to Petropavlovsky Cathedral. Louis Réau tells us that Louis XIV disliked the palace of St Germain-en-Laye because, from it, he saw the towers of St Denis, burial place of the kings of France; and he remarks that the Russian tsars were less fearful or less superstitious than the Sun King. A visitor in 1859, C. P. Smyth, was struck by the sight which the tsars had daily before them, and 'especially by night, when the golden tower rears itself like a pale tall spectre in the sky; and marks the position of the humble plot where their predecessors lie below, and where they too must come in their appointed course, and lay them down in their cold and narrow graves.'

The Jordan Staircase
(figure 5, no. 4)

On entering, one first seeks out what is sometimes called the Ambassadors' Staircase (since they climbed it to present their credentials), but more often the Jordan Staircase, because the reigning sovereign descended it on 6 January each year for the ceremony of Blessing the Waters of the river Neva. This commemorated the Baptism of Christ, and was justly described by Mrs Disbrowe (wife of the English Minister Plenipotentiary at the Court of St Petersburg) in 1826 as

a very extraordinary ceremony, and certainly very unseasonable. The whole court in general attends . . . The Emperor must, and all his attendants and priests, without hats, fifteen degrees below freezing point, imaginez, in the open air upon the river. A hole is cut in the ice, and formerly the devout used to plunge into the water and bring their children to be dipped. It has happened that the shivering priests let the unfortunate little creatures slip through their icy fingers under the ice. 'Mais quel bonheur l'enfant alloit tout droit au paradis' was the consoling reflection for the superstitious.

Smyth adds the information that from the same ceremony came the holy water held in every church to be used for baptism and for sprinkling worshippers with a bunch of basil, and that 'vast quantities of the fluid are carried away in bottles to every household, to serve during a whole twelvemonth in curing diseases and driving away evil spirits.'

The Jordan Staircase was restored by Stasov, keeping Rastrelli's plan, measurements and general design, so it remains a triumphant piece of Russian Baroque (**I**). Instead of the original pale pink columns on the upper floor, Stasov used monolithic grey polished granite columns from the quarries of Serdobol, near Lake Ladoga, with gilded bronze capitals and bases. The balusters of the handrails were changed from gilt to marble, to give white a dazzling pre-eminence, combined with gold. The gilded appliqué decorations are in plaster, as are many of the sculptures – though

WINTER PALACE
I The Jordan Staircase, by Rastrelli, restored by Stasov after the fire of 1837
II The boudoir of Maria Aleksandrovna, by Stakenschneider
III The Malachite Room, by Bryullov
IV One of the side wings on Palace Square, with a carriage-ramp entrance. The golden lantern is over the cathedral

some are marble figures taken from the Summer Garden. The original ceiling painting was destroyed in the fire; but another was brought out of the *fonds*, slightly smaller, and enlarged in the same style by Soloviev.

The Malachite Room (**III, 20–22**) is one of several whose rebuilding was entrusted to Stasov's chief colleague, A. P. Bryullov (he also handled the reconstruction of the service areas of the ground floor). Bryullov designed the room within the dimensions of the former hall, by Ricard de Montferrand; and he retained the original placing of columns and fireplaces. Its great interest lies in the decorative quality of the malachite, used for eight columns and eight pilasters – which do not themselves support the weight of the low vaulted ceiling, glittering with stamped and gilded papier-mâché (**20**). Malachite is also the material of the room's most striking ornaments: a large bowl supported by winged figures in gilded bronze (**III**), and great torchères and vases, notably an immense vase on a dark red marble pedestal.

Malachite, so typical of Russia, has a typically Russian history. In the early eighteenth century a certain blacksmith, Demidov, so pleased Peter the Great with his weapons that he was given land near Moscow to establish forges. These in turn succeeded so well that he was granted virgin territories in the Urals. Two generations later the Demidov family began mining operations, and discovered iron, platinum, precious and semi-precious stones, including large deposits of malachite. The Demidovs were so delighted with this stone that they used it to decorate one of their own rooms; and this was the prototype of the Malachite Room in the Winter Palace. Great skill is needed to work malachite, for it is cut in thin plates, mounted on special clay, and arranged to form reversed duplicate designs – each craftsman using his own taste. Most of it was made up at the State Malachite Works at Peterhof. All known veins are now exhausted.

Antonio Vighi painted the murals representing Science and Art. There are two entrancing cabinets made up of incrustations of glass and semi-precious stones from the Urals on a glass base, a technique known as Florentine mosaic (**III, 22**). These little jewels were made in the Stone-cutting Factories at Peterhof, and at Yekaterinburg in the Ural Mountains. The Malachite Room served as drawing room for Aleksandra Feodorovna, wife of Nicholas I. One reads that it was decorated with screens, jardinières, raspberry-coloured upholstery and curtains, 'sharp striking combinations of colours being to the taste of that time'. Today's taste is apt to find the malachite exciting enough in itself.

In contrast, a remarkably simple room, decorated by the architect Meltzer in 1894, is the Small White Dining Room, just large enough for a family dining-table to hold six at the most (**23**). The only colour is in the eighteenth-century tapestries of St Petersburg manufacture. There is an English chandelier of the same period with a concealed musical box: when wound, the whole chandelier revolves and plays a tune. The peaceful amusements of this private dining room of the imperial family were broken at the Revolution. The Kerensky government took over this and the Malachite Room for their meetings; and there, a plaque records, on 25–26 October 1917 (7–8 November by the new calendar) the Red Army and Navy stormed the Winter Palace and arrested 'the Counter-Revolutionary Bourgeois Provisional Government'.

The boudoir (**II**) was restored after the fire by A. P. Bryullov, but by the middle of the nineteenth century it was redecorated by Stakenschneider for Empress Maria Aleksandrovna. He was the architect of the neo-Baroque palace for Prince Beloselsky-Belozersky (**X**), and he adopted the same style for his interiors. Here, the lines of the alcove moulding upheld by caryatid busts, of the carved gilded frames to the wall panels and of the wrought-iron railings echo the exuberance of Rastrelli, a century earlier. The drapery and panelling are of crimson brocade. The floor is of inlaid wood in a bold geometric design.

Every great eighteenth-century palace had its own church, often incorporated into the building. The gilded lantern dome which one sees from Palace Square,

The Malachite Room
(figure 5, no. 1)

Cabinets in the Malachite Room

The Small White Dining Room
(figure 5, no. 2)

The boudoir

SUMMER PALACE
V   The ballroom of Catherine I. On the back wall, beyond the tall stove covered with Delft tiles, is a mirror-stand partly carved by Peter the Great (see plate 7). The portraits are of Peter's sister Natalia (left) and his wife, Catherine I

The cathedral
(figure 5, no. 7)

rising above the roof-top (**IV**), marks the position of what in old engravings is sometimes called the *Grande Chapelle*, but is known in Russia as the cathedral (**26**). After the 1837 fire Stasov rebuilt it, keeping all Rastrelli's measurements and many of his designs. Over the inside of the entrance door is a large initial E topped by a crown with a cross, standing for Empress Elizabeth, for whom Rastrelli did his finest work. The gilded decorations are in carved wood and plaster: some ornaments that resemble marble are actually papier-mâché. Stasov's restoration was completed with great speed, within a year, and is effective, though the religious atmosphere is now deliberately disturbed by the introduction of showcases.

The Military Gallery
(figure 5, no. 6)

The prime purpose of the Military Gallery is to display the portraits of the 332 generals who fought in the war against Napoleon. Originally there were six rooms in this space; but after Russia's victory in 1812, Rossi was commissioned to celebrate it by the creation of this gallery. (For his original design, and the Gallery today, see plates **28, 29**.) As absolute monarchs were also supposed to command the armies in the field, pride of place goes to Krüger's portraits of Alexander I of Russia and Friedrich Wilhelm III of Prussia, and to Krafft's portrait of Franz I, Emperor of Austria. But Prince Mikhail Larionovich Kutuzov, the Russian commander (obstinate as a rock) and the Duke of Wellington get handsome treatment. Curiously enough, an English artist, George Dawe, was invited to Russia to execute this huge assignment. He supervised the work of his collaborators, Polyakov and Golik, and himself painted nearly half the portraits. Most were drawn from life; others, of generals who had died, were painted from existing miniatures or drawings; thirteen blank spaces, bearing only names, represent dead generals of whom no likeness could be found. The Gallery was opened in 1826. Only eleven years later it was destroyed by fire, but the portraits were saved by soldiers of the guards regiments, and Stasov rebuilt the Gallery to Rossi's design, with only minor alterations.

The Small Throne Room
or Petrovsky Hall
(figure 5, no. 5)

Another hall rebuilt after the fire, and badly damaged again in the last war, is Petrovsky Hall, or the Small Throne Room (**27**). Each time it has been reconstructed exactly to the original designs of Montferrand, who also built the final, present version of St Isaac's Cathedral.

Petrovsky Hall was first carried out in 1833. It was intended as a tribute to Peter the Great, and behind the throne hangs a portrait of the youthful Tsar, painted in 1730 (five years after Peter's death) by the Venetian painter Amiconi for the Russian ambassador in London, Prince Antioch Kantemir. The Tsar is accompanied, in the picture, by an encouraging young mythological charmer sometimes described as Minerva, and sometimes as the Spirit of Russia.

The throne itself was made in London by Nicholas Clausen, a refugee silversmith who had fled from France after the revocation of the Edict of Nantes. It is a splendid piece of work, in silver gilt on a wooden frame. The arms end in eagles' heads, and the legs in eagles' claws, clutching balls. The imperial arms are applied in silver gilt at the top of the throne, and are also embroidered on the back. The footstool is of matching design. There is no record of when the throne was ordered or delivered. It stands in a recess below a finely decorated half-dome. The roof of the hall is gold-painted with tiers of double eagles, diminishing in size towards the centre, to give an effect of height. The walls are covered with crimson velvet, heavily embroidered with silver thread, now much tarnished. These hangings were made in France, but the silver torchères and wall brackets were the work of Buch, made in Petersburg in 1791–1802. Two painted wall panels, by Barnaba Medici and Giovanni Scotti, show Peter's great battles of Poltava and Lesnoye.

The Pavilion Hall
(figure 5, no. 10)

One fine piece of rebuilding was not part of the reconstructions after the fire: it took place more than a decade later, in 1850–58. This is the Pavilion Hall (**30, 31**), which like the Military Gallery swallowed up six of the original rooms, including a winter garden. Its German architect, Stakenschneider, is said to have wanted to create a romantic and oriental atmosphere. He took as his theme 'Bakhchisaraysky Fontan', from Pushkin's poem (made into a ballet for the Bolshoi in the 1950s).

Water from four little fountains on the end walls drops from cup to cup, tinkling a tune as it falls. Though these represent 'the fountain of tears', the whole atmosphere is light and gay: white fluted columns, pale pink marble wall panels, white marble stairs to a gallery with a delicate gilded railing, a host of crystal chandeliers hung on pale orange satin sashes. The octagonal mosaic floor is a curiosity. It is a greatly reduced version of a floor found in Rome at the time, during the excavation of some baths (and now in the Vatican): four masters of mosaic work from the Academy of Arts were sent to Italy expressly to copy it.

Coming down to earth, we see what is called Room 159 of the Hermitage (**32**), which now holds one of the best groups of Petrine furnishing to be found. On one wall is an early eighteenth-century tapestry of Peter I on horseback, made in the St Petersburg Tapestry Works, which he himself had set up under the direction of masters from the Gobelins factory. The large oval table, painted with a design using various wood-colours, as if it were inlaid, was made in Archangel, where Peter spent some time. The set of chairs and the brass candlesticks complete the period picture. (In the next room are the famous, somewhat unnerving, life-mask of Peter, taken by Rastrelli *père* in 1719, and the life-size figure made by Rastrelli immediately after Peter's death in 1725, in plaster, wood and wax. The figure is dressed in the unexpectedly pastel-coloured costume Peter wore for the coronation of his wife as Empress Consort, in 1724: pale blue jacket and breeches embroidered in silver, white lace cravat and pale pink silver-embroidered stockings. The hair may well be his own.)

The study of Nicholas I and that of his son Alexander II no longer exist as such, but contemporary drawings have poignancy and human interest. Nicholas' study was drawn by A. Kolb immediately after the Tsar had died there, in 1855 (**33**). This most militaristic, autocratic and unlikable man had the redeeming feature of driving himself as hard as he drove others. A traveller, Bremner, writing in 1839, says, 'The Emperor, who finds time for everything, has actually been at immense pains in drilling the public dancers – having condescended to give instructions himself to the leaders of the female regiment in the *Revolt of the Seraglio*. He is frequently behind the scenes, and always visits the stage between the acts.' Another traveller, Leitch Ritchie, remarked in 1836, 'The Emperor, after coming home, perhaps from the theatre, sits down to work, and never thinks of going to bed until all is finished, if he should sit up till 4 o'clock in the morning.' His couch was the iron truckle bed shown here, in a room as spartan and as charmless as his own character.

The study of Alexander II was also drawn just after the Tsar's death: this time in 1881, by the English artist Edward Gow (**34**). It is the epitome of a late nineteenth-century room, such as might have been found in any upper middle-class home anywhere in Europe. The walls are hung with family portraits, and the desk, tables and even the door are smothered with family photographs drawn with such realism that every subject could be identified with a magnifying glass.

The corner of the billiard room of Nicholas II (**35**), with its intimate group of Neo-classical furniture – sofa, curved-back chairs and marble-topped table supported by winged figures – has the reassuring, human scale of the Small White Dining Room (**23**).

The 'Hermitage' of the late eighteenth century was not only Catherine the Great's art gallery, but her favourite place to entertain the men of letters and the art connoisseurs whose company she particularly enjoyed; such men as Diderot, Baron Grimm, and the Prince de Ligne. Here informality was not only encouraged but enforced. Her famous ten rules, hung up for all her guests to note, were precepts for social revolution, in those days of etiquette, as well as guidelines for civilized society. They go from Rule 1, 'To leave every kind of rank at the door, likewise hats, and, above all, swords', through Rule 4, 'To sit, to stand, to walk about, as each thinks proper, without regard to other people', to Rule 9, 'To eat of the sweet and the savoury, but to drink with moderation, that each may always find his feet on going

Room 159 (figure 5, no. 3)

The study of Nicholas I

The study of Alexander II

The billiard room of Nicholas II

out of the doors', and Rule 10, 'All wrangling to end in the room; and what goes in at one ear should go out at the other before the party goes out of the door.'

Now, one passes from what was the 'Old Hermitage' across an enclosed gallery, where the windows filling the walls on both sides are of thick bevelled plate glass. This gallery bridges the Winter Canal, and leads into the theatre of the Hermitage, built by Quarenghi (**36**). He had made a profound study of Palladio, and was naturally influenced by the Teatro Olimpico at Vicenza; but being a man of excellent judgment he simply took from it principles of proportion and decoration of the walls, using marble columns, niches containing statues of Apollo and the Nine Muses with, above them, medallions of celebrated playwrights and composers. Lo Gatto describes the theatre as 'a wonderful solution of the complex problems of the site, of comfort and elegance' and says that, in this field, Quarenghi already had the experience of a large theatre project at Bassano, which was not executed because it was too costly. He adds that this is the only Russian theatre of the eighteenth century which has come down to us intact today. Quarenghi himself, in the preface to his volume of designs for the theatre, writes that it 'was designed for the private use of Her Majesty and her Court. There is enough space to put on the most magnificent spectacles, and it does not in this respect fall behind the most famous theatres. All the seats are equally well placed, and anyone can sit wherever he pleases.' He took care of the acoustics by placing above the stage and orchestra resonant barrel vaults of pinewood.

The Hermitage Theatre was for the private audience of the court and their friends. Small groups of the best foreign and Russian actors appeared there; and sometimes amateur performances were given, with the casts drawn from imperial and noble families. The irreverent young Englishman who wrote *Letters from the Continent* confirms both the 'magnificent spectacles' and the private atmosphere of the court when he reports in 1790,

On Saturday next there is to be a grand play. It is written by the Empress, and is called *Olga*, it is a tragedy with choruses, like the ancients, with a kind of Greek music: there are no less than *thirty* personages in the play; two emperors, and the rest of proportionate rank; the suite consists of *six hundred* people, who are all to be on the stage at once: it must be a marvellous sight, I think . . . When the play is over . . . the wittiest thing would be to call for the author, as they do in Paris, 'L'auteur, l'auteur!'

At the opposite end of the scale the *Deux Français* report of the Hermitage, 'The Empress often passes whole days there . . . the society is infinitely select; often a comedy is put on for a dozen spectators, or even fewer.' Now the theatre is used for lectures on art.

Life in the Winter Palace reflected the personality and tastes of the ruling sovereign. Elizabeth loved huge receptions and masked balls, and made a speciality of transvestite entertainments. As a young woman, she was a beauty; and the men's dress of the time, with knee breeches and silk stockings, gave her the chance of showing her shapely legs. Everything luxurious and ostentatious attracted her; she was so fond of clothes that fifteen thousand dresses were reported to be hanging in her closets when she died.

Catherine the Great's habits (as Georges Loukomski writes) were a mixture of pomp and simplicity. Usually she went through the dining room to reach the cathedral (**26**), where she took her place near the lantern. But on feast days she made a state entry from the Great Throne Room, or St George's Hall (**24**), preceded by her court. She wore all her orders, and also a small diamond crown. The whole imperial family accompanied her. On solemn occasions she took her meal on her throne in St George's Hall, and was served by the highest ranks of the empire. On ordinary occasions she arrived for her two o'clock dinner followed by one or two small English dogs, which she fed while she herself ate slowly. The conversation was free and gay, and usually in Russian. When Catherine needed to give a great reception, no one could do it better. Archdeacon Coxe writes during her reign,

PETRO PRIMO
CATHARINA SECUNDA
MDCCLXXXII·

1

2

3

4

5

8

9

10

11

13

12

15

14

16

17

18

19

20

21

24

25

29

32

33

34

35

The richness and splendour of the Russian court passes description. It retains many traces of its antient Asiatic pomp, blended with European refinement. An immense retinue of courtiers always preceded and followed the empress; the costliness and glare of their apparel, and a profusion of precious stones, created a splendour, of which the magnificence of other courts can give us only a faint idea . . . Amid the several articles of sumptuousness which distinguish the Russian nobility there is none perhaps more calculated to strike a foreigner than the profusion of diamonds and other precious stones, which sparkle in every part of their dress. In most other European countries these costly ornaments are . . . almost entirely appropriated by the ladies; but in this the men vie with the fair sex in the use of them. Many of the nobility were almost covered with diamonds.

(No wonder that the 'Lombard' was filled with diamonds in pawn: see page 201.)

Yet Catherine far preferred quiet evenings of conversation with a circle of interesting friends; she was assiduous in affairs of state; and her love-life, almost to the time of her death, was an occupation in itself.

Paul I, determined on a style as different as possible from his mother's, introduced discipline even into social life, and lavished his greatest attention on military matters (see page 179). But when palace receptions were considered essential, they were still splendid. In 1796, at the marriage of his second son Konstantin Pavlovich, the whole population was entertained with fireworks on the river, oxen, pigs and poultry roasted in Palace Square, and fountains running with red and white wine.

His successor Alexander I was anxiously preoccupied with the wars against Napoleon. Neither he nor his wife enjoyed entertaining on the grand scale; but tradition determined that every New Year the doors of the Winter Palace should be thrown open, and anyone could enter without ceremony. Loukomski tells us that the whole palace was lit, and that *tableaux vivants* were arranged, reproducing the masterpieces which hung on the walls. 'More than 30,000 people of all classes poured in, without any pushing, in perfect order.' The emperor appeared, and dancing went on through all the state rooms. Even in 1839, Bremner, travelling in Russia, writes that court entertainments surpassed anything to be seen in the rest of the world.

The vast size and splendour of the apartments, lighted by thousands of costly lamps – the ceiling and doors one blaze of gilding – the roofs supported by columns of the rarest materials . . . the walls covered with crystal mirrors that multiply the object a thousand times . . . the richest furniture that artist's skill can provide . . . in short, whatever the most uncontrolled fancy can imagine or the most boundless wealth can command, are here assembled with a profusion that dazzles even the accustomed eye.

The splendour dimmed as the century proceeded. Alexander III was, by nature, careful to the point of parsimony; and he continued to make his home at Anichkov Palace even after his accession to the throne. Nicholas II came to dread his capital, and spent most of his time at Tsarskoye Selo, or in the Crimea.

Now, up to '30,000 people of all classes' – the same number that used to attend imperial receptions, and the greatest number it is normally felt can be safely admitted at one time – pour into the palace to see the Hermitage collection. They still come in 'without any pushing, in perfect order'. The winter holiday season is as busy as the summer. One bitter January the turnstile keepers reported that the agreed maximum had been reached. The doors were closed. An hour later, someone thought to wonder whether anyone might be waiting outside. They looked out, and saw a patient line stretching along the embankment in the snow. Regardless of numbers, the doors were thrown open, the people brought in and thawed out with hot tea . . . It is clear that the profusion offered by the contents of the Winter Palace still dazzles even the accustomed eye.

23 The Small White Dining Room, by Meltzer
24 Design by Quarenghi for the end wall of the Great Throne Room (compare plates 19 and 25)
25 Drawing by Sadovnikov showing St George's Hall (the Great Throne Room), as restored by Stasov and Yefimov after the fire of 1837
26 The palace cathedral, by Rastrelli
27 Throne alcove in the Small Throne Room, or Petrovsky Hall, by Ricard de Montferrand
28 The Military Gallery, by Rossi
29 Design by Rossi for one of the end walls of the Military Gallery
30, 31 The Pavilion Hall, by Stakenschneider. Plate 31 shows the area beyond the columns on the right in plate 30
32 Room 159 of the Hermitage, with furnishings of the time of Peter the Great
33 The study of Nicholas I, drawn after his death in 1855 by A. Kolb
34 The study of Alexander II, drawn after his death in 1881 by Edward Gow
35 Neo-classical furniture in the billiard room of Nicholas II
36 Theatre of the Hermitage, by Quarenghi

II Palaces in Leningrad (continued)

Anichkov Palace

In early views of Petersburg, such as that of Makhayev (**38**), of 1761, the Anichkov Palace stands alone on the bank of the Fontanka, with an almost empty Nevsky Prospekt behind. Indeed, when Elizabeth I bought the land in 1741 it was a country estate. Her intention was to build a palace for her lover Aleksey Razumovsky, a man of remarkable sweetness of character and lack of ambition. He had been discovered by an imperial courier on a wine-buying mission, who heard him singing in the village choir in his native Ukraine and was so impressed that he brought him to Petersburg as a chorister for the Winter Palace chapel. Razumovsky's beautiful voice and handsome looks attracted the attention of the future Empress; and there are good grounds for believing that he became not only her lover but, later, her morganatic husband.

The palace owes its name to its site, in an early settlement where a Colonel Anichkov had been in command. The Empress commissioned the architect M. G. Zemtsov to draw up plans, but he died two years later, in 1744. Though it is possible that Rastrelli was then brought in, frequent alterations and rebuilding after fires have left no trace of this early work. One thing seems certain, and that is that Zemtsov's assistant, G. D. Dmitriev, took over the construction, and probably carried out his master's plans with certain modifications. The palace was built in the rich Baroque style which was then in the ascendancy. Its original form was a three-storeyed centre block with two lower wings ending in three-storeyed pavilions, each decorated with gilded onion domes. The pediments were adorned with gilded statues holding shields which bore the monogram EI under a crown. The main entrance was on the Fontanka, and not, as now, on Nevsky Prospekt. The art historian Uspensky gives a formidable list of leading craftsmen and decorative painters who devoted themselves to the palace, all under the direction of the Building Chancellery.

In 1750 the palace was presented to Razumovsky; but his relationship with the Empress kept him at the Winter Palace, and he used Anichkov mainly for festivities. In 1755, on his name day, he gave a banquet, with the Empress, the Grand Duke Peter and the Grand Duchess Catherine among the guests. Italian music was played during dinner, for Razumovsky had a passionate love of music, and did much to encourage Italian opera in Petersburg.

The French ambassador Merci describes how, after the death of Elizabeth in 1762, Razumovsky left the Winter Palace and settled at Anichkov; and how Peter III loved to spend the evening there. 'After supper,' he says, 'as soon as we rose from the table a large quantity of pipes and tobacco were brought in, and anyone who wanted could smoke. Then the Emperor would start some gambling game in cards and even we – the foreign ministers – were invited to take part.'

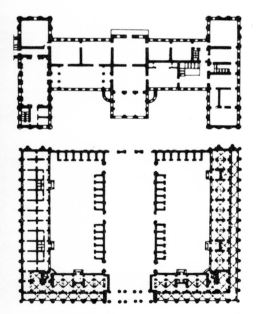

6   Anichkov Palace (top) and Cabinet. Nevsky Prospekt runs along the right, the Fontanka along the bottom. The range along the Fontanka is Quarenghi's original colonnade (figure 7); between it and the palace are the wings added when it became the Cabinet of Alexander I. Facing it, in the centre of the palace façade, is the vestibule

7 Quarenghi's design for the central portico in his colonnade of shops

Razumovsky died in 1771, and the palace remained in the hands of the Treasury until 1776, when Catherine II gave it to Potyomkin. He was chronically in debt, and soon sold it to the merchant Nikita Shemyakin; but Catherine – long-suffering in this respect – bought it back and presented it to him again. It is not thought that he actually lived there; but he gave great celebrations in the garden pavilion which had held Razumovsky's much-prized collection of paintings. Uspensky describes one particular fête in 1779, which foreshadowed Potyomkin's celebration at Tavrichesky, twelve years later (see page 82): the huge gallery was decorated with tropical plants and sweet-smelling flowers, rare works of art, and wonderful lighting and ornaments.

It was during Potyomkin's ownership, in 1778, that the architect I. E. Starov (who built Tavrichesky) changed the appearance of Anichkov by adding a third storey to the wings and replacing the onion domes with classical cupolas. The garden façade, glimpsed from Ostrovsky Square, still preserves Starov's idea. It was a measure of Potyomkin's standing, and effrontery, that having twice been given the palace, he sold it once more in 1785 – to the Treasury, who proceeded to hire it out for private receptions.

In the early nineteenth century a new addition was made to the Anichkov complex. The wide space between the palace and the Fontanka was to be partly occupied by a double colonnade, to contain a series of shops to display the products of the Imperial Factories. These manufactured the porcelain, glassware, bronze-work, tapestries and silks with which the imperial palaces were furnished; but they also accepted private orders. In 1803 Quarenghi was given the commission for this building (40) – partly, perhaps, as consolation for his bitter disappointment at seeing the building of his Exchange on Vasilyevsky Ostrov stopped by Alexander I, when it was nearly completed. (Its columns appear in the foreground of Paterssen's engraving of the Winter Palace from across the Neva, plate 16.)

Quarenghi's design for the colonnade at Anichkov had a balustrade and an impressive row of statues along the roof. Perhaps he had Canova in mind as the sculptor of those figures. At any rate, he wrote to Canova about the building. He describes the decoration of the main palace as 'Corinthian', but says he finds the Ionic order suits his building better, 'being subordinate to the other'; and that, to give character and variety to this order, he employs a Doric entablature. He then quotes examples from antiquity of styles being mixed in this way, and says that no man of talent can follow rules pedantically. He tells Canova that, as Anichkov is in a fashionable part of the city, he has designed arcades for the morning promenades; and he makes the admirable statement, 'I know too well the limits of my talent, to have the presumption

Quarenghi's colonnade, or Cabinet of Alexander I

71

to believe this building to be free of faults, and I regard it as an unvarying principle, that nothing contributes as much to the perfecting of human knowledge as wise and well-reasoned criticism, without hatred and without envy.'

Quarenghi's beautiful shopping colonnade had only been open for four years when two events caused major redevelopments, both there and in the main palace. The latter was handed over to one of Alexander's sisters, Grand Duchess Yekaterina Pavlovna, on her marriage; and the Emperor decided that his 'Cabinet', or administrative offices of state, needed extra space. The architect Luigi Rusca was employed on both schemes. He carried out elaborate and extensive redecorations in the palace. A great part of his work was destroyed by fire in 1812, but one room at least survives: the Colonnade Hall, probably inspired by Starov's at Tavrichesky (53), which he had just been restoring, but naturally on a much smaller scale. He also took down the cupolas from the end pavilions, completely changing the silhouette. Quarenghi's colonnade was now designated as the Cabinet of the Emperor. The shops were removed, and Rusca enlarged the building by adding two wings, jutting out towards the palace. In 1855, in the interest of still more working space for the Chancellery, part of the colonnade was filled in; but in spite of all, the building that throws its reflection in the waters of the Fontanka is still handsome (40).

In 1816 Anichkov underwent more alterations, in preparation for yet another owner. The Grand Duchess had sold the palace back to the crown after her second marriage. It was decided that it should become the home of the heirs to the throne, beginning with Alexander I's brother, Nikolay Pavlovich, since the Emperor was childless. Extensive restorations were needed in any case, after the fire of 1812. Now it was the turn of Carlo Rossi to take a hand. Characteristically, he seized the opportunity to give himself space for a great town planning project. He drastically reduced the size of the garden, building two charming little pavilions in compensation. He made major alterations to many rooms, and was probably responsible for the classical ceilings and friezes that survive. The land which Rossi took from Anichkov formed the site for his Aleksandrinsky (now Pushkin) Theatre, his Public Library, and Ostrovsky Square in which they stand.

In 1817 Grand Duke Nikolay Pavlovich moved in, and he lived in the palace until his accession in 1825. Indeed we are told by Smyth that it was a 'retreat to which he afterwards carried his Empress, in 1837, on the night of the destruction of the Winter Palace by fire'. Alexander II also lived there, as heir to the throne, and the future Alexander III, occupying it as Grand Duke, became so fond of it that he remained there after his accession, only living in the Winter Palace when state functions made it necessary. It was here that he built up the collection intended as the nucleus of a national museum. He wrote excitedly in 1872, 'On 26 February I received from the Tsarevna as a gift two superb large cloisonné vases, and also from the Emperor and Empress two large cloisonné dishes, so that my collection grows little by little.' Old photographs show a fantastic medley of paintings, sculptures, *objets d'art*. The tables and desks are laden with *bibelots*; pictures are propped on chairs and easels. Eventually all this was to be sorted out when his son Nicholas II opened the Russian Museum of Alexander III, in the Mikhaylovsky Palace (page 92).

The entrance vestibule

In 1875 the architect K. Rahau added a projecting vestibule at the courtyard entrance, with a winter garden above it, which effectively spoilt the façade, but which has great charm: it is painted a fresh green with white stucco panels and frieze (39). In 1886 M. E. Mesmacher redecorated a series of rooms which are among those few which have been preserved. Nicholas II, as heir apparent, lived at Anichkov, and after his accession, when he married Princess Alix of Hesse, he took her there as his bride. His mother, the Danish Princess Maria Feodorovna, lived there until the Revolution.

The last phase in the chequered career of this palace came in 1935, when it was made the headquarters of the Leningrad Young Pioneers. The vestibule and staircase, four state drawing rooms, the winter garden and the Colonnade Hall remain decorated and furnished as in the time of the tsars. The Blue Salon (**41**) is decorated in Rossi's style, with classical motifs used for the *grisaille* frieze, the panels over the doors, and the figures which support the mantelpiece. The furniture is also of the period of Alexander I. The same blue and gold silk covers the walls and makes the curtains. The chandelier is of crystal and bronze. The rest of the palace is given over to a wide range of activities – ballet and other forms of dancing, sciences, carpentry, music, languages. In Alexander III's study youngsters (90% boys) play serious chess. Every day hundreds of children run full tilt past pink Venetian glass torchères and Chinese vases standing on the floor; yet nothing is damaged. These latest owners enjoy their palace at least as much as did their imperial predecessors.

The Blue Salon

Yusupov Palace

The Yusupov family possessed four houses in Petersburg during parts of the eighteenth and nineteenth centuries. (Quarenghi built them a beauty on the Fontanka in 1790; but as early as 1810 it became the property of the Institute of Road, and then Railway, Engineers.) The palace shown here is on the Moika, where there were many large country estates in the time of Elizabeth I and Catherine II. The site originally belonged to Count P. I. Shuvalov, and he had built a small two-storeyed house in stone, which was a rarity at that date. During the 1760s Prince Yusupov bought the property and engaged Vallin de la Mothe to enlarge it. This excellent architect had only arrived in Petersburg in 1759, when Count I. I. Shuvalov, President of the newly created Academy of Arts, invited him to take charge of the architectural side of its activities. His masterpiece is the building of the Academy itself, on which he worked with his cousin Jacques François Blondel and the able Russian architect, Kokorinov. He also built the Old Hermitage for Catherine the Great. He was fully occupied as professor of architecture, so Yusupov Palace is one of the few private commissions he executed in Petersburg. Vallin de la Mothe enlarged the original house by bringing forward the centre of the main façade by means of a six-columned portico, which united the two lower storeys, and adding a third, attic storey, above the cornice and entablature.

It was unheard of for a wealthy Russian family of those days to leave a house un-altered for some sixty years; but no major rebuilding is recorded until 1830, when A. A. Mikhaylov II was asked to extend the façade along the bank of the river. This extension contains a large hall supported by white Corinthian columns, and with elaborate sculptural and papier-mâché ornamentation. At the same time Mikhaylov completely redecorated an enfilade of state rooms on the first floor, making Red and Blue Drawing Rooms with fine cupola ceilings by Giovanni Scotti, and a ballroom decked out with artificial marble. Less than thirty years later Ippolito Monighetti was asked to rebuild the staircase (**42**). It is curious that this assignment should have occupied him from 1859–62, and that at just the same time – around 1860 – he had a similar commission, to build the White Vestibule and staircase at Yekaterininsky Palace (**76**). It was an era following the long reign of Neo-classicism, when architects turned nostalgically towards Baroque; and this trend is reflected in both of Monighetti's staircases. At Yusupov, the highly decorated ceiling over the stairs was painted by Toricelli.

In the late nineteenth century a long narrow wing was built from the corner of the palace to run back to the garden, ending in a theatre. R. Lyall, after a tour in 1816, wrote, 'Many of the nobles fit up private theatres, at which their own servants are the actors; so that taylors and shoemakers, and musicians and dancers, body-servants and lackeys, sempstresses and chamber-maids etc. during day, in the evening become kings and queens, lords and ladies.' In wealthy families who cared greatly about their productions, a special troupe of gifted serfs would be trained to entertain their masters; and sometimes the masters and their guests would take the stage themselves.

The name Yusupov is generally associated with a later event – the murder of Rasputin in December 1916, in a basement room of the palace, by Prince Felix

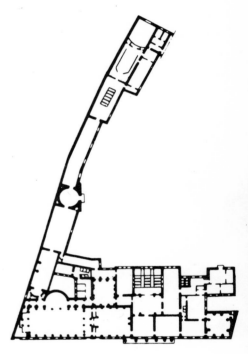

8   Yusupov Palace at first floor level. At the bottom is the façade on the Fontanka; the grand staircase is in the centre of the opposite side; at the end of the long wing is the theatre

Yusupov, Grand Duke Dmitri Pavlovich, a member of the Duma called Purishke-vich, and a doctor. The lurid tale is too well known to need retelling, except to say that Rasputin did not in fact exhibit such superhuman powers of survival as he was credited with by the horrified conspirators, who saw him emerge unharmed after eating a large piece of poisoned cake. The doctor who had prepared it the day before did not realize that a quantity of sugar would largely neutralize the cyanide; and the others were so unnerved by Rasputin's reappearance that their shooting was wild. Still alive, he was dumped through a hole in the ice – not of the Moika but of a small channel called Zhdanovka; and the truly horrific end to the tale was the finding of his frozen body, gripping the supports of a bridge, yards away, under the ice.

In the first years after the Revolution, the palace, with its great art collection, was open to the public; but then the treasures were divided between the Hermitage and the Russian Museum in Leningrad and the museums in Moscow, and the building was handed over to the Union of Workers in Education. Rooms damaged in the last war, by direct hits from bombs and shells, were faithfully restored; so now this House of Teachers is one of the handsomest of the professional clubs in Leningrad.

Marble Palace (Lenin Museum)

Catherine the Great showed an altogether excessive generosity towards her lovers. (The young author of *Letters from the Continent* wrote bitterly about his visit to Petersburg in 1790, where he lost more than he could afford at cards, 'I wish I had the millions the Empress has given away in diamonds, merely since she has been on the throne.') But Grigory Orlov had a special claim on her. Not only was he her lover for a longer period than any other – twelve years – but it was he who, with his younger brothers Aleksey and Feodor, led the coup which put her on the throne; and who – with her tacit consent, if not connivance – quickly despatched her husband Peter III, to whom a faction might have rallied if he had remained alive, in prison (see page 236). She had also borne Orlov a son, Aleksey Bobrinsky, and two daughters.

So, having proved the skills of the Italian architect Antonio Rinaldi at Oranien-baum (see chapter six) she gave him the important commission of building a palace in the heart of Petersburg, for the man who was regarded almost as a consort (though her head ruled her heart sufficiently to deny him that position). Heinrich Storch, writing a *Picture of Petersburg* in 1792, says of Catherine, 'She was indulgent in love, but implacable in politics, as pride was her strongest passion, and as in her the lover was always kept in subjection by the empress.'

The exterior

Rinaldi began the work in 1768. The site is one of the finest in the city: one wing of the palace runs along the Neva quay not far from the Winter Palace, the other along Bolshaya Millionnaya, the Petersburg phrase for 'Millionaires' Row' (**44**). The remarkable feature of the Marble Palace is the materials of which it is built. Both then and later, even the finest palaces were made of brick covered with stucco and painted. But, during that period, quarrying operations in the Urals and in Siberia had revealed a wealth of marble and semi-precious stones, and Catherine was determined that this palace should employ them for the first time in the history of Russian architecture. In the *Voyage des deux Français* (1790–92) it is remarked that the Marble Palace and St Isaac's Cathedral were the only stone buildings in Petersburg. (A small stone palace built by Count Shuvalov had been swallowed up in the 1760s by the new Yusupov Palace: see page 73.)

Rinaldi showed his fine taste by modifying the exuberant Baroque elements which had marked the style of his interior decoration at Oranienbaum (XXV–XXX, 144–162), and treating the rich materials with a strict Neo-classical aesthetic. There is positive severity in the façade of the Marble Palace, the ground floor of which is of granite, while the upper floors are faced with Siberian marble (**44**). Instead of Rastrelli's profusion of columns and curved mouldings, here the surface of the walls is only broken by the flattest of pilasters with Corinthian capitals, simple block mould-ings around the windows, and chaste garlands. Along the edge of the roof, above a solid parapet, is a range of urns. Inside the U-shaped courtyard, the severity is some-what lessened by the use of columns in restrained groups, and by a projecting feature above the main entrance that holds a large clock below garlands and scrolls (**45**).

The exterior simplicity gives way, little by little, in the interior. A drawing by Rinaldi shows a section through the palace, with the entrance at the left (**48**). The entrance hall, bottom left in the drawing, is faced with veined blue-grey marble: it has a series of fine arches, and groups of martial trophies in relief (**46**). These reliefs, and others throughout the palace, are by F. I. Shubin and M. I. Kozlovsky, leading sculptors of the period. The blue-grey marble of the entrance is continued in the balustrade and ornamental framework of the ceremonial staircase (**46**, **48–49**), which leads up to the Great Hall or ballroom (**47**). Here Rinaldi suddenly felt free to use all the wonderful coloured marbles which were being transported to the capital. Pink, green, yellow and grey, with a touch of lapis-lazuli blue, are used with such mastery that there is no sense of garishness. On one side of the hall there are two large reliefs in white marble, on a classical theme, with sprays of laurel below and looped swags with an eagle above. An immense oval painting covers the ceiling.

Going further up the stairs, one finds the walls painted in pale grey-blue with white stucco reliefs and swags, giving a Wedgwood effect which is surprising from an Italian architect (this appears at the top in Rinaldi's drawing, plate **48**). An occa-sional magnificent doorway in dark veined marble can be seen on the landings. Niches which once held statues now contain large vases depicting Lenin in various situations (compare plates **48** and **49**) – for this is now the Lenin Museum.

Although the Neva banks were lined with buildings, there were few private houses on Palace Quay, the very centre of the city; so Prince Orlov and his house-hold will have enjoyed the sight of the multitude of small boats which, Granville tells us in 1828, reminded him of Venice, and which were recorded by Andrew Swinton in his *Travels* of 1792.

In the Summer evenings, when the weather is calm, the citizens of Petersburg delight in sailing upon the Neva in their pleasure boats. The boats of the nobility are very elegantly ornamented. The company are seated in the stern, under a canopy of silk or other stuff, and have with them musicians, or frequently the party themselves perform upon different instru-ments. The rowers are all chosen from among such of their servants as have the best voices, and either sing in concert with the instruments, or without them. When they have rowed their boat against the stream, beating time to their songs with the oars, they allow her to drive with the current, fixing their oars in a horizontal position from the boat's sides; and the rowers collect in a circle. It is at this period that they exert their vocal powers, and make such exquisite harmony, as to draw the inhabitants to the galleries of their houses upon the river's banks, and the foot passengers to the water's edge, to listen to the music; and many follow the boat, to enjoy their native tunes... When the concert is ended, the audience upon the streets goes away, repeating the songs, and echoing them into every quarter of the city ... These concerts often continue to ten and eleven o'clock at night, and when silence reigns upon the face of the waters, it is beyond the power of description to convey any idea of the pleasing effect they have upon the mind.

Those travelling on the river would, in their turn, have looked up at the façade of the Marble Palace and have read the inscription which Catherine wrote to be carved on its wall: 'In grateful friendship'.

In the manner of the day, she presented Orlov not only with the palace, but with the contents – including the great Orlov Service, of more than 2500 pieces, made by the famous French silversmith Jacques Nicolas Roettiers in 1771–75. Catherine bought it back from the heirs on Orlov's death in 1782, when the palace reverted to the crown (pieces are now in the Metropolitan Museum, New York, and elsewhere). When Paul I came to the throne in 1796, he put the palace at the disposal of the de-posed King of Poland, Stanislas Poniatowsky, who had been his mother's lover.

In 1828, Granville wrote that, although it was nominally considered to be the

The entrance hall and staircase

The ballroom

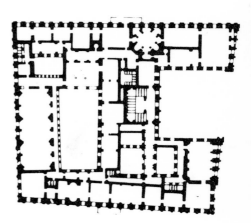

9 The Marble Palace at first floor level. The Neva façade is at the top, that on Bolshaya Millionnaya at the bottom. The staircase is near the inner-most face of the courtyard

palace of the Grand Duke Konstantin Pavlovich, it was not inhabited by any person of distinction. He quotes Storch, who visited it in 1792 and wrote enthusiastically, 'The prodigies of enchantment which we read of in the Tales of the Genii are here called forth into reality, and the temples raised by the luxuriant fancy of our poets may be considered as a picture of the marble palace which Jupiter, when the burden of cares drives him from heaven, might make his delightful abode.' Granville comments dryly, 'Nothing of what remains in the apartments, except indeed some exquisite fresco paintings, reminds me of such Olympian magnificence ... This palace, which was erected for one Imperial favourite, witnessed a few years afterwards, within its splendid chambers, the death of another. They have since remained largely uninhabited.'

A few years later, in 1836, Leitch Ritchie saw the palace in a state of neglect. 'The hall and staircase are entire; the rest of the interior, ruins ... As I ascended, the flapping of wings above my head proclaimed that doves, if not owles, now roosted in the chambers of princes ... I am only surprised that the progress of decay has been so rapid in so short a time.' In fact, 'ruins' was an unduly strong word to use. It is most unlikely that the actual fabric was affected – built, as it was, of exceptionally durable materials. But the decoration of unlived-in and unheated houses quickly deteriorates. As for the doves or 'owles', they seek refuge from the cold in any empty building. Visitors to present-day Leningrad are always distressed at the broken windows which give Rastrelli's marvellous Smolny Cathedral an air of neglect. It has not yet reached the top of the long list for restoration but, time and again, the windows have been reglazed – only to be broken each winter by a suicide squad of pigeons, who hurl themselves against the glass to force an entry.

In any case, in 1859, Professor Smyth noted that the Marble Palace 'is just now being fitted up once again, to serve as the residence of another Grand Duke Constantine, viz. the eminent naval one.' This was a brother of Alexander II. Since shortly before the last war it has been the Lenin Museum.

Chesme Palace and Church

When carriages were the only form of transportation, stages had to be arranged along the roads, not only to change horses but to rest the travellers. The imperial court, en route from palace to palace, occupied stages that were themselves palaces. Such a one was Chesme. It is one of the few that survives and, later in its career, history gave it special significance.

It stands on the original route from the Winter Palace to Tsarskoye Selo and, when it was built between 1774 and 1780, it consisted of a palace, service offices and a church (VI) set in a large park. The architect was Yuri Veldten, director of the school of architecture at the Academy of Arts. He was a man of great versatility, and for this ensemble he indulged in the fantasy of imitating the palaces on the Bosphorus: as Louis Hautecoeur reminds us, in *L'Architecture classique à Saint-Pétersbourg*, the curious mixture of Eastern and 'Gothick' forms known as the Turkish style was fashionable in Western Europe at the time.

The palace (not yet restored) is in the form of an equilateral triangle with a round tower at each corner. Originally these towers supported smaller towers, topped with green domes *à la turque*. In the centre was a spacious round hall with a kind of keep above it. The windows were given a Gothic lancet form, and there were battlements on the walls. A spiral staircase in one of the towers led up to the main hall: this had oval windows in a low cupola, whose inside surface was decorated with moulded plasterwork, and painted with wreaths, garlands and rosettes. The treatment of the walls, panelled with mouldings, was characteristic of early Neo-classicism; and the colour scheme of green, yellow and cherry-red was typical of the time. The hall was decorated with bas relief portraits of tsars and grand dukes by the sculptor F. I. Shubin, removed in 1930 to Oruzheynaya Palata in the Kremlin.

The church (seen from the west in plate VI) was built in 1777–80 on a quatrefoil

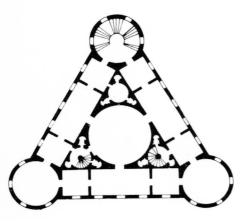

10 Chesme Palace at first floor level

VI CHESME PALACE CHURCH by Veldten

76

plan, with apses at the four points of the compass. Above each apse is a dome crowned with a domed and pinnacled tower, and there is a larger version in the centre, to compose the five domes prescribed by the Orthodox Church.

The site of the palace had a Finnish name, Kekerekeksinen, meaning 'frog marsh', and at first the palace was given a Russian approximation. Catherine II ordered from Wedgwood a dinner service for the palace, with a design of frogs. In 1780, after the naval battle of Chesme, on the coast of Anatolia, in which Aleksey Orlov defeated the Turks, the ensemble was renamed Chesme. Wounded veterans of this battle were buried in the churchyard when they died. In 1836, when the first Russian railway was being built between Petersburg and Tsarskoye Selo, it was decided to enlarge the palace complex as a hospital and almshouse for veterans of the war against Napoleon.

Meanwhile Chesme had had its historic moments. Granville writes of his visit in 1828, when he found in the central rotunda 'full-length portraits of all those Sovereigns . . . who were contemporaries with the conqueror of that great sea-fight, and who despatched these representatives of their persons to testify their approbation of Catherine's measures, and their joy at her success against the Sultan.' (He adds that they were not very good portraits.) He goes on to describe the strange tragedy by which Alexander I, who had accompanied his invalid wife to a resort on the Sea of Azov, died there of a fever, and how his death was soon followed by that of the Empress:

The Imperial apartments, at present, are in a dilapidated state, and entirely stripped of furniture. Silence reigns where the voice of revelry once sounded . . . Tchesmé, which had never received within its decorated halls its late Sovereigns while living, was destined to open its gates to admit them when dead. In September 1825, the Empress Elizabeth passed by this Imperial palace on her way to Taganrog, and was followed soon after by her Imperial consort . . . In less than eight months after, their mortal remains alone revisited this same spot, and found shelter for the night within the palace, but in a reversed order; for those of his Majesty had the fatal precedence on their return home, and were followed by the remains of the Empress two months afterwards.

Now the palace stands abandoned on waste land bordered by faceless apartment blocks. But miraculously, the fanciful 'Gothick' church, with its grooved walls, sharp pointed arches and toothed parapet, is freshly decked out in pink and white like a young girl's birthday cake – making one hope that one day the palace and what is left of the park may be restored, to bring a welcome note of fantasy to an utilitarian scene.

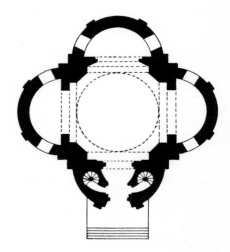

11   Chesme Church. At the bottom is the entrance in the west side, seen in plate VI

Tavrichesky Palace

In the 1770s Rastrelli's Smolny Cathedral and Convent stood among fields which sloped down to the Neva. Kikina Palata (3) was not far away. There were barracks for a regiment of guards, but little else. It was in this district that Catherine the Great chose a large area in which to build a palace for the man who had supplanted Orlov in her affections – another Grigory, Potyomkin. Potyomkin's successes in the Crimea, or Tauris, led to his creation as Prince of Tauris in 1787, an honour reflected in the name of his palace: Tauride or Tavrichesky. The palace was designed by I. E. Starov and built between 1783 and 1789. Starov was one of the first crop of Russian architects to be trained at the Academy of Arts, which had been founded by Elizabeth in 1757, towards the end of her reign, but only became a force under Catherine. Its chancellor during this long and fruitful period was Count Betskoy, illegitimate son of Prince Trubetskoy, from whom he took the last part of the name, as was customary. The director of its school of architecture was Vallin de la Mothe, who had been brought from France by Elizabeth in 1759.

Starov's design shares with Kamennostrovsky Palace (IX) the distinction of being one of the earliest purely Neo-classical buildings in Russia; and like all styles which herald a new epoch, its influence was widely felt. Maria Gibellino Krasceninnicowa,

VII   TAVRICHESKY PALACE by Starov: the centre of the main façade in *Architettura Russa* (1963), writes that even in the most distant Russian provinces villas were built in a similar style, from the closing years of the eighteenth century well into the nineteenth. The palace has a façade which is extremely simple, but in no way severe. The central block, only one storey high, though with two rows of windows, has a portico of six unfluted Doric columns supporting a pediment (**VII**). From this run single-storeyed wings which end in two-storeyed pavilions with Ionic porticoes. The central dome is so flattened that at one time the palace was called 'Pantheon' after its Roman original. Though without a trace of ornamentation, the façade charms by its excellent proportions, by the nicely calculated relationship of the wings to the main building, and by its use of Petersburg's favourite colour scheme, which has a look of spring even in the snow: daffodil-yellow walls, white columns and green roof.

The façade

The young Englishman who wrote *Letters from the Continent* remarked, in November 1790,

> The finest *skeleton* of a house (for there is nothing but bare walls) is Prince Potyomkin's . . . there is no end to the rooms, and they are all immense as himself . . . There is . . . a winter garden so large that there are several walks in it, with a temple in the middle, in which there is a statue of the Empress. . . . Most probably, however, it will never be finished, as he has sent for his gardener and architect, and is building a palace and laying out gardens at Jassy [now in Rumania].

The palace *was* finished and, in its day, evoked long passages of purple prose from all who had the good fortune to visit it; but its great days were few. Potyomkin died in 1791, aged fifty-two, having had barely a year to enjoy his completed palace. Even in his lifetime, those *Deux Français*, who missed nothing on their journey in 1790–92, and whose dry approach is welcome amidst all the adulation, wrote, 'In the absence of the prince this house is almost abandoned; in one room we found a servant lying at full length, with his greasy hair and in his boots, on a white satin sofa.'

The personality of Potyomkin dominated not only the Empress but the epoch. *Letters from the Continent* contain the passage,

> I live in hopes that Prince P will come here before I go away: all those who appear of great consequence now, shrink into nothing, and scarcely dare sit down in his presence, without his permission; he certainly is the most powerful subject in Europe, and one of the most singular of men. When I came here, the Court had not received any news from him, for near six weeks: at last a courier arrived: away flew the news to the Empress and the Privy Council, who waited with violent impatience for an account of some important victory; when, behold! the courier had been despatched to bespeak an *eel-pye* at a famous pastry-cook's, and as soon as it was ready, set out again for the army, with the eel-pye carefully packed up.

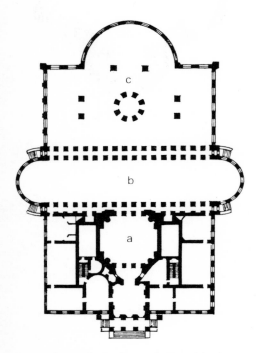

12 Central section of Tavrichesky Palace in its original state, showing the pillars and circular 'temple' in the Winter Garden (*c*) and its connection with the Colonnade Hall (*b*) and Cupola Hall (*a*)

Of Catherine and Potyomkin, Masson writes in *Secret Memoirs of the Court of Petersburg* (1800), 'These two great characters seemed formed for one another; their affection was mutual; and when they ceased to love, they still continued to esteem each other: politics and ambition united them, when Love had dissolved his bonds.' He chose all her subsequent lovers, except the last, the insufferable Platon Zubov, who took advantage of his position to tyrannize her court. Masson describes the Empress in 1796, the last year of her life, 'at her palace of Tauris . . . which she had purchased; and in honour of the celebrated favourite, whom she mourned, she gave his name to this palace where she resided in the spring and autumn.'

On the death of Catherine, her son Paul I immediately revenged himself on almost all the people and even the buildings which his mother had cherished. He quartered a regiment of Horse Guards at Tavrichesky, and turned the Colonnade Hall into stables. His mother's statue, by Shubin, which had queened it in the Winter Garden, was thrown out (it is now in the Russian Museum: see plate 65). He had the furniture carried off to his new Mikhaylovsky Castle, and the many treasures were taken to the Winter Palace and the Hermitage.

After Paul's death in 1801, the Italian architect, Luigi Rusca, was set the task of restoring the palace. During this work he found it necessary to raise the level of the main floors by about two feet, and this upset the architectural balance by diminishing the height of the massive colonnades which were the great feature of the three halls (**52, 53**). Work went on for a number of years, and in 1828 the Empress Mother Maria Feodorovna is reported as living there occasionally. Some of the treasures must have been brought back after Paul's death, when members of the imperial family were using the palace once more, for Sir Robert Ker Porter, in his lively letters to a friend, *Travelling Sketches* (1809), writes of the vestibule, 'where are some of the finest specimens of antiquity which have been preserved'. He goes on to complain, however, that with the antique statues 'are mingled the monstrous associates of modern ill-fashioned cupids, negroes, fantastic heads, and hideous whirligig pedestals of fifty-coloured marbles. . . . My disgust at this sight, can only be compared to your sensations, should a group of asses burst in with their horrid brayings, amidst the soul-entrancing sounds of spheric harmony.'

The final destructive blow fell in the early years of this century when the Duma (Parliament) was set up in an attempt to save the Monarchy by an appearance of constitutional reform. After brief sessions at the Winter Palace, the Duma was accommodated at Tavrichesky, in the vast Winter Garden whose praises had been sung by so many writers. For this purpose, a wall was built where there had previously been an open colonnade. The Duma was short-lived (1905–17) but naturally this huge assembly hall has been kept for use as a conference and exhibition room. The palace has become the High School of the Leningrad Communist Party.

Parts of it remain to give a notion of what it once was. From a vestibule, one passes into the Cupola Hall (**50–52**), a very large octagonal room that rises the full height of the palace under the flattened 'Pantheon' dome. The walls are ornamented with sixteen giant Ionic columns, and there is a high gallery, intended for an organ and orchestra. This gallery can be seen, with three men standing in it, in a drawing by Danilov (**52**) which shows the hall as it originally appeared. In about 1819 Giovanni Scotti, a member of the famous painter-decorator family, altered the interior by adding paintings in grisaille that include a deep frieze of classical subjects, foliage surrounds to the oval stucco medallions in the pendentives of the dome (**50**), and panels in the four corners (**51**). Below the latter there are handsome Neo-classical stoves in cream-coloured ceramic, with a moulded design of Hercules slaying the Hydra. From the dome, painted in *trompe-l'oeil* grisaille to give the effect of coffering, a gigantic chandelier of gilded bronze hangs on sashes of bois-de-rose silk.

The Cupola Hall

The special feature of the interior is that, without benefit of doors, one steps through an open range of columns – visible in the background in the Danilov drawing – into the great Colonnade Hall (**53**); and, as Starov designed it, one crossed the hall, passing through another open range of columns, into the Winter Garden. This was supported by a forest of pillars disguised as palm trees. The Colonnade Hall is now blocked off by the wall of the Assembly Room behind; but it is still a splendid sight, about 124 feet long and 56 feet wide, all in white, with eighteen Ionic columns running the whole length down each side, and a range of many-tiered chandeliers down the centre, each tier ringed with double eagles. A grisaille frieze runs round the ceiling. The ends of the hall are rounded and pierced by two rows of windows. The Russian nineteenth-century statesman and author Derzhavin wrote,

The Colonnade Hall and Winter Garden

With the first step appears a long oval hall, or more exactly an area which could comfortably hold five thousand people. It is divided lengthways by thirty-six columns in two rows, and gives the impression that some gigantic force transferred the whole of nature into this space. Through the columns one beholds a vast garden. Spring reigns everywhere, and art and nature vie with one another in beauty. Everywhere there is great taste and magnificence; and nature and art triumph together.

In looking at it one remembers its finest hour – the famous reception which Potyomkin gave for the Empress in the New Year of 1791. Heinrich Storch, in his

Picture of St. Petersburg (1792), writes,

He found the plan of an entertainment which should afford him an opportunity of testifying his gratitude to the exalted authoress of his prosperity, in his own house, in presence of the assembled court. It was grand and extraordinary, like all his other plans. A whole month elapsed in preparations; artists of all descriptions were constantly employed; whole shops and warehouses were emptied of their goods . . . some hundreds of persons assembled daily to work in preparing the banquet . . . About six in the evening the company assembled in masquerade habits.

Masson, in his *Secret Memoirs*, continues,

The empress entered the vestibule to the sound of lively music, executed by upwards of three hundred performers. Thence she repaired to the principal saloon, whither she was followed by the crowd; and ascended a platform, raised for her in the centre of the saloon, and surrounded by transparent decorations. The company arranged themselves under the colonnade, and in the boxes [at the tops of the columns on the left, in plate 53] and then commenced the second act of this extraordinary spectacle. The grand dukes Alexander and Constantine, at the head of the flower of all the young persons about the court, performed a ballet. The dancers, male and female, were forty-eight in number, all dressed in white, with magnificent scarves, and covered with jewels, estimated to be worth about ten millions of rubles . . . The company then removed to another saloon, adorned with the richest tapestry the Gobelins could produce . . . a magnificent stage appeared at the end of the apartment. On it were performed two ballets of a new kind, and a lively comedy . . . This was followed by . . . an Asiatic procession remarkable for its diversity of dresses, all the people subject to the sceptre of the empress being represented.

Storch resumes the story:

A brilliant illumination now struck the amazed eye wherever it turned. The walls and columns seemed to be all on fire; large mirrors fixed in different parts, or placed as pyramids or grottos, multiplied the effect of this unusual sight, and even the whole park seemed to be strewn with sparkling stones. A table spread in a manner corresponding with the splendour of the festivity now awaited the company. Six hundred persons sat down to it, and the rest were served at the side and among the pillars of the hall. No other vessels or implements were used but of gold or silver.

Every visitor was ravished by the beauty – and warmth – of the Winter Garden, whose walls were painted with trees between the windows, giving an illusion of leading into the park. This was laid out in the English manner which so delighted Catherine, and was designed and supervised by an Englishman, Gould, for whom Starov's assistant, the architect Volkov, built what is still called 'The Gardener's House'. It was Volkov, too, who designed the fine wrought iron railing which divides the palace courtyard from the street (**VII**).

Through the nineteenth century everything was so well maintained that in 1842 J. G. Kohl wrote, 'The hothouses and orangery of the Taurian palace, which are among the most spacious in Petersburg, supply the imperial table. I visited them on 28 February. Thirty rooms of various dimensions were filled with flowers, vegetables and fruit trees. The vines are planted in long rows, and form alleys of luxuriant overhanging foliage . . . There were fifteen thousand pots of strawberry plants.'

There is no trace now of any of this luxury. A modest piece of land surrounds the palace, and the grounds and lake now form a Children's Park.

Kamennostrovsky Palace

VIII. MIKHAYLOVSKY PALACE (RUSSIAN MUSEUM) by Rossi: an end bay in the White Hall

As the Neva flows through Leningrad it branches into a number of streams, large and small, among which are numerous islands. Kamenny Ostrov, or Stone Island, was first the property of Count A. P. Bestuzhev-Ryumin, who was Chancellor to Elizabeth until towards the end of her reign and was later recalled to the same post by Catherine II. In 1765 the island, with Bestuzhev's wooden villa and decorative pavilions in a fine park, was bought by the Empress as a home for the heir to the throne. It was not in her nature to take over other people's property without altering

it to her own tastes; but her son Paul was only eight years old at the time, and it was not until 1776 that a new palace began to take shape.

There are a great many arguments about the architect responsible for Kamennostrovsky Palace, as there are in the case of Mikhaylovsky Castle (see page 87); but in spite of the difference in style between the two buildings there are those who believe that they were both designed by Vasily Bazhenov. Authorities point to the pure Neo-classicism of his Pashkov House in Moscow ('Old' Lenin Library) and of his project for a palace in the Kremlin, never executed. Bazhenov spent some years in Italy and was basically a classicist, though he had the versatility of imagination to enter into Paul I's desire for a 'fortress' when he designed Mikhaylovsky Castle. Curiously enough it seems definite that, just as the Mikhaylovsky Castle project was carried out by another architect (Brenna) so Kamennostrovsky was executed by someone else – this time the tireless Veldten.

The palace is a two-storeyed building in yellow and white stucco, with wings which embrace a courtyard that leads directly to the garden. The courtyard façade has a portico of six Tuscan columns. The opposite façade, on the Little Nevka, a branch of the Neva, has an eight-columned portico (**IX**). This palace was finished in 1781, two years before Tavrichesky (VII, 50–53) was begun, so it represents one of the earliest examples of Neo-classicism in Russia. Its composition is extremely simple and well-proportioned, and the details are very restrained. The architect, whoever he may have been, turned his back on Baroque exuberance and took firm steps along the path of Neo-classicism which led on for over half a century.

During the nineteenth century the interiors were considerably modified, but still some of the original decorations remain. The finest room in the palace is the Oval Hall, which has white stucco bas reliefs on a light blue ground, porcelain stoves, doors with decorative lintels, and caryatids bearing lamps. It has been carefully restored, though the palace is now a sanatorium for the Air Force.

The charming garden was reorganized by Thomas de Thomon, on an informal landscape plan which is still preserved. Possibly the same architect designed the handsome garden gate, an arch with fluted Doric columns.

The palace gate lies down a short cul-de-sac from Kamennostrovsky Prospekt and is not open to the public; but where the main road skirts the garden one can see the attractive little chapel in eighteenth-century 'Gothick' style standing on the roadside.

The *Deux Français*, who visited the palace in 1791/92, were excellent examples of early journalism, for they found their way everywhere, even into grand-ducal bedrooms. They wrote of the palace,

It is extremely pretty, especially on account of the site; one goes up a few steps to the ground floor, and finds first a fairly big antechamber, with arabesques, then a salon of oval shape, whose length makes it look rather narrow; the decoration is very simple. At the right a room with a communicating door into a charming little theatre . . . The bedroom of their Highnesses is very prettily furnished; there is a very beautiful mantel of marble and porphyry: on a table, a marble bust of the Grand Duchess, which is an excellent likeness. . . . The façade on the garden is ornamented with columns . . . at the end of the garden there is a little brick chapel; the gothic style which they have tried to imitate, makes a pretty effect.

After the death of Paul the island became the private property of Alexander I, who often spent part of the summer there. On 8 August 1812, it was the scene of a historic meeting between the Emperor and Prince Kutuzov, at which plans were made for the war against Napoleon, resulting in the French retreat that winter.

One piece of good fortune about the site of Petersburg is that since the Baltic is tideless, the lower reaches of the Neva have none of the rise and fall which leaves ugly mud and debris exposed. *The Englishwoman in Russia* – 'a Lady ten years resident in that country' – wrote in 1855,

St. Petersburg never looks so beautiful as on a summer's night; the buildings are then seen to great advantage. The peculiar twilight of these latitudes casts a softness yet a clearness over

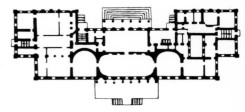

13 Kamennostrovsky Palace. The garden front is at the top, the façade on the Little Nevka at the bottom. The Oval Hall lies just inside the portico on the Nevka side

IX KAMENNOSTROVSKY PALACE by Bazhenov and Veldten: façade on the Little Nevka
X BELOSELSKY-BELOZERSKY PALACE by Stakenschneider: façade on the Fontanka

them, of which those who have not seen it can have no idea; the utter silence of a great city in what seems broad daylight gives a mysterious feeling to the heart, and subdues the thoughts. I was never more struck with the beauty of St. Petersburg than once when, on returning from a party at a late hour, I was crossing the upper bridge of Kamanoi Oustroff: the long line of palaces fading away in the distance, the magnificent quays, the calm river, the unbroken stillness, all produced the effect of a fairy scene, as if they were fabrics of a vision too lovely to be real, erected on the enchanting shores of a lake of liquid silver.

Beloselsky–Belozersky Palace

When one first sees this palace one imagines it to belong to the period of Rastrelli. In fact it dates from just a century later, when Neo-classicism had run its course and there was a swing back to Baroque.

The head of the Beloselsky family in the time of Catherine the Great was Prince Aleksandr Mikhaylovich. When Paul I took the Order of the Knights of St John under his protection he made the Prince its commandant, and in honour of this post he revived the ancient title of the principality of Belozersky.

The Prince's second wife, Princess Anna Grigoryevna, came from the family of Myasnikov who had fabulous fortunes, and her share made the Beloselsky-Belozerskys one of the richest families in Russia. In 1797 she bought from the Narishkins a small house on the corner of Nevsky Prospekt and the Fontanka; and three years later she asked Thomas de Thomon to build her a new palace, making its main façade on Nevsky. De Thomon's design would have been entirely Neo-classical in style, for he was a contemporary of Quarenghi (one can still see his work in the Naval Museum, originally the Exchange, on Vasilyevsky Ostrov). Nothing however remains of this palace, for the Princess's daughter-in-law had other ideas. Her son, Espere Aleksandrovich, married Yelena Pavlovna Bibikova, of another well-known family. He died young, in 1846 (in the same year as his mother) leaving a son, Konstantin Esperevich, who was only three years old. It was in the name of this child that Princess Y. P. Beloselsky-Belozersky commissioned the architect Staken-schneider to enlarge the palace. He added new wings to the courtyard and changed the whole appearance fundamentally. He was an admirer of eighteenth-century Russian Baroque and he remodelled the exterior and interior of the palace on those lines.

In 1884 the palace was sold to the imperial family, and became the home of the Grand Duke Sergey Aleksandrovich, brother of Alexander III. Four years later he partially rebuilt and extensively redecorated it, while preserving the essentials of Stakenschneider's design. The grand staircase has a wrought-iron balustrade with his initials; its walls are finished with pilasters, and with niches in which caryatids support candelabra. (The Grand Duke was made Governor of Moscow by his nephew, and was assassinated in 1905.)

The palace is painted deep red, a colour used in some of the earliest palaces of Petersburg and which glows richly in the waters of the river. It is now the head-quarters of the Communist Party for the Kuibishev district of Leningrad.

Mikhaylovsky Castle (Engineers' Castle)

This remarkable building, with its sinister history, sprang from a chain of circum-stances which might have come from a psychiatrist's case-book. To set the scene one must go back to the birth of Paul in 1754, over forty years before the castle was begun. After nine years of childless marriage between Elizabeth's nephew and designated heir, Grand Duke Peter (later Peter III) and Grand Duchess Catherine (later Catherine the Great), she gave birth to a son, Paul. Elizabeth had insisted that the confinement should take place in her own Summer Palace in Petersburg, a sumptuous building, though of wood, designed by Rastrelli. Immediately the boy was born the Empress carried him away. Catherine's *Memoirs* tell how she lay alone, exhausted after her ordeal, without anyone even to give her a glass of water. She never saw her son, as a child; and when she made her coup seven years later, she refused to be merely a regent on his behalf, but took the throne herself; so it is scarcely surprising that they were permanently estranged. Added to this was the fact that Paul was almost certainly not the son of Peter III (whom Catherine vowed had never consummated their marriage) but of the young man who was perhaps her first lover, Sergey Saltykov.

Paul I, soon after his accession in 1796, seems to have felt compelled to wipe out his birthplace, and, in doing so, to fulfill his desire for a place where he would be safe from all enemies. He was already developing paranoid tendencies. He suspected everyone of treachery, and at the same time maintained a regime of such severity that he was gradually forcing loyal and even affectionate members of his entourage – such as his sons – to fear for their lives, and to look for a way out by taking his. Paul announced that the Archangel Michael had appeared to him in a dream and told him to build a church on the site where he was born. Down came Elizabeth's Summer Palace, and in its stead Paul commissioned a castle, incorporating a church dedicated to St Michael (hence 'Mikhaylovsky' Castle).

There is great, continuing argument about the architect to whom the new building should be attributed, but the balance appears to be in favour of Vasily Bazhenov. Bazhenov is a mysterious and tragic figure. It has been asserted that he could have vied with the most illustrious of the foreign architects working in Russia, but that his talent was misunderstood and thwarted. He was the pupil of Vallin de la Mothe and of Chevakinsky, and he became an assistant to Rastrelli. He was then sent by the Academy of Arts to continue his studies in Paris and Italy, where he was greatly admired. On his return to Russia he was constantly given commissions by Catherine II, only to see them taken away and given to others, or simply never executed. The former was the case with his project for Smolny Institute, later given to Quarenghi; and the latter, with his immense project for a palace in the Kremlin. Even Tsaritsino, a huge palace in the Gothic style near Moscow, was never completed because Catherine lost interest and grudged the money for it. It seems likely that Bazhenov designed the Kamennostrovsky Palace (IX), but even that has been questioned.

Typically, Paul turned to an architect whom his mother had mistreated. There is a letter from him, instructing Bazhenov in his requirements for the castle; and there is little doubt that it was Bazhenov who drew up the remarkably original plan for the building. The difficulty arises from the fact that Bazhenov was already, at sixty, a sick man. He constantly begged to be excused from working on the castle, and certainly the architect who was finally in charge of the construction was Vincenzo Brenna. Undoubtedly, too, Brenna was not content merely to carry out another man's design, but made his own modifications. It has been suggested that what Bazhenov designed was an uncompromising fortress, and that Brenna softened it by extraneous ornamentation.

Mikhaylovsky Castle stands four square, with each façade treated in a completely different way; yet it makes a convincing and impressive whole, and has the unifying features of a heavy cornice running round the entire building, and of the colour, a deep salmon red.

The main façade, to the south (56), has a stone centrepiece framed by paired Ionic columns below a pediment that contains a relief symbolizing the glory of Russia. This central feature is further decorated by tall obelisks, and its military character is stressed by the use of rusticated masonry and carvings of martial trophies on either side of the door. Except for this entrance, the entire building is of stucco on brick. The west façade contains the church of St Michael, which forms a long semicircular projection, ending in a small dome and gilded spire. The north-western view from Marsovo Pole, or Field of Mars (54), shows this spire as one of Leningrad's landmarks and gives a glimpse of the north façade on the Moika, facing the Summer Garden. Its central element has a raised attic storey with reliefs between caryatids, and a portico of paired Tuscan columns. The east façade is on the Fontanka, and is screened by trees. The site was thus protected by rivers on two sides: on the other sides Paul had

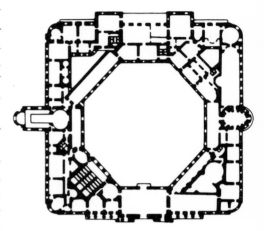

14   Mikhaylovsky Castle at first floor level. The main façade is at the bottom (south); the projection on the left contains the church

The exterior

View from Marsovo Pole

Statue of Peter the Great

canals dug (now filled in) to complete the moat, and drawbridges made, so that the appearance was truly that of a fortress. The rest of the space was laid out as the drilling ground which formed the mainspring of the Emperor's life.

In front of the main entrance stands an equestrian statue of Peter the Great, by the sculptor Carlo Rastrelli. The statue shows the Emperor in Roman armour, wearing a laurel wreath and a majestic but ferocious look, every inch the conqueror (**55**). For some reason it was not erected at the time; and when Catherine planned a statue to the memory of her great predecessor, this seemed unsuitable. She wished to present Peter as a law-giver and reformer, and briefed Falconet to this effect (for his statue, see plate 1). Paul, to whom the military character of Rastrelli's statue would naturally appeal, and who delighted in taking a different course from his mother, placed the statue outside his new castle. He mounted it on a plinth, with bronze reliefs of Peter's greatest battles, and rivalled the brevity of his mother's inscription on Falconet's statue by a two-word Russian inscription which can only be translated clumsily as 'To a great-grandfather from a great-grandson'.

Inside the walls of the castle – closed to the public – is an effective octagonal court-yard. Réau, in *L'Art russe*, says that the castle was constructed in feverish haste from materials snatched from everywhere: incorporated into the frieze there is even a biblical inscription intended for Rinaldi's new Cathedral of St Isaac. Paul pillaged the homes of his mother's lovers for furniture and decorations. One of his more harmless manias was 'to have his cipher of P I surmounted with a crown, affixed in every part of the building; for what reason he never declared, only it was his will: and now over every corner, frieze, door, window or lattice-hole, are these imperial letters multiplied without end. A person once attempted to count them, and left off perfectly weary and in despair, after he had numbered 8000.' So Ker Porter noted in 1805. This cipher appears in plate **56** above the trophies on the obelisks flanking the entrance.

What with the haste of building, and Paul's insistence on the site being made an island, the structure was pervaded by damp. In *Palmyra of the North* (1942) Christopher Marsden says that large iron plates were heated and fastened to the walls to draw out the moisture; but when Paul moved in, in 1800, contemporaries reported that the rooms were thick with fog and the hangings with mould.

By now, the Emperor saw enemies everywhere. He put his two eldest sons under house arrest. He challenged the Governor-General of Petersburg, Count Pahlen, who was in fact the head of the conspiracy; but he was quick enough to tell Paul that he had indeed penetrated a conspiratorial group, and was secretly compiling a dossier. When Paul began demanding details, everyone knew that the time had come. Count Pahlen ordered that men of the Semyonovsky Regiment, adherents of Alexander, should replace Paul's own Gatchina Regiment as guards. One night in March 1801, several conspirators, led by Catherine II's last lover, Platon Zubov, entered the castle, found their way to Paul's bedroom, strangled him with a scarf and beat in his skull with a paperweight. It was given out that he had died of apoplexy, but the truth was widely known.

After this terrible deed, no member of the imperial family wished to set foot in the castle. Alexander I announced that the staff were at liberty to take whatever they pleased; so valuables disappeared by the cartload. Shortly afterwards the castle was handed over to the School of Military Engineers, and became known as Engineers' Castle. It is now occupied by various state organizations.

Let Pushkin have the last word. As a young man he often stayed with the brothers Turgenev in their house at No. 20 on the Fontanka Quay, and there, from their windows, he saw Mikhaylovsky Castle,

> . . . sleeping in the fog enveloped
> Deserted tyrant's monument
> Discarded palace given to the past.

Yelagin Palace

The islands in the Neva, which were described more fully in the section on Kamennostrovsky Palace (pages 82–86), were regarded in the eighteenth and nineteenth centuries as a country retreat. The one we are concerned with now took its name from an early proprietor, I. P. Yelagin, who was marshal of the court to Catherine II. Alexander I bought the island in 1817 with the intention of making a home for the Empress Mother Maria Feodorovna.

This was the first independent commission given to Carlo Rossi, who was to have as great a role as Rastrelli and Quarenghi in giving Petersburg its special architectural character. He was the son of an Italian ballerina who often danced in Petersburg. Italian biographers say his father was Italian, from the Ticino, but Russians think privately, if not officially, that he was the son of the Emperor Paul. At all events he showed early talent. He studied in Russia with Brenna, then went with him to Italy, where he absorbed the spirit of ancient Rome before returning to become the greatest exponent of the style known as Alexandrian classicism, after the Emperor Alexander I. This style owed more to Rome than to Greece, and is thus distinguished from the earlier Russian classicism of the reign of Catherine the Great. Rossi was a great town planner as well as architect, and his principal complexes – the General Staff building facing the Winter Palace (18); the Senate and Synod building looking on to the Falconet statue of Peter the Great; Aleksandrinsky Theatre, Ostrovsky Square and the perfect Theatre Street (now named after him); and Mikhaylovsky Palace (the Russian Museum, 60–65), with what is now called Arts Square, are areas that retain the stamp of Rossi's genius.

When Rossi received the commission for Yelagin he was 'young and handsome, . . . had a foreign name – all great advantages'. The task that faced him was a difficult one, for he was ordered to give a new exterior and interior aspect to a building of the previous century, and to adapt it to the needs and tastes of the Emperor and his mother. He was considered by them and by outside opinion to have carried out his brief brilliantly.

The whole palace is set on a wide stone terrace fenced with cast-iron railings. The principal façade has a central portico of Corinthian columns, reached by a double ramp for carriages, with columned porticoes at the sides. Rossi's favourite Renaissance-type lions, with their paws on a ball, guard the entrance. The garden façade (57) has a deep central bay encircled by columns, and two porticoes at the sides with paired columns, echoing the arrangement at the front. Long flights of steps, punctuated by marble vases, lead down through the gardens to the banks of the Nevka – a branch of the Neva – opposite the Kamenny and Krestovy islands.

For the interior Rossi used a variety of materials with great skill and taste. He chose rare woods for the furniture and inlaid floors, and used natural and also artificial marble in a wide range of colours. He decorated the mahogany doors with gilded bronze ornaments and made much use of mirrors, and of crystal for the chandeliers and light brackets. He began a close and sympathetic association with sculptors and artists who were to work with him at Mikhaylovsky Palace and other buildings. The ceiling and cornice of the vestibule are painted in *grisaille*; there are four female figures in relief, holding bronze candelabra, that were sculpted by S. S. Pimyonov the elder. In the Oval Hall, set round with sixteen Ionic columns and roofed with a decorative cupola, V. I. Demut-Malinovsky and Pimyonov executed sculptures and bas reliefs between the columns. The prettiest room is the Empress Mother's work-room (59), where the background is all in white stucco. The walls are painted with groups of girls in fluttering draperies, by Vighi after Rossi's designs, and there are allegorical subjects along the frieze and on the ceiling. The whole palace is light, pretty and charming.

Altogether nine or ten rooms have their decoration restored but not their furniture, which was dispersed at the time of the Revolution and never reassembled. The only room restored on the first floor is the Cabinet of Alexander I. He was a devoted son, who went to see his mother at Pavlovsk every day when he was at

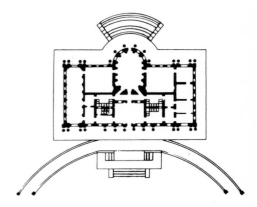

15 Yelagin Palace. The main entrance, approached by ramps, is at the bottom; at the top is the garden front, with its curved centre

The garden façade

The Empress Mother's work-room

Tsarskoye Selo, and no doubt he often visited her at this new palace, which greatly pleased them both. In 1822 A. Bulgakov wrote to his brother, 'Now the Palace of Yelagin belongs to the Empress. The idea of furnishing it with objects made in Russia is a very happy one. It is like an exhibition. The Empress will no longer have to go so far; the journeys to Pavlovsk and Gatchina must, with the years, tire her more and more.'

After her death the tsars used the palace to house distinguished visitors. Now it is a day club for workers, who put their names down and are given a day off to take their wives and families to Yelagin. Exhibitions are mounted in some rooms. The semi-circular room above the Oval Room, which was once a chapel, is used for dances. Rooms which have not been restored are used for chess, table tennis, cards and other amusements. The children go boating on the lake, and all assemble for a meal in the former imperial kitchens, which are now a canteen.

These kitchens are highly original, for they occupy a separate building that is semi-circular in plan (58), set around a courtyard. The entrance is framed by a six-columned portico. The rest of the exterior wall is solid, decorated with statues in niches, as all the windows open inward on to the courtyard. For the layout, Rossi took the most expert advice, including that of Signor Riquetti, *maître d'hôtel* of the court, Signor Belardelli, head confectioner, a coffee-master and the official taster.

Rossi already thought in larger terms than the construction of an individual building. With the collaboration of Joseph Bush, son of the gardener in charge of Tsarskoye Selo, he landscaped the whole island of Yelagin into gardens and park, with lakes fed by streams from the Nevka, a horseshoe-shaped stable building, orangeries and pavilions. On feast days and Sundays, the guards' band in splendid uniforms used to give concerts to a crowd described as being 'from all classes of society'.

From early times the population of Petersburg had the habit of going to Yelagin to watch the sunset. Professor Smyth, about 1860, describes how he drove out of Petersburg until he reached an open beach where carriages were drawn up and

owners were enjoying on foot the pure, balmy air, and the exquisite western scenery . . . Across the mouths of the Neva, you looked right away to the Gulf of Finland, decorated with its many sails, whilst the waters were rich reflections . . . of all the transcendent glory of the twilight sky above them. 'La pointe d'Yelaguine' is this delectable land's end termed; and we needed good Russian horses, and a northern twilight, to bring us back to our houses at a moderate hour.

Now, though the life of Petersburg has changed, the sun continues to sink behind the Gulf of Finland, and people 'from all classes of society' continue to watch it, and afterwards to return rather more quickly to their houses, by a good Russian bus.

The kitchens

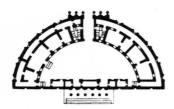

16 The kitchens of Yelagin Palace

Mikhaylovsky Palace (Russian Museum)

After Yelagin, Rossi was offered the unique opportunity of building an entirely new palace for the youngest brother of the Tsar, Grand Duke Mikhail Pavlovich. Lo Gatto (in his excellent section on Italian artists in Russia) says that the idea had been in the air for some time. Paul I and, after him, Alexander I, had put aside a sum of money each year: when, in 1818, it had reached nine million rubles, Rossi was given the order to prepare plans. As at Anichkov (see page 72), he visualized the palace as part of a great piece of town planning, to include the square, of which the palace would occupy one side, and the neighboring streets. Much has been spoilt by demolitions and additions – though these acts are infinitely less frequent in Leningrad than in other cities of the world – but the palace keeps its external splendour and much of its interior decoration.

With A. B. Granville, writing only two years after the completion of the palace in 1825, we can share the privilege of being taken round by the architect. He writes,

Mons. Rossi was so kind as to accompany me . . . and presented me with some original drawings . . . This magnificent structure presents a façade 364 feet in length [61] and consists of a main body . . . and two projecting wings . . . which form a spacious court . . . separated from the street by a lofty railing of cast iron . . . Upon the basement story is placed the state floor, of the Corinthian order, with an octastyle portico . . . of the greatest beauty . . . The wings are of the Doric order.

The garden façade of the palace (**60**) is, if anything, even grander: above a rusticated basement floor, an unbroken range of twelve Corinthian columns forms a loggia between two monumental, pedimented end blocks.

The garden façade

Continuing in the tradition of the eighteenth-century architects, Rossi designed every detail of his buildings: the mural and ceiling paintings, the floors and fireplaces, the chandeliers, wall brackets and every piece of furniture. His White Hall, the principal room of the palace, is preserved in its entirety with its Kozlovsky sculptures, its reliefs by Pimyonov the elder and its murals by Vighi (**VIII**). The carved and gilded furniture, upholstered in pale grey-blue, is a set consisting of four sofas, two double-sofas, forty chairs and six marble-topped tables (**62–64**). Moving inside on his tour, Granville exclaims,

The White Hall

It is impossible to do justice in words to the imposing effect of the grand staircase, around three sides of which extends a wide gallery with handsome columns, supporting the highly ornamental roof, raised to the height of the entire building. Ornamental modern painting has seldom, if at all, been carried out to such perfection as in this case by Scotti, Vighi, and Medici. The ceilings . . . are exquisitely beautiful . . . The floors are inlaid with handsome woods from Carelia, as well as from foreign parts. The walls of the largest rooms are of scagliola, imitating the yellow siena, the porto venere, the verde antico, or the finest polished and white carrara marble. The Great Hall [or White Hall] is that on which Signor Rossi has bestowed all his ingenuity, *estro architettonico* and classical taste. It is an oblong apartment of considerable length, supported at each end by two detached Corinthian columns and an architrave . . . [The ends of the room beyond the columns, **VIII**], covered with beautiful, even, and highly polished scagliola, of a dazzling . . . white, are embellished by groups of figures, four feet high, painted in oil, the production of Vighi.

The scagliola which so impressed Granville resulted from the discovery of a particular sort of white alabaster near Kazan. He recounts how George IV of England asked for a specimen of it, painted in oils – as in the palace – and showed it to his architect John Nash. Granville goes on to say,

Nothing can be more creditable to the mechanical skill and handicraft of the Russians, than the vast and rich assemblage of a variety of objects contained in this palace . . . On the day of its inauguration the late Emperor [Alexander I], standing at the great entrance door, under the portico, received his Imperial brother, and having offered him bread and salt on a golden salver, according to the ancient manner of the Russians, welcomed him to a mansion, which was to be hence forward his own.

Alexander gave his brother more than bread and salt. Mrs Disbrowe wrote in 1825, 'Yesterday we went in a body . . . to see the gold and silver plate, china and glass, given to the Grand Duke Michel, with a new palace by the Emperor; very handsome, but nothing extraordinary, a great many naked ladies as handles and pedestals, the good things in the dishes are to keep them warm, I suppose.' The Grand Duke was the only member of the imperial family of that time who was spoken of as 'literary'. Perhaps he had acquired these tastes from his wife, the Grand Duchess Yelena Pavlovna – a princess of Württemburg – who was intelligent, cultured and an excellent hostess. During their occupancy of the palace they had the nearest thing to a 'salon' which had been seen at Petersburg. Mrs Disbrowe, seeing the imperial family enter Moscow in 1826, described the Grand Duchess as 'a blaze of beauty and health and cheerfulness'.

The palace is now the Russian Museum; but visitors do not always realize that it became a museum a number of years before the Revolution. At the Anichkov Palace Alexander III had amassed an art collection which he always dreamed of housing in a Russian Museum (see page 72). While still heir to the throne he bought the Kokorev collection of Russian paintings. He hoped to buy Tretyakov's collection,

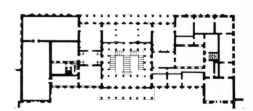

17 Mikhaylovsky Palace at first floor level. The façade on Arts Square is at the bottom, the façade on the park at the top. Just inside the park façade, in the centre, is the White Hall, divided by columns into three sections

91

but was foiled by its owner's intention to found his own museum, as a gift to the city of Moscow. At an 'Exhibition of All the Russias', held in Moscow in 1885, his ideas were strengthened, and he bought ten paintings, saying 'These are for the future Museum'. He searched for a suitable building to house them, and had almost decided to build afresh, when he died. One of the first things his son Nicholas II did after his accession was to make his father's dream a reality. In 1895 the crown bought the Mikhaylovsky Palace, and the Tsar renamed it 'The Russian Museum of the Emperor Alexander III'. Gradually Petersburg's national collections were re-arranged, and the greater part of the ikons, Russian portraits and Russian paintings of the eighteenth and nineteenth centuries were established in the Russian Museum. The room shown in plate **65** contains a display of portraits by Rokotov, and Shubin's statue of Catherine the Great from the Winter Garden of Tavrichesky (see page 80). The setting is second only to that of the Hermitage collection at the Winter Palace.

The Rokotov Room

Stroganov Palace

The Stroganovs were one of the great families of Russia from the fifteenth century right through to the Revolution. They won almost universal respect for their gifts of character and ability, and for their outstandingly cultivated tastes. They held high posts in government administration. They first come into view in the early eighteenth century. Of two brothers from this period one, Sergey Grigoryevich, was a close companion of Yelizaveta Petrovna (later Elizabeth I) and commissioned from Rastrelli the palace whose façade on the Moika is shown in plate **37**. He was a great lover of art, and so particularly required a large picture gallery to house his collection. On his death in 1756 – only three years after Rastrelli had begun the building – the Academic Gazette gave him an epitaph which anyone might envy: 'He was an eye to the blind, a leg to the lame, and a friend to everyone.'

His son, Aleksandr Sergeyevich, continued the building of the palace, which was completed in 1760 and is as fine as anything Rastrelli achieved. Perhaps the refined taste of his clients inspired the architect, who certainly realized that a private house, even of palace proportions, was not the place to shoot off all his decorative ammunition, as he did at the Winter Palace and the Yekaterininsky Palace at Tsarskoye Selo. In any case, the result is perfection. The entrance, on Nevsky Prospekt, is through a plain wide arch, with banded rustication like the rest of the lower floor. The only plaster decorations, apart from the lion and human masks which top each stucco window frame, are a pair of terms supporting the central window. In the broken pediment above is the family crest. There are columns between the windows of the *piano nobile* and a cluster of columns above the entrance.

The palace has a fine corner position, with one façade running along the quay of the Moika. It is painted a deep green, against which the white columns and plaster-work show up handsomely; but when it was painted in Rastrelli's original colours, bright orange and white, it must have been dazzling. In fact Rastrelli made great play with colour, often using not merely one but two – such as turquoise and green – always with white. As it costs no more to paint in one colour than another, it would bring great excitement to the palaces if such colour schemes were used again. Rastrelli himself wrote a description of Stroganov. He was especially pleased with the great hall, which had large winged male figures each side of the mantel, their torsos rising out of scrolls and fronds. He also described a gallery glittering with mirrors, and a grand staircase richly decorated with plaster ornaments.

Aleksandr Sergeyevich Stroganov was honoured by four sovereigns. He was made a count by Elizabeth, when she sent him as ambassador to Vienna. Catherine II made him a senator. Paul I made him President of the Academy of Arts and Director of the Public Library. Alexander I made him a member of the general management of all schools, and of the State Council. He was a patron of writers and artists. He had a large collection of paintings and prints, medals and coins – about sixty thousand items. His library was considered one of the finest in the country.

38

38

39

40

41

44

45

48

49

50

51

53

55

Façade principale du Château St. Michel sur la Grande entrée.

Главной фасадъ Михайловскаго Замка съ большаго Подъъзда

56

57

58

60

62

63

64

66

67

Aleksandr Sergeyevich has another claim to fame. It is generally supposed that he was the father of A. N. Voronikhin, whose mother was a serf on the Stroganov estates. The count took a great interest in his education and, sensing his talent, sent him travelling abroad to study as an architect. With him he sent his legitimate son, Pavel Aleksandrovich, a much younger boy, to be educated in France. Sir Robert Ker Porter, admiring Kazan Cathedral in Petersburg, in 1805, wrote, 'The architect of this great design was formerly a slave of Count Stroganoff. But that nobleman, out of respect for his talents, gave him his liberty. Indeed no generous mind could have done otherwise; it would have been sacrilege to the image of God in man, the richly endowed soul, the creative power of genius! to have trammelled it with the degrading reflections of bondage.'

The almost universal story of destructive fires was repeated at the Stroganov Palace towards the end of the eighteenth century. When the French Revolution broke out both Voronikhin and young Stroganov returned to Russia; so the former was on hand to design the new interiors which the palace needed. The most interesting of these were the Picture Gallery and the Mineral Cabinet. Both these rooms, and Rastrelli's Great Hall, still exist, maintained in their decoration but shorn of their treasures. The Picture Gallery has bays at each end, divided from the central part by an entablature supported by two Ionic columns. A barrel roof covers the central section, and the paintings were effectively shown on the long wall facing the windows.

A. B. Granville noted in 1827, 'The collection of the late venerable Count [Aleksandr Sergeyevich] Stroganoff though less remarkable for the number than for the extreme choice of its pictures and antiques, contains valuable productions of the Italian masters, which even the galleries of the Hermitage cannot boast.' The *Deux Français* remarked,

Count Stroganoff has the only collection of paintings that is really worth mentioning, although not very large, it deserves great attention, and could not be bettered in any country. [He] has had drawings made with great care of a *voyage pittoresque de Russie*; it is not complete; but such as it is, in views, plans and costumes of different peoples, there are already about four hundred plates; it is much to be hoped that, by having them engraved, he will give the public the pleasure of this precious work.

The writers must have been speaking of the Mineral Cabinet which Voronikhin designed for the palace when they wrote,

There are many things to see, such as . . . all sorts of precious stones. In this salon are twelve columns of stucco imitating granite. In the small circular gallery above, pieces of natural history, mined gold, silver, lead, iron, stones, petrified wood, shells etc.; a beautiful piece of Siberian malachite . . . cost 2500 rubles; all is well chosen, and those which are not perfect are put elsewhere, and not exposed to the gaze of the curious.

The Stroganovs owned over twenty-four million acres in the Urals, which included important mining interests, and the count wished to display these, both decoratively and for study. Voronikhin's solution was to divide the height of the room into two parts, with a gallery lit by a cupola in the upper part, and a library and showcases on mining subjects below.

Throughout the nineteenth century, Stroganovs continued to take part in politics, education and the arts. One founded the Petersburg Archeological Society; another gave his enormous library to the new university of Tomsk. The family continued to live at the palace till the Revolution. Now one can walk from Nevsky Prospekt into the courtyard and sit on a bench under the trees – but no further, for it is a government office. Yet there is news of discussion on moving this office elsewhere, and then the palace could be opened to the public as a museum, which would be a wonderful addition to the city's monuments.

18 The Picture Gallery in the Stroganov Palace, by Voronikhin

Sheremetev Palace

Count Boris Petrovich Sheremetev commanded a force which made Russian history by capturing the almost impregnable fortress dominating the junction of the Neva and Lake Ladoga, a fortress which Peter the Great triumphantly renamed Schlüsselburg (Key Town). In 1712 he built a one-storeyed wooden house on the Fontanka. His elder son increased the size of the house but kept it to one storey. His second, much younger son, Count Pyotr Borisovich (1713–88) was a more flamboyant personality. In 1743 he married Princess Varvara, daughter of Prince A. M. Cherkassky and his wife, who was a Trubetskoy. The new Countess Sheremetev had been a maid-of-honour to Empress Anna Ioannovna, and was lady-in-waiting to Elizabeth. She brought a vast fortune to a husband who already owned sixty thousand serfs, had a strong liking for the good life and a great taste for the arts.

Not long after the marriage Count Sheremetev commissioned Savva Chevakinsky to design a new palace, which he called 'Fontanny Dom' after its site on the Fontanka. Chevakinsky was a colleague of Rastrelli, and a very gifted architect. He designed a Baroque palace with white stucco ornamentation on a yellow ground, and the familiar green roof. The central pediment of the portico displays the family emblem: a pair of lions holding palm branches in their mouths. At each side is a pavilion. (This arrangement can just be glimpsed through the railings in plate **69**.) The whole complex makes a charming group on the quayside, opposite Mikhaylovsky Castle.

In the meantime, from one of the serf families on the Cherkassky estate, two interesting young men made their appearance. The elder was Feodor Petrovich Argunov, whose talent had been spotted at the age of eleven, when he had been sent away for training as an architect. The younger was Ivan Petrovich, who was only sixteen when he arrived in Petersburg. Feodor was thought to be sufficiently experienced to superintend the construction of Chevakinsky's plan for the palace. He carried out this work, and also built pavilions in the garden to his own designs – a Grotto, Hermitage and Chinese Summer House, none of which survive.

The interior of the palace consisted of the usual series of halls, drawing rooms, bedrooms and cabinets, which L. V. Antonova tells us were almost continuously redecorated every time the fashion changed. Starov, Quarenghi and Voronikhin are all thought to have worked on the decoration at various times. One great room remains – once the ballroom, all painted white with moulded plaster ceiling, cornice and panels between the windows. A lower cornice projects like a narrow gallery all round the room, and holds a range of close-set candles encircled with crystal drops. Big brackets for holding lustres curve out from the walls, but the light fittings are there no longer. It must have been a splendid sight on a gala evening, when the Count and Countess gave one of their numerous balls, concerts and dinners, at which the Empress Elizabeth was often a guest.

In the meantime the younger Argunov had been sent to study as a painter under Georg Grooth. He learnt conventional portraiture, but soon developed his own style. Instead of flattering his sitters with accepted platitudes, he made masterly character studies. He established his authority as a portraitist, but too much of his time was taken up in buying precious objects for his patron's museum – for Count Sheremetev had been gripped by that fever of competition which ruined so many noble families, but which his fortune could and did sustain, all the way to the Revolution.

Fontanny Dom was altered in 1837 by I. D. Corsini, who installed the impressive high cast-iron railing and gates through which one now sees the palace façade (**69**). In 1867 N. L. Benois added courtyard buildings in the Baroque style of the palace. The interior cannot be restored to its former beauty, or opened to the public, until another home has been found for its present occupants, the Office of Arctic Exploration.

Shuvalov Palace

The Shuvalov family had been prominent in the time of Peter the Great, but their real fortunes dated from the moment when two young officer brothers, Aleksandr and Pyotr Ivanovich, helped Peter's daughter, Yelizaveta Petrovna, to seize the throne in 1741 (see page 121). The younger was the abler and the more unscrupulous. Elizabeth, tireless in amusement, was lazy in matters of state; and Count P. I. Shuvalov obtained a position where no military or economic decision could be taken without him. He built himself a house of stone, a luxury almost unheard of in Petersburg at the time; and he died owing the state one million rubles. Meanwhile a third brother, Ivan Ivanovich, grew up as a remarkably handsome and brilliant man. He became the Empress's lover, a situation accepted in friendly fashion by her previous lover (and almost certainly morganatic husband), Razumovsky. More important, he was a considerable statesman and a wise patron of the arts, of education and science. It was by his initiative that the Academy of Arts was established in 1757. With his friend, the great scientist and inventor, Lomonosov, he founded the first university in Moscow. He was unselfish and unbribable, and refused all honours offered to him. He became the much-loved friend of Catherine the Great, and survived her by one year.

For the origins of this Shuvalov Palace we must turn to another great family, the Narishkins, from whom had come Peter the Great's mother. In 1790 a Countess Vorontsova built a small villa on this pleasant site on the Fontanka. At the beginning of the nineteenth century, L. A. Narishkin acquired the villa and a large piece of ground; and seemingly in 1821–22 he enlarged the villa by building on the Colonnade Hall, a ballroom and a hall for a museum. It has been suggested that Quarenghi worked on the interior of the palace; but he died in 1817 – so that either the Narishkin building operations were earlier than stated, or another architect must have been used. The Colonnade Hall is indeed a fine design, not unworthy of Quarenghi. Its columns are faced with artificial marble and have Corinthian capitals. The whole hall is in tones of white, beige and gold. (Until the Revolution Count Shuvalov held a fancy dress ball there, each year, in the costume of one epoch or another. Photographers were invited to attend, and wore full evening dress.)

The daughter of L. A. Narishkin married Pyotr Pavlovich Shuvalov in about 1844; and her father handed over the house to her on their marriage. The young couple immediately started rebuilding and enlarging it. The present façade (68), with its Renaissance character, was designed by the architect N. E. Yefimov. It has a frieze containing cupids in niches, and is painted an unusual pale grey-green. The principal rooms were designed by the architect Bernard Simon, in the eclectic style of the mid-nineteenth century: each room echoes a different period – Gothic, Renaissance, Baroque, Neo-classical. One feels a traveller in time, passing through them. The staircase hall is unusual, with its intricate arrangement of columns and lintels on the first floor, below a dome rising to the full height of the building (66). The Red Drawing Room has a Renaissance character: red brocade walls and pelmets, white barrel roof touched with gold, and fantastical gilded wood brackets carved with huge bats (67). High on the walls just below the ceiling are the Narishkin arms in moulded plaster.

The Shuvalov family had acquired one of the great Russian art collections; and after the Revolution the palace was opened to the public as an 'exhibition of bourgeois living'. Seventeen rooms were shown, filled with paintings, porcelain, glass and carved ivory. In 1925 all these treasures were handed over to the Hermitage, and the palace was occupied by the Engineering and Technical Workers. During the last war there was extensive damage from incendiary bombs. In 1965 the whole palace was expertly restored and opened as the House of Friendship, and now the members of the many Soviet Friendship Societies entertain their foreign guests there. It is a splendid setting, which will be remembered by many visitors.

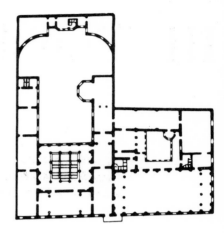

19   Shuvalov Palace at first floor level. The façade on the Fontanka is at the bottom; the grand staircase is in the centre of the left-hand section

The façade

The grand staircase

The Red Drawing Room

III Tsarskoye Selo

TSARSKOYE SELO – 'Imperial Village' – seems an appropriate name for a place which was the home of tsars and empresses over a period of two hundred years. In fact it is a Russian corruption of the original Finnish place-name, Saari Mojs, meaning 'High Place'. Saari became Sarskoye, and the rest followed. 'High Place' is relative, but the land stretching back from the Gulf of Finland is predominantly flat, so that every piece of rolling country brings wide views and a sense of fresher air. The court and the noble families delighted to leave Petersburg in the summer months, just as, today, every Russian who can afford it escapes to his *dacha*.

Tsarskoye Selo (now called Pushkin: the poet was educated there) lies about fifteen miles south of Leningrad. It is a town now. There are two palaces, Yekaterininsky (or Great Catherine Palace) and Aleksandrovsky, in their own parks (figure 21), divided only by a traffic-free road. The first is the older and more famous of the two, and one can see over that large part of its superb interior which has been restored; whereas only the park of Aleksandrovsky can be visited. It is therefore with Yekaterininsky that we are most concerned.

Alexander Benois, in his lavishly illustrated book on Tsarskoye Selo, written in 1902, makes a comparison with the history of Versailles: both started as small country houses, serving mainly as hunting pavilions; then turned into larger houses for summer entertaining; and finally became palaces on the grandest scale, incorporating the whole mechanism of government.

Tsarskoye Selo had its modest beginnings in 1718, when Peter I's wife, Catherine, decided – during one of his frequent absences – to build a small stone house on the site. She employed the German architect Braunstein, who also worked at Peterhof and Kronstadt, and surrounded the house by the Dutch type of garden, with formal parterres, clipped bushes and a canal, which was specially admired at that time. Peter is reported to have been enchanted by it; but all the same his passion for the sea took him more often to his country palaces on the Gulf of Finland – Peterhof and Strelna.

In 1728, the year after her mother Catherine's death, and while her half-brother Peter II occupied the throne, the palace was handed over to Yelizaveta Petrovna (later Empress Elizabeth) who was only nineteen. She had spent very little of her childhood there; but when it was her own she became greatly attached to it, and it is to her that we owe the magnificent exterior which we see today. She gave the Yekaterininsky Palace its name by placing, in the pediment, the monogram of her mother Catherine I 'of eternal and happy memory'. Yelizaveta Petrovna behaved with great caution during the reigns of Peter and of her cousin Anna Ioannovna: she had an excellent claim to the throne, and she knew she was under surveillance.

On the death of Anna Ioannovna in 1740 she was again passed over in favour of

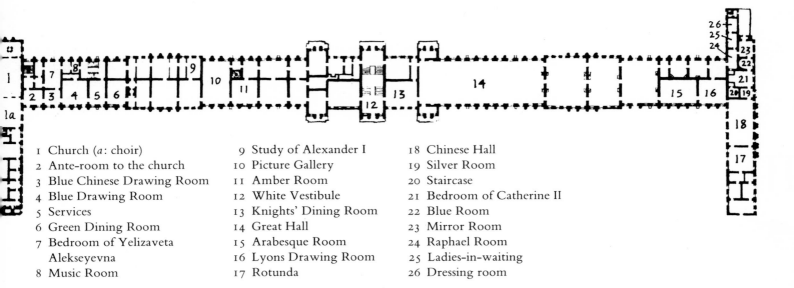

1 Church (a: choir)
2 Ante-room to the church
3 Blue Chinese Drawing Room
4 Blue Drawing Room
5 Services
6 Green Dining Room
7 Bedroom of Yelizaveta
　Alekseyevna
8 Music Room

9 Study of Alexander I
10 Picture Gallery
11 Amber Room
12 White Vestibule
13 Knights' Dining Room
14 Great Hall
15 Arabesque Room
16 Lyons Drawing Room
17 Rotunda

18 Chinese Hall
19 Silver Room
20 Staircase
21 Bedroom of Catherine II
22 Blue Room
23 Mirror Room
24 Raphael Room
25 Ladies-in-waiting
26 Dressing room

the infant son of Anna Leopoldovna and her husband the Duke of Brunswick (she was descended from another branch of the Romanov family: see genealogical table, page 282). The child was to reign as Ivan VI under the regency of his mother. The army – which played as powerful a role in eighteenth-century Russian politics as it has since played in other parts of the world – preferred the younger daughter of Peter the Great and persuaded her to make a bid for the throne. Full of apprehension, Yelizaveta Petrovna agreed to a night coup, which passed off peaceably. The infant tsar was imprisoned with his parents in the fortress of Schlüsselburg, and there he remained until he was murdered by his guards twenty-six years later.

It is understandable that not until she was proclaimed Empress in 1741 did Elizabeth feel able to put into practice the ideas that must long have been in her mind. That same year Zemtsov, who had been associated with many of Petersburg's early buildings, was commissioned to work on a new project; but he died only two years later, and Kvasov, a young, comparatively unknown architect, was called in. A model of his project for the palace (**71**) shows that he was thinking on the Baroque lines which Rastrelli was to perfect later; and indeed it bears a considerable resemblance to the central section of the Great Palace in its final form (**72**). Benois describes the scene in the 1740s: 'The whole building site looked like a camp, with strange people wandering about, soldiers and labourers carrying wood, bricks, iron. Before one part of a building was completed, another was started. It looked a complete chaos . . .' The rôle of Bartolomeo Rastrelli, at this point, was confined to that of interior decorator and designer of pavilions in the park – the Hermitage, Grotto, Monbijou, and Katalnaya Gora, only the first two of which survive.

Chevakinsky was commissioned to build the church, which Elizabeth wished to have incorporated into the palace (**XI**). A great deal of her thought went into this. It is reported that at dinner she pronounced against a recommendation from the various Italian masters assembled, that the *iconostasis* should be of marble, and decided that it should be in the traditional carved and gilded wood. She watched over the painting of the icons; and, having obtained the instructions of the Holy Synod as to their correct placing, she ordered that the best should be placed low down, and the others above, where they would be less noticeable. In the spring of 1749 she chose the interior colour scheme to be deep blue walls with gilded decorations: by the autumn she wanted to change to carmine and silver; but, being told that most of the work was completed, she sensibly agreed to leave it as it was. So it has remained, restored after the fires of 1820 and 1863, and after the destruction of the last war (**75**).

But one rebuilding during her reign was not enough. All the time, Rastrelli was

20　Yekaterininsky Palace at first floor level. North is at the left; the lower edge of the plan is the garden front. The Agate Pavilion and Cameron Gallery lie beyond the projection of the upper right hand corner

Kvasov's model

The church
(figure 20, no. 1)

121

emerging as the architect of genius who was to set his stamp on the era. He was building palaces in Petersburg for Counts Stroganov (37) and Vorontsov; he had built the large wooden Summer Palace for Elizabeth on the site now occupied by Mikhaylovsky Castle (see page 86); he was working on one of the many phases of the Winter Palace (16–18). Elizabeth realized that she would never be satisfied with mere alterations to her palace at Tsarskoye Selo: it must be a complete rebuilding. Architect and patron were ideally suited to one another; and the result, even after all the vicissitudes of the past two hundred years, is triumphant.

The exterior

Rastrelli's ideas, chiming in with those of Elizabeth, were on the grand scale. First of all he raised the height of the whole building – wings as well as central structure – and made one incredible façade a thousand yards long (**72, 74**), ornamented with columns and pilasters and decorative frames around the windows, stretching from a five-domed church at the northern, or Petersburg, end (**XI**) to a single-domed pavilion at the far end, under which rose the main – indeed the only – grand staircase. He therefore forced everyone to experience the stupendous length of the palace on arrival. In a great arc round the courtyard Chevakinsky, in collaboration with Rastrelli, spread a range of charming one-storey buildings to house court officials. The main gate into the vast courtyard (**70, 72**) was made by Cordoni to Rastrelli's design. Through the fine gilded wrought-iron work, surmounted by a double-eagle and crown, one glimpses the palace façade. Two smaller wrought-iron gates, bearing the initial E of the Empress, give access at each side of the yard. All the gateposts are painted in the deep bright blue which Elizabeth herself chose for the palace walls, a beautiful background to the white columns, and unexpected after the yellows, greens and reds of Leningrad and its environs.

The garden façade

The garden façade (**74**) has a central porch ornamented with Neo-classical sculptures. In front of it is a formal garden: from above, one sees arabesque scrolls of low fresh green, enclosing beds coloured deep grey and red. On descending, one discovers that these 'beds' are filled with chippings of anthracite and brick.

In 1755 Elizabeth issued the very practical instruction that any demolition of old structures should take place only in the wet season, so that the new gilding should not get dusty. For above every window of the whole complex Rastrelli had set his characteristic plaster decorations, of masks and heads and fronds in endless variety, which were all gilded with pure gold leaf – as were the massive Atlas figures by the German sculptor Duncker, shouldering their burden, and a range of statues and urns standing along the roof, behind a balustrade. At the end of a drive through the quiet countryside from Petersburg the effect must have been electrifying.

Another result of placing the grand staircase at the extreme end of the façade was that, on climbing the stairs, the visitor was faced with the interior counterpart of the immense façade he had passed in the courtyard: a dramatic progress, unbroken by any turning, through a golden enfilade of huge halls.

The Great Hall
(figure 20, no. 14)

In decoration, as in architecture, Rastrelli and the Empress were in sympathy. He gave her the perfect setting for the receptions, balls and fêtes in which she delighted. His Great Hall, or Gallery, was about 260 feet long, with each of its long walls almost filled with two ranges of windows giving views on to the park and gardens. Between the windows were tall mirrors, framed with elaborate arabesque carving in gilded wood (fragments of Rastrelli's decoration, temporarily re-erected, can be seen in plate **77**). The mirrors were personally ordered by Elizabeth from the gilder Leprince, to be sent 'from overseas'. The three pairs of double doors at each end of the hall were also framed in carving and flanked by mirrors; and above each mirror and door were Rastrelli's favourite pair of stucco figures in white and gold – cherubs, or female shapes in various attitudes – who peopled the great heights of the hall, above the heads of the throng below. Mirrors and gilding glittered in the light of fifty-six chandeliers and innumerable wall-bracket candelabras. All this went in the war, but the restorers have been working on it for several years, and one day it will re-open, to astonish us all.

The scene described by La Meselière on a visit to Petersburg in 1757 in fact took place at the wooden Summer Palace which Rastrelli had built for the Empress in the city; but it could just as well have been a ball at Tsarskoye Selo. He wrote,

Lords and ladies glittering with jewellery and gorgeous apparel filled the rooms . . . The beauty and sumptuousness of the furnishings were astonishing, but they took second place to the delightful impression produced by four hundred ladies, most of them very beautiful and richly dressed . . . This cause for admiration gave way to another: an effect of night falling, through the sudden and simultaneous lowering of the blinds – remedied instantly by the brilliance of 1200 candles, which were reflected on all sides in the pier glasses . . . Double doors were flung open and we saw a dazzling throne, from which the Empress, surrounded by her officers, entered the ballroom . . . which was very large; one could dance twenty minuets at a time . . . The festivities lasted until three in the morning.

In the centre of the Yekaterininsky Palace was a Chinese Room, ornamented with lacquer panels and brackets holding a rare collection of Chinese, Japanese and Saxon porcelain. What remains is simply an exhibition display. Next came the Knights' Dining Room (**78**), which Rastrelli decorated in 1750. The Russian word *Kavalersky* means something which belongs to an order of knighthood. When we reach Pavlovsk we shall see that the Kavalersky Zal, or Hall of the Knights, there was designed for the receptions of the Knights of St John of Malta (see page 178, and plate 112). At Tsarskoye Selo it has a looser interpretation, signifying a dining room where the sovereign would hold special dinner parties, probably devoted, on occasion, to an order of knighthood. Coxe, in 1784, describes Catherine presiding over a gathering of the Knights of St Andrew, instituted by Peter the Great in 1698, and thus the earliest order of the Russian Empire. Curiously – since Russia only adopted Christianity in the tenth century – there was a tradition that the Apostle Andrew had found his way to the Russian borders. Coxe writes,

The Knights' Dining Room (figure 20, no. 13)

Her Majesty had on a robe of green velvet, lined and faced with ermine, and a diamond collar of the order. The dress of the knights was splendid, but exceedingly gaudy and inelegant. They wore a green velvet robe, lined with silver brocade, a coat also of silver brocade, waistcoat and breeches of gold stuff and silk stockings, a hat à la Henry IV ornamented with a plume of feathers, and interspersed with diamonds. As the order of St Andrew is the most honourable order in this country, it is confined to a few persons of the first rank and consequence.

The gilded carving of the Knights' Dining Room is delicately suited to the size of the room, and so are the tiered wall-bracket lights, graduating from five candles to one. The dinner service, in green and brown on white, depicting hunting scenes, was made in the St Petersburg Imperial Porcelain Factory in 1760. The way in which the white cloth hangs to the floor and is draped into knots caught up round the oval table is characteristic of Russian dining rooms of the time. Dutch tiles still hold their own, in the corner stove. The ceiling painting, of Apollo driving his chariot, is by an unknown artist of the early eighteenth century.

The Picture Gallery (**82**) is decorated according to the taste of the period, by literally papering the walls with paintings, divided from one another only by gilded frames. The paintings are good, if minor, works of the seventeenth and early eighteenth centuries – French, German, Italian, Dutch and Flemish; but their individual character is entirely subordinated to their value as decoration. One large battle scene shows Peter the Great at Poltava. A pair of magnificent Dutch-tiled stoves soar from gilded legs to the height of the gilded cornice. Tall mirrors between the windows hold candelabra. The whole ceiling is one huge painting stretched out above an elaborately inlaid wood floor. The four double doors, surmounted by carved decorations, are in white and gold.

The Picture Gallery (figure 20, no. 10)

Nowhere is there a trace of an early bedroom; yet we read that there were a great number – because Elizabeth moved from room to room during the night, seldom sleeping soundly until dawn. In a despatch four years after Elizabeth's completely successful coup, the English minister, Lord Hyndford, wrote that she continued in fear of a plot to overthrow her: 'Elizabeth is a prey to such terror that she rarely stays more than two days in the same place, and few people know where she sleeps.' She seems the last person one would have suspected of night fears; but her own coup had taken place at night, and 'uneasy lies the head . . .'

The Amber Room
(figure 20, no. 11)

The Picture Gallery and the Knights' Dining Room are the only Rastrelli interiors visible at present. Catherine II replaced some, to make the palace more suitable to her needs. The others were destroyed in the war; and their scale and richness makes them daunting subjects for even the intrepid Russian restorers. The most famous of all – the Amber Room – is impossible to restore, since the amber was removed by the German occupying force in 1944 and its whereabouts have never been discovered. The room had come into being through the envious eye of Peter the Great who, on a visit in 1715 to Friedrich Wilhelm I of Prussia, admired in the little palace of Monbijou a room which was panelled with amber, finely carved by a Dresden master to the designs of Schlüter. On such occasions hosts have often felt bound to act with oriental courtesy and present the admired object. So the amber was removed to St Petersburg to be installed in the Winter Palace, and tradition has it that the Kaiser received in return 'fifty-five guardsmen of exceptional stature'. In 1753, at the height of the rebuilding of Tsarskoye Selo, it was decided that something splendid could be done with the amber. A small closely-panelled cabinet had no place in Rastrelli's scheme. He treated his find as a precious material, interspersing its panels with mirrors, and making it the ornament of a large hall. It was Persian amber, of a deep honey tone, and those who saw it before the war say that, as one entered the room, the whole air turned to gold. Now only a few small amber *objets d'art* remind one of this lost glory.

The ceilings of Rastrelli's halls were executed by the finest decorative painters of the day; and of these Valeriani and Tarsia were outstanding. Unfortunately ceilings were especially vulnerable to the fires of peace and war, and little of their work remains. Krasceninnicowa emphasizes the great influence which Valeriani in particular had on the development of Russian decorative painting. He arrived in Petersburg from Italy in 1742 and began almost at once to paint ceilings for the Yekaterininsky Palace, Peterhof and the Winter Palace and also, according to the cultivated eighteenth-century custom, was invited to design the decoration for the popular masked balls at court and for Elizabeth's coronation festivities.

In all this perpetual building and decorating Elizabeth took a close personal interest which was second only to that of her successor, Catherine II. The main difference between them, in this respect, was of taste – the taste not only of two very dissimilar women, but of different epochs. There is nothing so dated as that which has enjoyed great success with the preceding generation; and the very exuberance of Baroque in the hands of Rastrelli – its scale, its drama and splendour – made its span of life shorter than that of more restrained styles.

Already, in Western Europe, the Neo-classical influence was strong, and its simple dignity struck a responsive chord in Catherine. Even so, it took a long time before she decided to act on her desires; and she was practical enough to realize that the outward aspect of the palace, and its enfilade of great halls, were still needed for state occasions and large-scale festivities. One thing she did without delay. The exterior gilding was beginning to look shabby, and was in any case not at all Catherine's style. She ordered that all the gilded plasterwork should be painted bronze colour; and so it is to this day. She also swept the statues and urns off the roof.

The need she felt (and one can scarcely wonder at it) was for some suites of rooms on a more human scale, where she could entertain in the intimate manner which she most enjoyed. Her visits to Tsarskoye Selo were a great joy to her; but only if they could take place in an atmosphere of informality. Her rules for guests at the Hermitage of the Winter Palace, including 'Disputes about prerogative, pride and such like . . . to be left at the door' were a great deal more stringent in the country. It is said that every time a lady rose to her feet on the Empress's arrival or departure she was fined a silver ruble.

It was already 1773, eleven years after her succession, before Catherine began to pursue her dream of building a *'maison antique'* in the park. Unluckily, she was advised by Falconet (then working on the equestrian statue of Peter the Great, I) and by Cochin, the engraver, to approach their compatriot Clérisseau. He, his head filled with his plans of Diocletian's palace at Spalato (and perhaps also with thoughts of the wealth of all the Russias) sent her a design for a gigantic palace at a gigantic price. He misfired badly; Catherine was furious, and all his efforts to mollify her – by sending her unsolicited drawings, for which she refused to pay – only drew down more wrath. (Yet she had reason for gratitude to Clérisseau, in that her most important architect at Tsarskoye Selo, Charles Cameron, had studied under him in Rome; and the great portfolio of drawings that Clérisseau had given her was at her disposal and at that of any of her interior designers.)

By 1778 Catherine's patience was exhausted. She wrote an agitated letter to her friend and art advisor in Paris, Baron Grimm:

At Tsarskoye Selo there is going to be a terrible upheaval in the private apartments. The Empress has no desire to remain any longer in two unworthy rooms; she is going to pull down the main and only staircase at the end of the house; she wants to live in the midst of the three gardens; she wants to enjoy from her windows the same view as from the main balcony. She will have ten rooms, and for their decoration she will ransack her whole library and give her imagination free rein, and the result will be like these two pages: that is to say, quite without commonsense.

Normally her excellent letters are direct and informal, and it was most unlike her to write to an old friend in the third person. Perhaps she had lost her temper with her house, her architects and herself. Exactly a year later, however, she wrote to Grimm on the same subject, but in a very different vein. In it she begs him to write to Reiffenstein, Director of the Russian Academy in Rome, to

find me two good architects, Italian by nationality and clever by profession, whom he will engage for the service of Her Imperial Majesty of all the Russias by contract for so many years, and that he will send them from Rome to Petersburg like a bag of tools. He is not to give them millions, but a decent and sensible salary, and he is to choose decent and sensible men, not types like Falconet – men with their feet on the ground, not in the clouds. He should send them to me or to Baron Friedrichs, or to Count Bruce, or to M. d'Eck, or to M. Bezborodko, or to the devil and his grandmother, just so long as they come; for all my architects have become too old, or too blind, or too slow, or too lazy, or too young, or too idle, or too stuck-up, or too rich, or too heavyweight, or too lightweight . . . in a word, anything you like except what I need.

This request produced one nonentity, Trombara, and one great prize, Giacomo Quarenghi, of whom more, in this section and elsewhere. They arrived only four months later, and in giving Grimm the news, Catherine writes, 'You know that the frenzy of building, here, is more violent than ever, and no earthquake can have destroyed more buildings than we are erecting.' She breaks into German to continue, 'Building is a devilish business; it eats up money, and the more one builds the more one wants to build. It is a sickness like alcoholism, and also a kind of habit.' And then she casually makes the first known mention of the presence in her capital of the man who was to leave his mark on Tsarskoye Selo and Pavlovsk. 'Just now I have secured mister Cameron, Scottish by birth, Jacobite by persuasion, great designer, who has absorbed the designs of antiquity, known for a book on the ancient baths; we are making with him here a terrace garden with baths below and gallery above; this will be something fine, fine . . .' Isobel Rae, in her researches for a recent book on Cameron, discovered that the 'Jacobite by persuasion' and other romantic details of Scottish descent had no foundation in fact: Cameron was a London Scot, who had studied in Rome. Many of the foreign architects imported into Russia by successive rulers had built little in their countries of origin. Many, like Cameron, had built nothing. Their genius blossomed in this new atmosphere, where there was space, money, enthusiasm, and the highly knowledgeable encouragement of patrons, from the imperial family downwards.

Catherine the Great was not only a remarkable ruler but a remarkable patron. Some critics suggest that her motives were more those of self-aggrandizement than of genuine passion for the arts. But posterity benefits,, or suffers, not from motives but from acts; and Catherine's acts were wholly beneficial in this respect. Also, it is difficult to believe that a woman as intensely busy as she could find time personally to seek out architects and artists, to brief them and supervise them, to be acutely aware of what they were doing, and to praise or criticize the results, unless her interest was genuine and profound. Louis Réau in *L'Art russe* writes of Catherine,

She is in the first rank of great builders . . . She liked to say that great buildings spoke of the greatness of a reign no less eloquently than great actions. Did she exercise a personal influence on the architects of her time? She was not an artist and did not pride herself on being one. She said cheerfully to Falconet, when he asked her advice, that she did not even know how to draw. But she had something which was more important than being able to carve, like Peter I and Maria Feodorevna – great good sense, and a natural taste for simplicity. In art, as in politics, she liked to go straight to the point.

It also speaks much for Catherine's relation to her architects that she continually mentions them by name in her letters to Grimm. It is true that much of that correspondence related specifically to art and architects, but the entirely human way in which she writes about them, whether in praise or displeasure, is a very welcome departure from the extraordinary anonymity in which are shrouded the vast building operations of Petersburg's first 150 years. It is rare to read any account which names an architect. It is only the name of the owner which is given, as if he or she had conjured up some new building by an act of will. The rival merits of architects seem never to have been discussed. No one congratulates himself, or is congratulated, on having secured the services of a man of outstanding reputation. Loukomski, in *La Vie et les moeurs en Russie*, states that architects, painters and musicians were not received in society unless they were under court patronage. His actual words are, 'They were put on the same footing as porters, barbers and lacqueys,' and he adds that this explains the success of certain architects to the detriment of others who had no support for their talent. It also explains the in-fighting which went on between them, which was as fierce as it is between commercial interests today.

A patron was a prime necessity for existence to an architect or artist. There were no public authorities, no business corporations, and no general public with adequate means. The *Deux Français* say of the sculptor Shubin, 'It would be impossible for him to live without commissions from the Empress' (Catherine II). They speak of Potyomkin as 'a great patron of the arts', but one who pays as generously as he makes artists wait for their money. Réau even says that theatres and museums were nothing but appendages of the Imperial House. '*L'Etat c'est moi*' could have been said with truth by the Russian tsars. The remarkable thing is that from Peter I through Alexander I (with only a short hiatus under Anna Ioannovna) this autocracy – together with a number of noble families through several generations – showed so much imagination and enthusiasm in the field of the arts.

Catherine was a shrewd operator; a great spender, but determined to get value for money. New talent was carefully tried out – but given its head, once it had proved itself. This was her method with her architects and her gardeners. (Louis Réau compares it to the way in which she tried out possible lovers on her ladies-in-waiting: but this was more comparable to that other royal habit of having a 'taster', to prove that dishes were not poisoned. Catherine's lovers were tested not for prowess but for health; she had a horror of syphilis.) So when Cameron came into her employ she set him to construct and decorate eight rooms on the site of a demolished Rastrelli hall at the northern end of the palace, leading towards the church.

The suite, known as the First Apartment, consists of the Green Dining Room (**XIII**), the Blue Drawing Room (**83**), the Blue Chinese Drawing Room (**XII**), the ante-room to the church (**XVII**), the bedroom (**XIV, 81**), the Music Room, and two service rooms. The last three are very small; and all are on an enjoyable moderate scale. They have been exquisitely restored since the war, and form a most beautiful sequence. (The bedroom is given the name of Yelizaveta Alekseyevna, wife of Catherine's grandson, Alexander I, who occupied this suite in 1815–1825.) For these, Cameron was given no special privileges in obtaining materials for decoration. The many-coloured woods of the inlaid floors were all of Russian origin (Rinaldi was busy exploiting them at Oranienbaum: see chapter six). The Imperial Glass and Porcelain Factories had been established by Peter I and Elizabeth I respectively. The Imperial Silk Factories were producing fabrics comparable with the French. The Imperial Bronze Foundries and the Tula Steel Works – both originally established for the manufacture of firearms – had developed an admirable sideline in decorative household furnishings of all kinds; even, in the case of Tula, of actual furniture. Plate **84** shows a fine group: a pair of chairs in chased and inlaid steel with double, curved bar backs and chased panels under the arms and on the splay feet, and a central table in the same design. This happy state of affairs continued well into the nineteenth century, when the Tula Steel Works conceived the unlucky idea of presenting a grand duke with examples of their furniture as a wedding present – a gift which received the cold response that they would do better to stick to firearms.

There were fine Russian cabinetmakers also. Foreign architects, including Cameron, taught the craft in their workshops. Typically Russian pieces in Karelian birch are shown in plate **85**: the desk, with statuettes and appliqué heads in gilded bronze, was designed by the architect Stasov for the study of Alexander I at Tsarskoye Selo; resting on it is a box made of malachite. Karelian birch gets its unusual mottled markings from the fact that it grows on the tundra, with a permanent bed of ice not far below the surface. Old trees grow thick, but very stunted; and this tortuous growth produces a unique pattern, in a wood which polishes as smooth as satin.

With the Green Dining Room (**XIII**) one comes straight into one of the most famous examples of Cameron's work still in existence. On a background of pale almond green, tall calm white figures look down from the walls, and delicate garlands trail from urns. Small pale pink medallions and bas reliefs are set among them; and pale pink, green and white are the colours of the painted door panels. The marble mantel is white; and so is the extraordinary bureau (**86**), carved from walrus tusks by a Russian master in Archangel, and inset with cameo-like portraits. The stucco wall reliefs were executed by the Russian sculptor I. P. Martos. The magnificent fender, sphinx firedogs and fire-irons were designed by Cameron and made at the Imperial Bronze Foundries. The clock and candelabra on the mantel are French. There are vases in the room from the Imperial Porcelain Factory, and simple white-painted chairs with green upholstery, designed by Cameron.

The Blue Drawing Room (**83**) has the always effective device of using the same flowered silk to cover walls and furniture and to make curtains. Here it is in deep blue on white; and the colour is emphasized by a pair of torchères in deep blue glass, made by the Imperial Glass Factory. The white marble mantels at each side of the room are supported by caryatids sculpted by Rachette. The gilded frieze contains numerous oval medallion paintings. On the walls there are portraits of Peter the Great, by Nikitin; Elizabeth I and Catherine II by unknown artists; Paul I by Roslin; and his wife, Maria Feodorovna. Cameron designed everything in the room except the French candelabra.

The Blue Chinese Drawing Room (**XII**) has walls covered with pale blue silk painted with Chinese scenes. The fireplace is the unrestored original. The small portrait of Elizabeth I as a naked child, by Louis Caravaque, represents the eight-year-old girl as Flora, and in some sense captures the sensuous, luxurious and wholly extrovert character of the woman she was to become. (There is a copy of this

The First Apartment
(figure 20, no. 2–8)

Tula steel furniture

Karelian birch furniture

The Green Dining Room
(figure 20, no. 6)

The Blue Drawing Room
(figure 20, no. 4)

The Blue Chinese Drawing Room
(figure 20, no. 3)

painting in the Divan Room at Peterhof; so Elizabeth was clearly pleased with it.)

The ante-room to the church (**XVII**) is a small room glowing with the splendid yellow silk, woven with peacocks, pheasants and swans, which covers walls, furniture and windows. This was not, as so often, woven since the war, in faithful imitation of some scrap found fluttering in the ruins; it was discovered in the vaults of the Winter Palace – a huge roll of the original silk, ordered at the time of the first decoration of the room, and put away with careful forethought for the redecoration which would one day be needed. The Rococo furniture was designed by Rastrelli.

At this point one can walk ahead to look down, from the choir gallery, at Chevakinsky's church which lies beneath the golden domes (**XI**). One immediately steps into purest Baroque (**75**), with springing angels, a great sunburst of cherubs, columns twined with leaves and berries, all in gold against royal blue. The contrast with Cameron could not be more dramatic . . . And then back again to Cameron; for, without descending yet into the church, one can walk back, and into the bedroom of Yelizaveta Alekseyevna (**XIV, 81**). Here Catherine the Great would have slept, until Cameron built the Fifth Apartment. It is an exquisite room, supported on fifty slender shafts of faience, in pistachio green and white, with twisted ribs, springing from stylized leaves on bronze bases. The sculptor was Martos. Cameron designed the whole room: the delicately painted doors; the painted Wedgwood-type medallions (real Wedgwood was used in his later rooms); the decorative fender of Tula metalwork (**81**); and the floor inlaid with a geometric and stylized flower design, using a variety of woods. The lantern with crystal drops is a typical work of the Imperial Glass Factory.

A corner of a Cameron room not yet fully restored is shown in plate **79**. This is the Lyons Drawing Room, so called from its original hangings of French silk. The table of semi-precious stones, with lapis lazuli top, was made by the Peterhof Stonecutting Works. The white and gold vase standing on it, supported by the Three Graces, came from the Imperial Porcelain Factory. The French chairs, with gilded frames, are covered in pale blue silk (more chairs from this set can be seen in plate **XIV**). Other chairs which Cameron designed for the Lyons Drawing Room suggest that the reaction to reptiles must have been different from our own (**80**): serpents were a favourite theme in furniture, and here two make their sinuous curves over the chair backs, while lizards crawl down the arms. The silk upholstery design of appleblossom and fruit is delicious by any standards. Some day the wall panels by Carlo Scotti, Cameron's chief decorative painter (and father of the talented and prolific Giovanni Scotti), will be repainted from his original drawings, and the room will once more look as it did when it took shape as part of the Fourth Apartment, in the 1780s. The other rooms in this group (there were no Second or Third Apartments) were the Arabesque Room, the Rotunda and the Chinese Hall.

Sadly, no idea can be given for the date at which one might hope to see a full restoration of the Cameron apartments. Judging by pre-war photographs and descriptions, the Fifth Apartment in particular – the Empress's private rooms – showed Cameron's powers at their height. These rooms must have been miracles of richness, refined by taste. Special features were the use of milky glass wall panelling, overlaid with delicate bronze motifs; of Wedgwood medallions, made for the purpose; of subtle muted colours; of violet glass columns, echoing those of the bedroom already seen (**XIV**). Only one thing is certain. When they are restored, we shall see them not as they had become after a century and a half of various occupants, of fires, rebuilding and neglect, but as nearly as possible as they were when Catherine wrote to Grimm in 1781, 'these apartments will be superlatively good. So far only two rooms are finished, and people rush to see them because they have never seen anything like them before. I admit that I have not grown tired of looking at them for the last nine weeks; they are pleasing to the eye.'

The state rooms and private apartments we have visited are on the first floor. The staircase by which we ascended was not Rastrelli's, which Catherine destroyed, nor

was it Cameron's smaller one, which disappeared in the war, along with his Fourth Apartment which was grouped round it: it was a much more recent staircase, which is yet extremely handsome (**76**). It was designed by Monighetti in 1860, when there was a revival of interest in Baroque, so that very suitably it draws its inspiration from Rastrelli. It is called the White Vestibule, and white it is – the walls, the carved wall-brackets, and the great carved doors, with the initials MA above them, for Maria Aleksandrovna, wife of Alexander II. The only colour is in the geranium-red curtains, and the collection of Chinese and Japanese porcelain for which the brackets were designed. There are three brackets at each side of the stairs: in the centre of each is a large plate; at each side, a vase; and above, three more vases. Lower down are a barometer and a clock, in lavish surrounds, facing each other. Their numerals and letters are painted in deep blue on white and gold plaques, set against a deep blue background.

Catherine the Great had wished for a *'maison antique'* and a 'terrace garden with baths below and gallery above'. She had to wait for these until her three sets of apartments in the Great Palace were finished; but, in 1784, Cameron moved at last into something that was to be entirely his own. The site had long been chosen at the far end of the palace, behind the south-east corner; Catherine would thus be able to step out from her favourite suite, the Fifth Apartment, on to a hanging garden which leads both to the Agate Pavilion and to the Cameron Gallery – called, in its early days, the Colonnade. You see this hanging garden in plate **87**. Across a wide gap, at the left, is the garden façade of the Yekaterininsky Palace; in the centre is the Agate Pavilion; and at the far right is the first column of the Cameron Gallery.

The Empress had always had in mind the idea of using Cameron's profound study of Roman baths to create a bath-complex at Tsarskoye Selo. The Russians shared with the Finns a habit of bathing which was unknown in the rest of Europe at that time. The Agate Pavilion (**87**) is often referred to as the Thermae, or as the Cold Baths – though it contained hot baths, too. The entrance from the hanging garden to the first floor of the Agate Pavilion is flanked with red-painted niches holding bronze sculptures, and there is a low green Pantheon-dome over the Ionic rotunda. Inside is an astonishing group of rooms in which Cameron used all the riches which Russia could produce. Not only is there a wide range of colours in marble, but also in jasper, agate and porphyry; and against these shades of green, red, golden brown and grey he set the blue of lapis lazuli, the emerald of malachite and the white of alabaster. The Great Hall (**88**) and the Jasper Hall use these semi-precious stones for whole columns with bronze Corinthian capitals; medallions and bas reliefs decorate the walls; marble figures flank the fireplaces, holding huge candelabra; and the ceilings are rich with painted stucco mouldings in plaited geometrical frames. Rachette and Martos were the sculptors here. The design of the floors resembles that of rooms in the palace – but where they are inlaid in wood, these are in vari-coloured stone. From this suite of rooms a staircase with steps of red agate and a balustrade of bronze led down to the ground floor, to dressing rooms and swimming pool (the cold bath), and then through a warm to a hot bath, rest and massage.

The other side of the hanging garden leads into the Cameron Gallery (**89–91**); and here Catherine found endless delight in the changing views – which she wanted Hubert Robert to come and paint. The upper floor of the Gallery has a walk on each side very like the deck of a ship (**91**): the centre section is glassed in to form a room in which the Empress could sit in bad weather, and where she often chose to hold large dinners; and this in turn shelters the open colonnade from side winds. The only decoration here is the austerely beautiful line of bronze busts – casts from the antique – of fifty-three philosophers and statesmen, plus Charles James Fox, whom Catherine honoured because he had spoken out in the English Parliament against war with Russia.

The lie of the land is the key to the whole arrangement (figure 22): at this point the ground dips sharply down to a lake below, so that the Gallery, jutting out from this slope, has a ground floor deepening throughout its length. Finally, even the ground floor finishes so high that the whole end of the Gallery is one great double staircase, leading down into a wide steep flight of steps, a few yards above the lake (**90**). On the side walls of the steps stand bronze casts of the Hercules and Flora Farnese. The Gallery is such a supremely successful architectural achievement that it is no wonder that it almost immediately won the honour, unique in Russia at the time, of being named after the man who designed it.

The last contribution that Cameron was able to make to the comfort of his patron is what we would prosaically call a ramp, but is generally referred to as the *Pente Douce* (which in Russian becomes 'pandus'). When Catherine became stout and rheumatic, the dramatic descent from the staircase of the Cameron Gallery was too much for her, and the climb back even worse. Yet she wanted to walk in the garden and by the lake and to return, unfatigued, to her first-floor apartment. Cameron's first project for the ramp, which leads from the hanging garden to the ground, had a pair of sphinxes at the foot and classical statues on pedestals all the way up. But commonsense – whether his or Catherine's – prevailed, and the *Pente Douce* is a simple sloping roadway, ornamented only with effective stands for flowers. Its rising arches are beautifully integrated with the ground floor of the Gallery, for which Cameron had used heavy blocks of rusticated, almost volcanic stone, such as he had seen in Roman baths (**89**). Each keystone is made impressive by a large mask in relief.

So now we have reached the lake – a considerable stretch of water, and a focus for several of the pavilions and monuments with which the park is strewn (figure 21). An eighteenth-century plan of the park, by the gardener John Bush, illustrates several of these follies (**73**). Catherine pokes fun at herself, writing to Voltaire in the 1770s: 'If this war [against the Turks] continues, my garden at Tsarskoye Selo will look like a skittle alley; for at each brilliant stroke I get some monument erected.' Already her predecessor, Elizabeth, had got Rastrelli to build several pavilions, including the

Grotto on the shore of the lake (**92**), and the Hermitage (figure 23), in the gardens. One monument Catherine refers to is the Rostral Column in the middle of the lake, celebrating the naval battle of Chesme. (The best-known rostral columns are in the centre of Leningrad, outside the former Exchange; they are an echo of the Roman practice of sawing up an enemy's ships after a naval victory, and embedding the prows in a victory column.) At the far end of the lake is the Palladian

Bridge (**93**) copied from the one at Wilton by V. I. Neyelov and his son, who were sent to England by Catherine II, to study architecture. Built in 1769–70, it is sometimes called the Siberian Bridge, being in grey Siberian marble on a red granite base, and it bridges a small bay where a stream runs in, in low waterfalls. A little further is

the Turkish Bath (**XV**), complete with marble baths and basins. It was built in the middle of the nineteenth century by Monighetti, and is the prettiest folly, in pink and white and yellow, with its mosque-like minaret, and arabesque moulding on the flattened dome.

Everywhere there are streams, pools and woods of mainly deciduous trees, which turn to glorious colour in the brief autumn. On one of these streams, quite near the roadway which is the only border between the two parks of Yekaterininsky and Aleksandrovsky, is the Creaking Pavilion (**XVI**), built by I. V. Neyelov, the son,

between 1778 and 1786. Apparently one of the practical jokes, so much enjoyed in the eighteenth century, was to design it with deliberately creaking floors. It is a charming piece of *chinoiserie*. Having arrived there, one has only to reach the road to be in the midst of a Chinese complex. Carried high on an arch that spans the road

is the Bolshoy Kapriz (**96**). This was built by V. I. Neyelov, with the help of an architect-engineer called Gérard. It was copied from a Chinese print showing an arch at Fukien, topped by a similar summerhouse. The only difference is in scale: the Chinese arch was so large that ships could pass under it.

A short way into Aleksandrovsky Park, we come to the remains of the Chinese

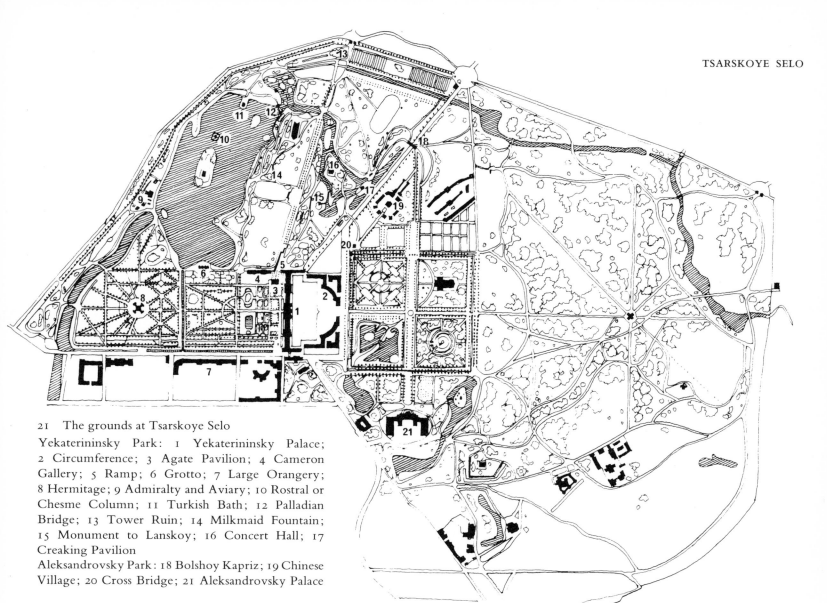

21 The grounds at Tsarskoye Selo

Yekaterininsky Park: 1 Yekaterininsky Palace; 2 Circumference; 3 Agate Pavilion; 4 Cameron Gallery; 5 Ramp; 6 Grotto; 7 Large Orangery; 8 Hermitage; 9 Admiralty and Aviary; 10 Rostral or Chesme Column; 11 Turkish Bath; 12 Palladian Bridge; 13 Tower Ruin; 14 Milkmaid Fountain; 15 Monument to Lanskoy; 16 Concert Hall; 17 Creaking Pavilion

Aleksandrovsky Park: 18 Bolshoy Kapriz; 19 Chinese Village; 20 Cross Bridge; 21 Aleksandrovsky Palace

22 The Cameron Gallery and ramp from across the lake (after Vorobiev). In the background to the left is Yekaterininsky Palace; to the right, the Agate Pavilion

Village (plate **95** shows Quarenghi's gouache of the scene). Looking at the present-day dilapidated cottages, with their television aerials, it is hard to go back two hundred years to the time when this project was first planned. Europe had developed a passion for things Chinese; and as there were few direct connections with China, apart from a limited trade, architects and designers studied Chinese art, and then let their imaginations roam. Chinese villages had already been built in Sweden at Drottningholm, and in Germany near Kassel; but the one at Tsarskoye Selo was of course to be the biggest and best. It is thought that the Neyelovs were the architects, inspired by Sir William Chambers and two English brothers called V. and D. Half-penny, whose popular book published in 1776, *Village Architecture in Chinese Style*, provided the design for the charming little Cross Bridge over the nearby Cross Canal. Chambers had actually visited China, had subsequently published *Designs of Chinese Buildings*, and had built the ten-storey pagoda in Kew Gardens. There were plans, never realized, for a similar eight-storey pagoda in the Chinese Village. When Charles Cameron arrived in 1779 the designs for the village were made, but he was entrusted with the actual building. It must have been an extremely pretty toy, with its dragons on the roofs, its Chinese motifs, and no doubt bright paint and gilding. Until the Revolution, members of the court lived there when the Emperor moved to Tsarskoye Selo for the summer. Now it is crumbling, and it is doubtful whether it will ever be restored.

And so we come full circle in the gardens, to the Aleksandrovsky Palace (**94**) except that one can only glimpse a flash of yellow and white in the distance, and not even walk up the drive. This is all the sadder as it is probably Quarenghi's master-piece (indeed, Lo Gatto calls it the finest, architecturally, of all the palaces in and around Leningrad); and though many splendid buildings by Quarenghi are to be seen in the city (such as the Smolny Institute and Assignation Bank), no other ex-ample of his domestic work – apart from the rather special case of the Hermitage Theatre in the Winter Palace (36) – survives.

Catherine II commissioned the palace for her eldest and favourite grandson, the future Alexander I, and presented it to him on the occasion of his marriage. Her expressed view that it would be a very handsome and pleasant place to live in was a considerable understatement. The palace is chastely Neo-classical, inspired by Palladio (as was Quarenghi's English Palace at Peterhof, totally destroyed in the last war), with no exterior ornamentation whatever – except for a fine double row of Corinthian columns across the courtyard, joining a pair of pavilions which are separated from the central block. It relies, with complete success, on the nobility of its proportions. Quarenghi also designed all the interior decoration. Lo Gatto found the palace 'splendid yet simple; luminous and airy; elegant and majestic'.

Grabar comments that though Rastrelli founded a whole school of architects and Quarenghi did not, his influence was no less important. He left instead 'a gigantic heritage which, even if in a fragmentary way, entered into the blood of the best builders of the succeeding epoch. This one sees with great clarity and strength in the art of Rossi, the last great European architect.' One can only hope that one day another home will be found for the organization which now occupies the Aleks-androvsky Palace, so that the town of Pushkin will again have two great and wonderfully contrasting palaces for our pleasure.

* * *

Tsarskoye Selo gave endless delight to the succession of empresses who lived there from the time Catherine I built her small Dutch house. Elizabeth, in addition to her revels, had the country taste for sweet-smelling grass, which she ordered to be strewn in her bedroom, and she loved birds: every palace had its aviary, in those days.

71

72

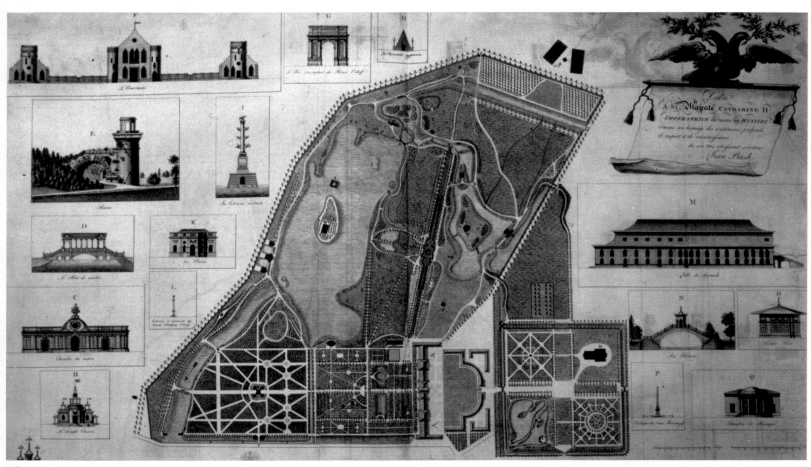

73

75

77

78

79

80

84

85

86

87

88

92

93

94

95

Catherine II felt it to be her happy domain. It was here that she was able to carry out her views on gardens – which were as different from those of her predecessors as were her views on architecture. In 1772 she wrote to Voltaire, 'I love to distraction gardens in the English style, the curving lines, the gentle slopes, ponds like lakes, archipelagos on dry land, and I hold in contempt straight lines and twin alleys. I hate fountains which torture the water and force it into a course contrary to its nature; statues are consigned to the galleries, halls etc. In a word anglomania rules my plantomania.' In Tsarskoye Selo her gardens were designed and supervised by John Bush from Hackney (whose daughter was to marry Charles Cameron).

One of the most fascinating accounts of life in the reign of Catherine the Great is to be found in the unpublished diary of Elizabeth Dimsdale. She was the wife of a Dr Dimsdale whom Catherine had made a Baron in 1768, after he had inoculated her against smallpox. The Empress invited him to come with his wife, in 1781, to inoculate her grandsons, and Elizabeth Dimsdale jotted down her impressions with vivid simplicity. Here she is at Tsarskoye Selo.

Mr Bush from England visited me and asked me to dine with him. We had rooms under the regal apartments, the best in the Palace except for the Empress's and Grand Duke's. Madam Naryshkina presented me to the Empress. I kissed her hand and she my cheek. Fine looking woman, not tall, fine expression, blue eyes and a sweet sensible look, a handsome person in her fifty-fourth year. The Duke is a little man, not handsome, the Duchess was gracious, they asked me to play cards, I declined. She is taller than I am, handsome, about 22 years. The two princes Alexander Pavlovich . . . aged 4 years. Constantine Pavlovich . . . aged 3 years. They are beautiful and sensible and clever. Empress allows 30,000 rubles a year for their clothes. We went for a walk with them in the garden, two Englishwomen who have charge of them are sisters. Mrs Guslar and Mrs Nichols, both civil. Empress ordered them to call [the princes] by their christian names only, as pride would come fast enough without encouraging it . . . Empress is very fond of them and cannot refuse them anything, nothing pleases them like soldiers and exercising. Each of them would have a regiment, twenty-four boys, two in turn to guard their apartments. Prince Alexander knows all the uniforms of the Empress's services, as much as the officers . . . [Elsewhere there was a Hermitage (figure 23) and in it] a sopha, I and the Princes and the English women sat on it, we were immediately drawn into an apartment. A room with large bow windows each made a room, a table in the middle which would dine 10 people and 4 small tables round it, and 4 dumb waiter plates with silver rims and something of the slate kind in the middle of them and a pensil fixed to each plate, you wrote on the plate what was ordered, then pulled another string and the plate sunk down and returned again with the order, dishes the same. The Empress neglects it, occasionally she dines if a foreigner is with her. Empress Elizabeth liked dining here.

This privacy from servants was the peculiar charm of all the Hermitages. The idea was taken from France. One finds it at Peterhof (131), and a table was arranged to come up through the floor even in one of the Hermitage buildings of the Winter Palace.

Catherine was at her nicest as a grandmother, and when her daughter-in-law gave birth to two sons in quick succession, Catherine monopolized them from an early age. Her own son Paul had been taken from her at birth by his great-aunt Elizabeth; and to take away Paul's sons in turn was a compulsive act of self-compensation. She writes like any fond grandmother, 'If only you could see how Alexander digs the earth, plants beans, cabbages, cuts with a scythe, works with the plough, sweating hard, then runs to the stream, then takes the net and with Constantine catches fish. He separates pike from perch because pike eat other fish, says Alexander . . . He takes a book with the same pleasure as he jumps into the boat.' One of her pages, Baschilov, wrote that on the walks in the park there were games of a military sort: two armies, one commanded by Alexander and one by Constantine. 'The armies were composed of grand duchesses, and ladies-in-waiting were the amazons. The Empress admired her grandchildren and rejoiced in the fact that she was Lord of half the universe. Often she admired the grand duchesses dancing Russian dances, *en sarafane* [national costume] to two violins.'

The Hermitage
(figure 21, no. 8)

Catherine loved walking with her greyhounds – the *doyen* of whom she called Sir Tom Anderson – whose mausoleum was another addition to the park monuments. She played ball, went on swings, and took a boat on the lake. She writes, 'The young people make me play and romp – or perhaps, if you like, it is I who make them . . .' Elizabeth Dimsdale describes the Katalnaya Gora built by Rastrelli but long ago destroyed. It was the precursor of the Katalnaya Gorka at Oranienbaum (XXXI, 140). She throws light on the mention of Catherine's pleasure in going on swings by saying that on top of the 'mountain' for sledges, 'two very high swings are placed and chaise to hold one person and two or three wooden horses so constructed anyone can ride round the mount, wheels underneath are worked by a horse with great swiftness.' Many travellers have commented on the Russian passion for swift motion, and clearly their 'ice hills', 'Russian mountains' and swings were designed for just this end.

But Catherine's pleasures were not all of such rustic innocence. In 1782 she had a young lover, Lanskoy, whom she adored. While he was only in his mid-twenties (and she was fifty-four) she made him a general, and strove to please him in every way. She wrote to the long-suffering Grimm saying that if he (the 'general') could have an enamel miniature of her 'he will leap like a buck, and the colour in his cheeks, which is always so beautiful, will grow brighter still, and his eyes, which shine like a pair of torches, will throw off sparks.' Two years later the young man died suddenly of a fever, aged twenty-seven, and Catherine went into a decline. Her alarmed staff quickly sent for Potyomkin – who, from the day when their own affair changed to friendship, chose all her lovers except the last insufferable young upstart, Platon Zubov. He found a successor. Catherine was not promiscuous: her lovers followed one another in an orderly sequence, as a kind of court appointment.

Indoors, there were games of cards and chess and billiards. When Catherine gave a big dinner, it would be in the Great Hall. Her one blind spot in the arts was for music. She writes to Grimm, 'I die of desire to listen to and love music; but however hard I try, it is noise and that is all . . . The only sounds I recognize are those of my nine dogs who, in turn, have the honour of entering my room; each one of whom, even from far off, I can recognize by his voice.' Yet one of the halls was made into a theatre, as a birthday present to her, and operas were performed as well as plays.

The men of the imperial family were less happy at Tsarskoye Selo. The only account of a visit by Catherine's husband, Peter III, during his brief reign, in 1762, speaks of his order to heat the rooms where there were stoves, and otherwise to cover the ceilings with felt, and heat by soaking the felt in wine and vodka. Intellect was not his strong point (if he had a strong point) and one can only imagine that he reasoned that liquor, which warmed human beings, would also warm rooms. The Grand Duke Paul detested Tsarskoye Selo, as he would have detested any of his mother's houses. He stayed at Pavlovsk, nearby, and later at Gatchina, further away. On one occasion only he stayed in the Yekaterininsky Palace, for two weeks – and all the time conducted military exercises: he thought that was what courtyards were made for.

Alexander I, however, had a great affection for the place where he had spent so much time as a child. This is an account of his routine, written in *Les Trésors d'Art en Russie* (a short-lived but highly informative art magazine) in 1904.

At 6 a.m. he took tea, and after dressing went into the park where the gardener, Liamine, waited – also swans, ducks and geese who, seeing him in the distance, gave loud cries. The Emperor fed them, gave his orders to the gardener, and continued his walk. At 10 a.m. he got back, and sometimes ate fruit . . . About that time Liamine brought fruit picked in the orangeries, and the Emperor sent it to those of the Court who were staying in the Chinese Village. Then he changed his clothes, and received his ministers and the Chief of the General Staff. At 3 p.m. he went to Pavlovsk to see his mother. At 4 p.m. he dined; and after tea at 9 p.m. he worked in his study. At 11 p.m. he took curds or plums, and went to bed, when he fell into a profound sleep.

Nicholas I ran Tsarskoye Selo with military efficiency. Kohl, writing in 1842, observed:

The gardens at Zarskoye Selo are certainly the most carefully kept in the world; the trees and flowers are watched and inspected with the most anxious minuteness. An old invalid soldier commands his five or six hundred men as gardeners and overseers. After every falling leaf runs a veteran to pick it up ... Every tiny leaf that falls in pond or canal, is carefully fished out; they dust and trim and polish the trees and paths in the gardens, as they do the looking-glasses and furniture of the saloons, every stone that is kicked aside is laid strait again, and every blade of grass kept in a proper position.

Finally, Aleksandrovsky Palace was the favourite home of the last of the Romanovs, Nicholas II. He and his family spent many summers there; they lived there altogether after his abdication in 1917, and it was from there that they set out to Siberia, on their voyage of no return.

23   The Hermitage, by Rastrelli. Like the Hermitage at Peterhof (plate 132) it was moated. Beyond it, in Makhayev's engraving, is the east front of Yekaterininsky Palace

IV Pavlovsk

To MOST visitors, and to most Russians, Pavlovsk is their favourite among the palaces. It is indeed the most privileged. In the first place, a very high proportion of its treasures escaped war damage. Apart from the sculptures, buried in the ground, some six thousand pieces were carried away to safety. Then, many of the rooms being small, and some relatively simple, it was felt that a given expenditure could produce more restoration than in palaces with large or elaborate rooms. So, at this date, Pavlovsk has risen from the ashes more completely than either Yekaterininsky or Peterhof.

Pavlovsk was built for Grand Duke Paul, the son of Catherine the Great. After his first wife had died, bearing a stillborn child, he had married Princess Sophia of Württemberg. All brides of members of the imperial family had to be of Russian Orthodox faith: if necessary, they were re-christened, and just as another Princess Sophia had become Catherine (the Great), Paul's wife took the name Maria Feodorovna. In 1777 their first child was born – the future Alexander I. Catherine was overjoyed; and to mark her satisfaction at the birth of her first grandson she presented his parents with an estate of about 1500 acres, some $3\frac{1}{2}$ miles south-east of Tsarskoye Selo. At that date the rolling country was thickly covered with forest, through which flowed the river Slavyanka. There were only rough track roads, the entire population of the two villages on the estate was 117, and the only buildings in the woods were two hunters' cottages called Krik and Krak. The new owners made Krik their dacha, and it became known as 'Their Highnesses' Cottage'.

Almost at once, building operations started which were at first modest. It was decided to build two wooden houses, one called Paullust (Paul's Joy) the other Marienthal (Maria's Valley). Catherine, who had just begun to employ the Scottish architect, Charles Cameron, and who greatly admired him, offered his services to her son and daughter-in-law, and Cameron began his association with Pavlovsk by building both these houses. It is said that Maria Feodorevna herself chose the site for Paullust: that it was an excellent choice is proved by the fact that, when the ambitious plans for Pavlovsk were made, the palace was built only a matter of yards from the original house. Cameron even preserved something of his original conception: the first 'maison de plaisance' had a lightly colonnaded dome much like that of Pavlovsk (**XVIII**).

During the first four years the Grand Duke and Duchess were only nominal owners: all their orders had to have Catherine's approval. She paid for the building of Paullust and Marienthal, but – in marked contrast to her lavish generosity to her lovers – she kept her son and daughter-in-law on a very tight rein. They wrote a humble letter of appeal to which she replied acidly, 'Dear children, You can of

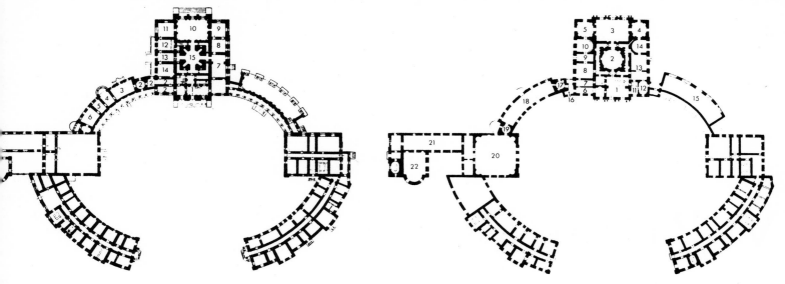

course imagine how unpleasant it is for me to see you short of money; I can only assume that you are continually being robbed, and that is why you are in need, although you lack nothing.' It was also a psychological and practical mistake on Catherine's part to land them with Cameron as their architect. If she had been honest with herself she would have recognized that her son disliked everything and everyone with whom she was associated. She would also have realized that she was putting Cameron in the impossible position of working for two sets of clients, all very positive and demanding people of very different tastes, and all expecting their work to have priority. It was a recipe for disaster, and disaster came – not to either owners or palaces, but to the architect. But that is a later stage of the story.

With great houses rising fast in Petersburg and Moscow and on country estates everywhere, it was not surprising that the heir to the throne and his wife soon decided that they ought to have something better than their first wooden houses. They must have felt that Catherine would be bitterly offended by any change of architect; so, although they did not care for Cameron's style of decoration, they asked him, in 1781, to design a palace in stone. They also commissioned several pavilions, which were, in those days, thought to be so important that their construction often preceded that of the main building. This was the case with Pavlovsk, where the first thing to be built was the Temple of Friendship (**114**). It seems to have been the notion of Maria Feodorovna to erect this as a hopeful gesture of affection towards her formidable mother-in-law, and it was planned to contain a statue of the Empress.

Strangely, the grand-ducal pair also decided, at almost the same moment, to make a prolonged tour of Europe. In their absence Catherine considered it necessary to keep an eye on developments at Pavlovsk; but, as she had a self-confessed mania for building, her duty was also her pleasure. She wrote to them in May 1782, while they were in Italy:

On the third we travelled to Pavlovsk, where on both sides of the road there was plenty of snow. At the gate of the garden I left the carriage and walked along the hill path. Having reached [Paullust] I found the rooms and furniture very clean and well kept. In the court they are removing the earth for the foundations of the new house and the wing on the left side. We then descended on a comfortable road near the Temple [of Friendship] built by Cameron. This structure is almost finished and its exterior is very charming. The interior, however, was full of scaffolding and this gave a depressing picture . . . From there we went over the bridge, passed the cascades and so to the chalet . . . There I sat down and found the view very pleasing . . . The meadows are not yet green and there is not a single leaf. From the chalet we walked towards the [Apollo] Colonnade, on which the work has already begun . . .

At the new gates which are standing at the exit from the meadow to the main road we passed through various equipment and materials. Here we took the carriage, having walked for a good two hours, having climbed steep and not so steep inclines, and were deadly tired. We said: What a pity that the proprietors are not here. They would have forced us to walk still more and would have shown us things in a more pleasant state, but whilst they are absent everything looks sad and empty and I had a pang of heart. Do return therefore as soon as possible, if only to remove that sad air from Pavlovsk. Your children are well, and they run so fast no one can catch them. Good-bye my dear children. I embrace you.

The Temple of Friendship
(figure 26, no. 2)

The Temple of Friendship (**114**) is surrounded by a ring of fluted columns, the first use in Russia, as Loukomski noted, of the Greek Doric order. Bas relief medallions inside the colonnade celebrate classical themes of affection, while dolphins, symbolizing friendship, alternate with wreaths in the frieze.

The Apollo Colonnade
(figure 26, no. 3)

The other early structure in the park referred to in Catherine's letter is Cameron's Apollo Colonnade (**115**). This was first built on the near side of the river, beside the park entrance, but – perhaps on Paul's orders – it was moved to a commanding position high on the far bank which runs steeply down to the river. Originally the statue, a copy of the Apollo Belvedere, was completely surrounded by columns joined at the top to form a ring. But nature decided to better art. In 1817, five years after Cameron's death, a tremendous storm swelled what was normally a trickle of water into a flood: the ground gave way and, with it, a section of the colonnade. Someone, presumably Maria Feodorovna, made the wise decision to leave it as it was. At first one thinks it a typical eighteenth-century folly, but it is better still: it is a natural ruin, and finer than when it was first erected.

Paul and Maria Feodorovna must have seen the early projects for the palace before they left on their travels. It was to have a main quadrilateral centre section, of three storeys, the upper two linked by the Corinthian colonnade of the central projection, which is surmounted by an architrave and cornice on the courtyard façade, and by a pediment on the façade looking over the park (**97, XVIII**). A lightly moulded frieze runs along the architrave and the walls of the building, and the windows of the *piano nobile* are finished with simple frames and pediments. The ground floor of this main building is treated very simply, as a base for the upper storeys, and the whole is topped by a flattened dome encircled by slender closely-spaced columns. This colonnaded drum is Pavlovsk's characteristic skyline, its simple classical equivalent to the Baroque cupolas of the Yekaterininsky Palace at Tsarskoye Selo (XI) and Peterhof (124). Springing from the central building were to be two low semi-circular galleries, ending in one-storey pavilions.

Exterior of the palace

The main outlines had been decided, but there were endless matters concerning the decoration of the interior which had to be referred to the owners (travelling incognito in Europe as the Comte and Comtesse du Nord), and Cameron had to keep sending them his designs and suggestions. It irritated him that they were showing them to foreign architects, and discussing them in his absence. It irritated him that they were buying all manner of decorative things – furniture, pictures, tapestries, statues, vases, clocks, candelabra, even whole fireplaces – without any regard for the rooms the objects were to occupy. Cameron was accustomed to designing everything himself, down to the doorknobs and fire-irons. It irritated him most of all that his patrons' frequent criticisms and alterations were sent to him not directly, but through the director of building at Pavlovsk, K. I. Kuchelbäker.

Maria Feodorevna, like so many wives, was the principal letter-writer, and her letters to Kuchelbäker are filled with warm appreciation and affection. Even Paul signed himself as to an old friend. Clearly they were fond of him and trusted him implicitly, and indeed he is described by contemporaries as the soul of honesty. All the same, it was galling to creative artists like Cameron, Quarenghi and the decorative painters that it was Kuchelbäker who had the ear of their patrons, who were ready to blame anyone but him when things went wrong, as they frequently did. Louis Hautecoeur quotes one of the Grand Duchess's letters: 'My husband consents, though regretfully, to having a vaulted ceiling in the bedroom, but on condition that it takes the least disagreeable form possible. So beg Cameron, in God's name, to try to do something good; above all that he takes care not to add any arabesque ornament.' (Since Catherine loved such ornaments, Paul hated them.) Hautecoeur describes how she set out to instruct Cameron, who had deeply studied antiquities in Italy while she was in the schoolroom. She says, 'The medallions, being part of the ornaments, ought all to be in white; to do the contrary is to ignore the rules of architecture. The background of the frieze and the frieze itself ought to be in white; it is nobler that way.'

'Noble' was the key word here. A younger generation was despising the exquisite coloured medallions and friezes which Cameron was making at Tsarskoye Selo (XIII, XIV) and was admiring a more austere classicism; and Paul, whose head was filled with ideas of military glory – though he never saw a battlefield – could not have enough of martial emblems. Cameron was being driven by Catherine at Tsarskoye Selo, and by Maria Feodorovna, whether absent or present, at Pavlovsk. Catherine was enchanted with his work; Maria Feodorovna lectured and snubbed him. He was overworked. If he appeared to neglect Pavlovsk, it was because he could not be in two places at once, and because, at Pavlovsk, he was expected to do anything and everything, whereas his work for Catherine was only of the highest order. For example, in 1784 Maria Feodorovna wrote to Kuchelbäker, 'The eternal slowness of Cameron becomes insupportable. Warn him for the last time that if he does not send plans for the stables, the job will be given to someone else.'

Kuchelbäker tried to paint a reassuring picture of the progress being made, but the Grand Duchess feared the worst. In October 1782, shortly before their return, she wrote, 'My dear Kuchelbäker, you are gradually preparing me for the fact that one day you will tell me that I shall find my house with no roof on it. This is your intention, is it not, my dear Kuchelbäker?' She went on to ask after the garden: 'Will it be planted with rare flowers?', the Colonnade, the poultry-yards, the woods; 'In a word, will I find a lot of new things?'

It was during 1784 that Maria Feodorovna became particularly agitated about the unfinished state of Pavlovsk: in that year, after the death of Orlov, Catherine had presented the palace of Gatchina to Grand Duke Paul. It had been built by Rinaldi a few years before the Marble Palace in Petersburg (44–49) – also a gift to Orlov from Catherine. Strangely enough, though Paul was taking over the palace of a man whom he had detested, as the murderer of his supposed father and the lover of his mother, he became devoted to Gatchina and preferred it to all his other homes. It lay considerably further from Tsarskoye Selo and from Petersburg, so he was able to feel the king of his castle; particularly since it is a severe and fortress-like structure, with towers on the wings. Rinaldi could not have built anything more to Paul's taste if he had been working to his orders. Splendidly decorated by Rinaldi, and partly redecorated by Brenna during Paul's ownership, the palace is now occupied by a government organization, and may not even be approached. Its movable treasures are mostly in Pavlovsk.

Orlov had maintained Gatchina superbly in every respect: his imperial mistress had always provided him with the money which she grudged to her son; and immediately a rivalry sprang up between the two palaces. Pavlovsk was Maria Feodorovna's great passion. Paul handed it over to her in 1788, and from his accession in 1796 it was to be hers officially. It was her creation, in the same sense as the Yekaterininsky Palace was the creation of Elizabeth and Catherine II. She applied to it her artistic sense, which was far from negligible, and her energy and devotion, which were immense.

Maria Feodorovna was one of those employers who think they can make people toe the line by playing off one against the other. She hoped to frighten Cameron by approaching Quarenghi (not yet working at Pavlovsk or Tsarskoye Selo) behind his back; but Quarenghi was a man of great dignity, who did not lend himself to intrigue. One of Cameron's colleagues, however, was not made in this mould: this was his assistant at Pavlovsk, Vincenzo Brenna. He was an architect and decorator with great gifts, but he was an opportunist. It was a cut-throat life between architects at court, and if anyone's throat was to be cut, it would not be Brenna's. To his patrons, he possessed the supreme advantage of being 'their man'. He had only worked in Russia since 1780, and never for Catherine.

Pavlovsk, with its moderate-sized central building and low curving galleries and pavilions, was originally a Palladian concept of great elegance. When Brenna displaced Cameron as chief architect, he overwhelmed it – during 1789–97 – with the weight of an additional storey on the south gallery and on both pavilions, two curved wings, two storeys high, which almost enclose the courtyard, and a further projection on the south side containing on its first floor the church, Throne Room and Hall of the Knights. The outer pair of wings always contained living quarters for the staff, offices for the palace administration and so on. The additional space built on to the original building of course made it possible to create many fine rooms for which there would have been no place in the original plan.

Brenna assembled a large and distinguished team at Pavlovsk. Voronikhin did some of his finest decorative work; Quarenghi designed at least two of the rooms; Rossi began his career there. The leading decorative painters and sculptors of the day worked on the palace.

The courtyard façade

The view from inside the courtyard (97) is still very beautiful and harmonious, partly because light trellis balconies have been retained, to curve along the first floors of the original galleries, screening Brenna's Picture Gallery and other halls on the left, and Rossi's Library on the right. The statue of Paul I (in German uniform) in the centre of the court is a cast of one at Gatchina, by Giovanni Vitale, and was only erected at Pavlovsk in 1872.

Cameron not only had to see all these changes being made to his architectural conception, but found that his contribution to the decoration of the palace was very limited. There is even argument as to what Cameron's share actually was. Most authorities credit him with the two finest halls – the Grecian and the Italian (101–103); though others go all the way from believing that slight changes were made by Brenna, to attributing the designs to him entirely. (Projects have been found, bearing Brenna's name; but he is suspected of having put his name to Bazhenov's designs for Mikhaylovsky Castle, and may not have been above doing the same with Cameron's designs at Pavlovsk.) But we should begin at the beginning – noting that, unlike Yekaterininsky and Peterhof, where one follows an enfilade of rooms on one floor, in Pavlovsk one has two floors to explore and, on each, two directions in which to go.

The Egyptian Vestibule
(figure 24, no. 1)

One enters the Egyptian Vestibule on the ground floor (98), originally designed by Cameron in 1786 with the participation of the sculptor I. P. Prokofiev, but entirely changed in character after a fire in 1803, which ruined much of the decoration of the central building. The Egyptian figures, painted bronze-colour and representing the months of the year, were designed by Voronikhin, though executed by Prokofiev, together with medallions showing the signs of the zodiac. Giovanni Scotti painted the ceiling and frieze to give the impression of moulding.

Turning left, we pass through an ante-room and rooms for the servants-in-waiting to the Pilaster Room, decorated in 1800 (99). Though sometimes attributed to Brenna or Voronikhin, the balance of opinion seems to come down on the side of Quarenghi as the designer of this distinguished room, which takes its name from its decoration of pilasters in artificial marble tinted a golden Siena shade, with white Corinthian capitals, against walls panelled with a similar composition in white. Reliefs, painted bronze, contain medallions. Scotti painted the ceiling. The large suite of mahogany furniture – some pieces supported on small winged sphinxes, others featuring the motif of carved and gilded snakes – was designed by Voronikhin and made in the Petersburg workshops of Heinrich Gambs.

PAVLOVSK
XVIII The central block, by Cameron, seen from across the lake. On the left is part of Rossi's library wing
XIX The Lantern Room, by Voronikhin
XX The Guryevsky Service in the State Dining Room

Beyond this, there is a room about which there is no dispute: it is the Lantern Room, regarded as Voronikhin's best interior (**XIX**). The 'lantern' is the projecting apsed bay window round which runs an Ionic colonnade. The arch dividing the bay from the rest of the room is supported on caryatids by the sculptor Demut-Malinovsky. There is brilliant contrast between the illuminated bay and the subdued light of the interior, furnished with the sombre brilliance of black and gold furniture designed by Voronikhin, whose imagination was given full rein in a small table (at the left, in the bay window) with claw feet supported on the heads of eagles. The low white cupboards hold jasper vases from the Peterhof Stone-cutting Works, and porcelain vases from the Imperial Porcelain Factory. The walls are hung with paintings that suit the small scale of the room, by Carlo Dolci, Guido Reni and Ribera.

The Lantern Room
(figure 24, no. 4)

Next door is Maria Feodorovna's dressing room, built to Quarenghi's design in 1800. The walls are faced with sections of white and pale coloured artificial marble, and Scotti painted the frieze and ceiling in *grisaille*. The room contains a fine toilet group, consisting of a great jug with gilded bronze handle which stands in a shallow ewer of deep blue and white, designed by Voronikhin and made at the Imperial Glass Factory. It stands on an octagonal table with a deep blue glass top and a single curved orange leg. The dressing table holds a thirty-four piece toilet set in apple green and white, made in 1800–1801 at the Imperial Porcelain Factory; its most remarkable feature is a pair of porcelain baskets with wide bands of pure gold, inset when hot. Armchairs and chaise longue, with serpent-head decoration, are upholstered in pink and green.

Maria Feodorovna's dressing room
(figure 24, no. 5)

From the dressing room we reach Maria Feodorovna's actual bedroom (**XXI**), as distinct from her State Bedroom on the first floor of the main building (**106**). The room was designed by Voronikhin in 1805. There is no longer a bed, but there are still the beautiful chairs and divan he designed for her, with gros point seats. Walls and ceiling are painted with flower garlands which hang down the walls, each side of the overmantel mirrors. The fireplaces themselves are of grey-green jasper, made at the Yekaterinburg Works in the Urals; and on them stand deep blue vases, gilded urns, and gilded bronze candelabra supported by cherubs. A chandelier in azure blue glass hangs on gilded chains. The mirrors between the windows each reflect a pair of white urns, classically ornamented in Pompeian red, black and gold, and an Egyptian figure in gilded bronze holding a circular candelabrum. The curtains are bordered with the original silk, taken down on the outbreak of war, and preserved in the cellars.

Maria Feodorovna's bedroom
(figure 24, no. 6)

Now back to the Egyptian Vestibule (**98**), to explore the range of rooms on the ground floor of the central block (7–14 on the plan, figure 24), which have recently been restored. There is a ballroom, only meant for small dances, with gilded mouldings in the form of stylized branches that weave their way along the frieze and around a mirror inset in the ceiling. The rosy-blue colouring of the room is typical of Russian classicism. Cameron's framed mirrors and classical reliefs on the walls were replaced by paintings by Hubert Robert – an essential ornament to any aristocratic house of the time. Out of twelve of his paintings at Pavlovsk, specially commissioned in 1784, four are here.

The ballroom
(figure 24, no. 7)

Next comes the drawing room. It contains three large tapestries from the famous *New Indies* series, woven at the Gobelins in 1780 to designs by François Desportes, and presented to Paul by Louis XVI. Their exotic – and highly fanciful – scenes of life in the New World were very much to the taste of the eighteenth century. The billiard room – a feature of many houses of the period – has nothing to suggest Cameron's hand. Paintings, here copies of Canaletto, are the main decoration. There are marquetry card tables, for the inveterate gamblers, made by Russian craftsmen at the end of the eighteenth century. A rare musical instrument, a clavichord with an organ, was made at Petersburg in 1783 and presented by Catherine the Great to Potyomkin.

The drawing room
(figure 24, no. 8)

The billiard room
(figure 24, no. 9)

PAVLOVSK
XXI The bedroom of Maria Feodorovna, by Voronikhin

The dining room
(figure 24, no. 10)

The dining room, largest of the ground floor rooms, has a simple decoration of white fluted pilasters against soft pistachio green walls. The frieze and cornice were replaced by Voronikhin after the fire. Doors open on to the park above the Slavyanka River; and the scenery is brought indoors by four large paintings of the park of Pavlovsk, done by A. Martynov in 1800. This was a popular room with all the owners of the palace. Maria Feodorovna made it a drawing room, to which she invited guests for literary evenings, improvised concerts and charades; and later in the nineteenth century Grand Duke Konstantin Nikolayevich made it his study. In the room now is displayed the Guryevsky Service, made in 1807–20 at the Imperial Porcelain Factory, and formerly on show in the State Dining Room, or Throne Room (**XX**). It took its name from Count D. A. Guryev, manager of the Cabinet of the Emperor Alexander I, who had charge of all the Imperial Factories, and who ordered the service for the Empress. It consisted of around a thousand items; and its great size, the elaboration of its sculptured figures (mainly by S. S. Pimyonov) and of its painted designs representing the Russian people, their costumes and activities, account for its many years in the making. (The crystal service which complements the porcelain was ordered by Paul from England.)

The Guryevsky Service

The Corner Drawing Room
(figure 24, no. 11)

The Corner Drawing Room, a conversion of what had been Paul's bedroom, was the first work of the young Rossi in the Petersburg neighbourhood. He already made a point of designing all the fittings to his rooms: here they include a suite of furniture in a special type of birch wood with a wavy pattern; a bronze chandelier in coloured cut-glass; and the curtains. The colour scheme is lilac-grey and violet, touched with bronze and gold.

The New Study
(figure 24, no. 12)

The New Study, one of Paul's private rooms, was decorated in 1800 by Quarenghi. Coloured prints by Volpato, copying Raphael's frescoes in the papal apartments in the Vatican, are mounted on the walls, and there is a painted border of *grotteschi* drawn from the ornaments of Raphael's Vatican Loggie. The General Study is full of portraits of the imperial family. The ceiling painting, designed by Brenna, shows Apollo and the Nine Muses: it is another of Scotti's *trompe-l'oeil* compositions, this time imitating bronze. Precious objects in ivory and amber are scattered on desks and tables.

The General Study
(figure 24, no. 13)

The Raspberry Room
(figure 24, no. 14)

The last room in this group is the Raspberry Room, Paul's private study, its walls decorated with panel-paintings by Shchedrin of views at his favourite palace, Gatchina (**100**). Paul ordered them for one of the halls of Mikhaylovsky Castle in Petersburg; they were painted in 1797–1800. The mahogany and bronze furniture here, and in many of the other rooms at Pavlovsk, was made by one of the most famous cabinetmakers of the time, David Roentgen, whose workshops were at Neuwied on the Rhine.

The State Staircase
(figure 25, no. 1)

Once more one has arrived in the Egyptian Vestibule: but this time one climbs the State Staircase, its walls decorated with a fresco by Gonzago (though some say, Scotti) to reach the State Vestibule, which is Brenna territory: his bas-relief groups of banners, weapons and armour were Paul's delight.

The Italian Hall
(figure 25, no. 2)

Now one does best to go straight ahead into the Italian Hall (**101**). It is the centre of the palace, and occupies the whole height of its top two storeys, including the cupola, from whose lantern windows light falls. A gallery breaks up this great height, and so does a series of arches above, and bays below – these last holding antique statues. The walls are covered with artificial marble. This hall scarcely suffered from the fire of 1803, as it was protected by the corridors all round; and though Voronikhin's hand is seen in some of the decorations, the conception of the hall, and the greater part of its decoration, is by Cameron. Fortunately, Quarenghi's magnificent doors in mahogany and rosewood, ornamented with inlay work and gilded bronze, remained unharmed.

The Grecian Hall
(figure 25, no. 3)

Going straight ahead again one comes into Cameron's Grecian Hall – the most beautiful in the whole palace (**102, 103**). It is magnificent in its proportions, its colour and its detail. Fluted columns and pilasters in verde antico artificial marble, with

174

white marble bases and white plaster Corinthian capitals, give this large oblong room the appearance of a Greek peristyle. The lighting is from two splendid hexagonal bronze lanterns, and from a host of small lamps, in the simple form associated with Greek temples, hung on groups of slender gilded chains. The walls are covered with white artificial marble, and copies of classical statues stand in niches. The two great fireplaces are particularly fine, in white marble with insets of lapis lazuli and bronze ornaments. On each stand French gilded bronze candelabra and clocks (the one in plate **103** is by Charpentier, made in the second half of the eighteenth century). A series of remarkable urns in porphyry and jasper and other semi-precious stones were designed by Voronikhin and made in the Stone-cutting Factories of Yekaterinburg and Peterhof. Voronikhin also designed the magnificent furniture, with winged gryphons forming the arms, and Beauvais tapestry covering.

Anyone who has seen the Great Hall at Kedleston in Derbyshire, decorated by Robert Adam in 1761, must be reminded of it when they see the Grecian Hall at Pavlovsk. Cameron would certainly have been aware of its design, even if he had never visited it. The similarity lies mainly in the use of fluted Corinthian columns in verde antico, all part of the material of Neo-classicism; and Cameron's Grecian Hall is so triumphant in its own right that one has no sense of plagiarism.

At this point, one can turn either right or left, to the ante-rooms which lead to the enfilade of Paul's rooms (the Hall of War) or to those of Maria Feodorovna (the Hall of Peace, **104, 105**). Brenna's is the hand here, and a very handsome pair of rooms he has made. Both are entirely in white and gold, with ornamental plaster coved ceilings – designed by Voronikhin after the 1803 fire – fine bronze lanterns, and antique busts on plinths. In the Hall of War, Brenna used the emblems of the Roman Empire – trophies, armour, weapons and lictors' fasces, to celebrate the mood of triumph in Russia after the victories over the Turks. In the Hall of Peace emblems with a pastoral air are chosen – cornucopias, garlands of flowers and musical instruments. These motifs are used for the wall mouldings and to ornament the splendid ceramic stoves which occupy one of the four bays in each room (plate **104** shows the stove in the Hall of Peace, decorated with cornucopias). The motifs, and the very idea of Halls of War and Peace, are borrowed from Versailles.

The Hall of War and Hall of Peace (figure 25, no. 4, 5)

One can walk back through either of these two series of rooms, Paul's or Maria Feodorovna's, but if we retrace our steps through the Grecian and Italian Halls, we can start on a tour of the private rooms through the words of Maria Feodorovna herself, written in 1795. Though some details may differ today, these rooms remain basically as she described them; and it is not often that one can be shown round a palace by its owner, from nearly two centuries ago.

Maria Feodorovna turns to the right as she comes out of the Italian Hall, where, she says, 'we sometimes dine', and enters 'one of my cabinets, with a fine cornice. Walls have the palest green tint. Some of my favourite pictures: Mengs, Greuze, Angelica Kauffman . . . Rembrandt, etc.' She continues,

Apartments of Maria Feodorovna (figure 25, no. 6–10)

From this cabinet one enters my dressing room . . . the ceiling vaulted, painted with a cradle of roses; the walls are divided into panels, painted with views of Pavlovsk in borders of roses; very pretty designs in doors; the furniture is covered with beautiful white toile, with rose borders, made at Mulhouse; the chaise longue and chairs, varnished white. The dressing table is of steel, made at Tula . . . a beautiful casket in mother-of-pearl, which I owe to the kindness of my good and excellent mother.

The next room, her State Bedroom, is a triumphant design by Brenna (**106**). It is said she never slept there: such rooms were the status symbols of the time. She tells us,

Maria Feodorovna's State Bedroom (figure 25, no. 8)

The bedroom is almost square; a fine cornice, painted ceiling; wall covering of white *pékin*, painted with different *trophées champêtres* after the designs of Willem van Leen, celebrated flower painter; pupil of Dirk Cuypers, and wonderfully executed; the brilliance of the colours gives the room an air of great freshness; gilded mouldings. The great bed, armchairs, chaise longue, carved and gilded in Paris, covered with white *pékin* painted in tempera like the wall covering. The bed is superb, perfectly draped, white *pékin* . . . with borders matching the wall hangings, the curtains of the windows draped . . . like the bed. Opposite the bed, a large mirror, in front of which is placed the beautiful toilet set which the King of France gave me.

This is a remarkable Sèvres set in blue, white and gold, which was ordered by Marie Antoinette as a gift for the 'Comtesse du Nord' during their visit in 1782. The pieces are decorated with chased gold, and enamel imitations of precious stones. Figures modelled in biscuit, after designs by Boizot, support the mirror. The sixty-four pieces of the set even include an eye bath identical with those we use now. The fireplace is of white Carrara marble with malachite pilasters and insets of jasper, agate and lapis lazuli. On either side of the bed, tripod tables in gilded bronze, azurite and malachite are patterned on those found at Pompeii. There is a chandelier in ruby-coloured glass, made in the Imperial Glass Factory. The decorative painting was 'wonderfully executed', as Maria Feodorovna says, by Mettenleiter.

Moving on, she continues,

Maria Feodorovna's boudoir
(figure 25, no. 9)

My boudoir [107], leading off the bedchamber, is long shaped, the vaulted ceiling painted in arabesques, the marble pilasters also [they were painted in Rome with motifs from Raphael's Loggie]. A beautiful cornice, and fireplace . . . the pediment supported by two columns of porphyry; the mantel ornaments are in porphyry and jasper, with a great marble vase in the centre. From the balcony I have a view of the little garden and of a large part of the park. There are fine porphyry topped tables [the legs have human feet and sphinx's heads] supporting three-legged stands, holding cut crystal dishes. The legs of the tables, ottomans, armchairs and stools have been carved and gilded in Paris. A bureau by Roentgen, for writing or drawing, standing. A table of porcelain made here.

The table (at the centre in plate 107) is supported by white porcelain figures, and was made in 1789 by the Imperial Porcelain Factory. The lyre-back chairs are part of a set in Paul's library (108). The whole effect – mainly designed by Brenna, with additions by Voronikhin – has a brilliant and stately air.

From her boudoir, Maria Feodorovna went into her library,

Maria Feodorovna's library
(figure 25, no. 10)

which has one curved wall hung with a [tapestry] which was given me by the King of France . . . This room, in a severe style, is very beautiful . . . That finishes my rooms on the first floor.

She omits to mention a large mahogany writing table with bronze fittings, made in 1784 by Roentgen, and its remarkable chair designed for her by Voronikhin, with back supports shaped like cornucopias to hold flowers, which she loved.

Maria Feodorovna then crosses over to begin the description of her husband's rooms. From the State Vestibule,

Apartments of Paul
(figure 25, no. 11–14)

one goes through the service room of his *valets de chambre*. From there one enters his dressing room . . . three tables of marble and bronze hold vase-candelabras, and work of mine in ivory and amber.

(Maria Feodorovna was skilled at such work, and gave her husband many examples.)

Paul's library
(figure 25, no. 13)

From this one enters a large room, divided by an arch, as the Grand Duke wished: the arch marked by two fine carved marble vases on pedestals. Beside the window there are marble tables ornamented with pieces of my work in ivory and amber. In the library [beyond the arch] the middle of the wall is filled by my portrait.

The portrait, shown in plate 108, is by the Austrian court painter, Lampi, who worked for a while in Petersburg. It represents Maria Feodorovna holding her own drawing of six of their ten children, with a bust of her husband, for good measure.

Along the walls runs a low bookcase, covered with marble plaques, and ornamented with marble busts. In the middle of the library is a round temple which I made in ivory, amber and gilded bronze, with an altar . . . Also a very large writing table, like one made by Roentgen. It stands on twelve ivory columns which I turned myself.

This temple can be seen standing, under a cover, on the bookcase at the left in plate **108**. Another temple that Maria Feodorovna made – square rather than round – is virtually a shrine to her family. Her description of it is particularly interesting, for it reveals the sentimental side of her character which was to have such an influence on the park at Pavlovsk (page 179):

in the pediment is a cameo of the Grand Duke set in white glass on which I have painted a trophy in monochrome . . . In the middle of the temple is an octagonal altar, made of amber and ivory; on the central face are my initials in a medallion painted on glass and set in amber; on the other faces are those of my seven children, beginning with Alexander . . . and ending with the late dear Olinka. I had made this gift last year [1794] to the dear Grand Duke when dear Olinka was still alive and when Annette was not yet born. I have painted all the ciphers of the children in roses and myrtle; mine is in little blue flowers. Above the altar is a little bronze statue with the attributes of conjugal and filial love.

Paul's library is hung with tall narrow Savonnerie tapestries illustrating the fables of La Fontaine, which were among the lavish gifts of Louis XVI. The chairs, with backs like golden lyres, were designed by Brenna – as was the whole room – in 1790. After the fire of 1803 Voronikhin had to replace most of the furnishings, but he was faithful to the original designs.

We continue, without Maria Feodorovna as guide, into the Tapestry Room, where a splendid hanging is mounted on the curving end wall (**109**). It is from the *Don Quixote* series, one of the most popular tapestry sets of the eighteenth century, woven at the Gobelins from designs by Charles Antoine Coypel. The set at Pavlovsk was made in 1780 and, like the *New Indies* tapestries on the ground floor, presented by Louis XVI. Two eighteenth-century Brussels tapestries, also on the Don Quixote theme, hang on the side walls. Voronikhin designed this room, with its wide richly decorated frieze and its chandelier of bronze and crystal. Beneath the Gobelins tapestry is a magnificent mahogany writing table ornamented with chased bronze and ivory cameos, made in Petersburg and intended for Paul's study in Mikhaylovsky Castle. The carved and gilded suite, made in 1784 in Paris by Henri Jacob, is among the finest furniture in the palace (parts of two settees are visible in plate **109**). Other treasures here are marble sculptures, table decorations in ivory and amber, rare clocks, and French and Japanese porcelain vases: in this one room are gathered fine examples of the arts of France, Russia, Italy, Belgium, Germany and Japan.

The Tapestry Room (figure 25, no. 14)

Now, having already seen the Hall of War, a counterpart of the Hall of Peace (**104, 105**), which lies beyond, we must return through the enfilade of Paul's rooms, and turn left into the Rossi Library, built over the curving northern gallery. It was commissioned in 1822–24: Rossi showed great sensitivity in architectural relationships, placing his structure between Cameron's central block and Brenna's pavilion and wing in such a way that it seems as if it were all one unified composition. His great room has long been open as an exhibition hall of furniture and pictures; its full restoration was completed too late to be illustrated here. It is a very large, gently curving room, with a barrel-vaulted ceiling painted in grisaille by Barnaba Medici, and five huge round-headed windows looking on to the park. The bookcases held upwards of twenty thousand volumes, many acquired by Catherine the Great.

The Rossi Library (figure 25, no. 15)

Retracing our steps, we cross the main block of the palace to reach the southern gallery, which was built by Brenna in 1797 (immediately following Paul's accession) mainly as an approach to the large hall which was originally called the State Dining Room but soon became the Throne Room. He used the curved space above Cameron's original one-storey gallery to make a Picture Gallery with three charming little passage-rooms at the ends. These passage-rooms are really ante-rooms for those waiting to be received by the Emperor. In the first of them is one of the most precious pieces of furniture in the palace (at the left in plate **110**): it is a secretaire by the great Louis XVI *ébéniste* Adam Weisweiler, decorated with his characteristic gilt bronze caryatids at the corners and with a splendid large Wedgwood plaque modelled by Flaxman in 1778.

The first passage-room (figure 25, no. 16)

177

The Picture Gallery
(figure 25, no. 18)

The Picture Gallery itself impresses more by its decoration than by its paintings, though these include Terborch, Metsu, Veronese and a Rubens sketch. They were mostly collected by the grand-ducal couple during their travels in Europe, and they give the impression of having been bought and displayed less out of love and knowledge than from convention. But there are fine tables; vases of crystal, porcelain and semi-precious stones; and a pair of magnificent silver torchères by Gouthière (**111**). Their great height is increased by setting them on plinths. A winged sphinx stands at each corner of the triangular bases, and eagles' heads support the branches of the candelabra. Elegant vases in brown porphyry with bronze garlands were made by F. V. Strizhkov, who discovered and first used the mineral riches of the Altai mountains in his work.

The State Dining Room
or Throne Room
(figure 25, no. 20)

The third passage-room links the Picture Hall with the State Dining Room or Throne Room, built and decorated by Brenna in 1797 (**113**). Thrones for the Emperor and Empress were placed there; but Paul's reign was short (see page 88), and a few years after his death the thrones were removed, never to be returned. Now, great curved tables are again set out with some of the palace banqueting porcelain (the Guryevsky Service, described on page 174, was formerly displayed here: see plate **XX**). The furniture of the room, carved and gilded, with embroidered upholstery, was made at Henri Jacob's workshops in Paris. The great arches over the windows and doors are supported by caryatids sculpted by I. P. Martos and M. I. Kozlovsky – who also decorated impressive stoves in the corner recesses. Huge deep blue Sèvres vases of the Louis XVI period stand on plinths. The ceiling is covered with an immense *trompe-l'oeil* painting, giving the effect of open sky above the arches of a classical building. The imperial scene-designer Gonzago (whose exterior murals are a striking feature of Pavlovsk) had planned this in the late eighteenth century, but it was never executed. After the Second World War, restorers found his drawing and it was decided to use it: so the room is now nearer than ever before to Brenna's original conception.

The Hall of the Knights
(figure 25, no. 21)

A pair of small rooms leads through to one of the great halls of the palace: Kavalersky Zal, or Hall of the Knights (**112**). The Order of the Knights of St John abandoned the island of Malta when Napoleon captured it, and sought refuge in Russia. Paul was pleased when they asked him to become their Grand Master, and in 1798 he instructed Brenna to prepare a hall specially for the court receptions of this Order. It is an extremely beautiful, very subtle and understated room. The walls are of palest green, with white plaster bas reliefs and friezes. The actual plaster mouldings, and the mouldings painted in grisaille on the ceiling, merge into one another. Apart from a few pieces of simple white-painted furniture, upholstered in green, the only decorations are Roman sculptures of the second and third centuries AD: some are original, some are casts. (As they were too heavy to be carried to safety in the last war, they were buried in the ground. When dug up later, a pencil inscription was found on the shoulder of one statue: 'We will come back and find you'.) The whole conception of the hall is so light and elegant, so quiet and unmilitary, that it has been said that Brenna employed Cameron's designs. If so, they must have been made earlier; for in 1796, within three weeks of the death of his mother, Catherine the Great, Paul I had not only dismissed Cameron from his service but deprived him of his house at Tsarskoye Selo, near the Orangery.

The Pavilion of the Three Graces
(figure 26, no. 4)

There must have been an unexplained softening of Paul's attitude in 1800, when Cameron was recalled to design the Pavilion of the Three Graces (**116**). This is a shapely portico of sixteen Ionic columns, with pediments at front and back, modelled by I. P. Prokofiev. The relief in one tympanum shows Apollo with his lyre, and attributes of art; in the other (seen here) is Minerva with emblems of strength and glory. The ceiling is ornamented with rosettes and acanthus leaves in high relief. Cameron himself had no part in choosing the central sculptural group of the Three Graces, by Paolo Triscorni after Canova, which was installed in 1803; but it makes an acceptable focal point to his last distinguished contribution to Pavlovsk.

During all the time that the palace was being built and decorated, work went on unceasingly in the park. Maria Feodorovna loved flowers and trees, and was as tireless in ordering them and asking after them as she was in her care for the palace itself. When she and Paul were in Vienna, she sent home a whole load of seeds. Bulbs and rare plants were ordered from abroad, mainly from Holland and England; oak trees came from Finland; limes from Lübeck. Proprietors of great estates in Russia sent fruit trees from their orchards and conservatories. Peasants, soldiers and sailors worked in their hundreds, planting them. Lakes were dug, so that the river Slavyanka provided decorative water effects through the whole valley, and the river itself was regulated with dams and crossed by handsome stone bridges. An example of the careful attention to detail, everywhere, is the attractive gateway shown in plate **117**, at a modest side entrance to the park. Built by Brenna and dated 1802, it is called the Theatre Gate, as it led to a wooden theatre (demolished in the mid-nineteenth century).

Cameron is generally given the credit for the construction of the gardens at Pavlovsk. Isobel Rae points out that J. C. Loudon, in his *Encyclopaedia of Gardening* (1850), suggested that 'Capability' Brown himself provided the plan – through his ex-pupil, Potyomkin's gardener, Gould. It is a fascinating notion, and certainly, as Loudon noted, the park at Pavlovsk 'presents the best specimen of the English style in the neighbourhood of the Russian capital'. But there is one great difficulty about accepting Loudon's suggestion: one can hardly imagine anyone less likely to be *persona grata* at Pavlovsk than Potyomkin's gardener. Paul had such a detestation of Potyomkin that he wreaked vengeance even on his house (see page 80). Louis Réau is surely right in claiming much credit for the painter Gonzago, because work on the park went on intensively, years after Cameron ceased to be employed at Pavlovsk, and Gonzago was an immensely gifted and versatile artist.

Maria Feodorovna, Réau writes, 'sowed her park with numerous pavilions. She loved to multiply monuments to her charming parents, her unforgettable husband, to her children; the weeping sentimentality of the Württembergian princess would have finished by turning Pavlovsk into a Campo Santo.' Luckily, the park was immense, and swallowed up these monuments, digesting them so thoroughly that unless one has the time and strength to take the fifteen-mile tramps on which its proprietor used to lead her family and guests, one cannot see more than a few of them. Apart from the Temple of Friendship, the Apollo Colonnade and the Pavilion of the Three Graces (**114–116**), all mercifully within quite easy reach, Cameron's Aviary, built in 1782, is also close by and well worth a visit. To an eighteenth-century park in Russia an aviary was an essential as a fish pond. The park buildings originally numbered about sixty: several of them, like the famous Rose Pavilion – once the family's favourite reception place – have disappeared.

Amid all these animated endeavours to decorate the palace and develop the park, Paul – having laid down the colours and designs which were, and were not, to be used – devoted himself to his own brand of parade-ground militarism. In 1785 he formed an artillery detachment at Pavlovsk, whose main duty seemed to be to fire two sets of salvoes per day – one at the Grand Duke's meal times, and the second when everyone was actually seated at table. He had an enormous parade-ground made in the park, and there he instructed his troops and held manoeuvres. Masson, in *Secret Memoirs of the Court of Petersburg* (1800), says of Paul,

Near Pavlovsk he had a terrace from which he could see all the centinels, whom he delighted to station about him wherever there was room for a centry box. On this covered terrace he spent a part of each day, and observed with a spying glass all that was passing about him. Often he sent a servant to a centinel, to order him to button or unbutton a little more of his coat, to keep his musket higher or lower, to walk at a greater or less distance from his centry box. Sometimes he would go himself nearly half a mile to give these important orders, and would cane the soldier, or put a ruble in his pocket, according as he was angry or pleased with him.

The park

The Theatre Gate
(figure 26, no. 7)

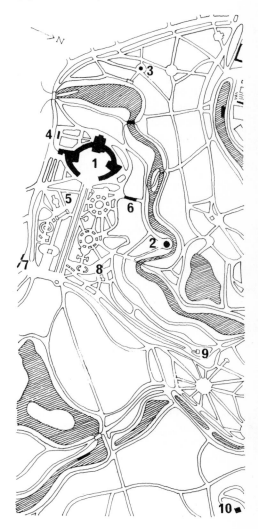

26	Part of the park of Pavlovsk
1	Palace
2	Temple of Friendship
3	Apollo Colonnade
4	Pavilion of the Three Graces
5	Aviary
6	Great Stone Staircase
7	Theatre Gate
8	Dairy
9	Monument to the Parents
10	Mausoleum of the Emperor Paul

Paul was not interested in other than military display, and his Empress had a strong feeling for economy and for homely, family-style entertainments, which were in marked contrast to those of their predecessors. One cannot imagine either Elizabeth I or Catherine II writing as Maria Feodorovna did in 1789, to arrange a fête at Pavlovsk, 'I have ordered to be sent from the town flower garlands with which the large hall [at Kamennostrovsky] was decorated by the previous owners, and I think that these very garlands will serve as decorations of the theatrical hall. One can tie them up with pretty bows made of coloured paper. I think one can decorate this hall almost without spending a kopeck.' These modest arrangements caused private amusement to the grandees of Catherine's court, who were used to festivities on a very different scale. A certain Admiral Shishkin later recalled the joys of social life at Pavlovsk in the reign of Paul, describing it as

uniform and boring. Usually, after dinner, we walked with measured, grave steps in the garden. After the walk, having rested for a while, we gathered daily for conversation, usually very tedious. There the Emperor, and grand dukes and duchesses, were sitting together and spent the time in dry uninteresting talk, and we sitting on stools round them, as if we were riveted like stone idols, the reason being that we could not converse or get up. This was not allowed.

Once more, Paul chose the opposite path to his mother, one of whose rules for receptions at the Hermitage had been, 'To sit, to stand, to walk about, as each thinks proper'.

The year 1801 was a tragic one for the Empress. She lost both her husband and a daughter, Aleksandra Pavlovna; and a second daughter, Yelena Pavlovna, died shortly afterwards. Maria Feodorovna began to erect what Réau called her 'Campo Santo'. The Mausoleum to Paul (no. 10 on the plan, figure 26) was designed by Thomas de Thomon, and built by Carlo Visconti, with sculpture by Martos. In the Monument to the Parents (no. 9) the sculptor was again Martos, and he also carved the memorial to Yelena Pavlovna.

Maria Feodorovna's character is something of a mystery. She had genuinely loved her husband. To the outside world he appeared as a petty and detestable tyrant, but he may well have shown quite another side to his family. She wrote, 'My children and their father make my happiness, but this is the only happiness I find in this whirlpool of the great world!' Whatever public face it was necessary to display, she must have known that her husband had been brutally murdered (see page 88) and that their eldest son, Alexander, was aware of the plot to replace his father by himself – even if it was put to him under the euphemism of 'abdication'. She had lost three out of her six daughters. Perhaps, being essentially a doer rather than a thinker – and in a situation where thoughts would have led to such agonizing conclusions – she threw herself even more fervently into activities of all kinds. The fire at Pavlovsk in 1803 was a further terrible blow. She wrote to Count Vorontsov in London to tell of the loss of statues, paintings, furniture, her library and collection of engravings. Her poplar trees near the palace, which she had planted and tended, and which had grown tall, had had to be cut down to prevent the fire from spreading, and this upset her very much. She begged Vorontsov to send her some more, 'half a dozen or a dozen of the tallest poplars you can possibly get'. The greater part of the restoration from fire damage was completed within a year; but for the rest of her life she never slackened in her pursuit of still greater perfection for her beloved Pavlovsk.

Masson writes of her in 1800, 'She is, perhaps, more careful of her time, and dedicates it to more useful purposes, than any lady in Russia. Music, painting, etching, embroidery, are the arts in which she excels . . . Reading and study are with her not so much a business as a recreation; and the management of domestic affairs, and the distribution of charities, serve happily to occupy her hours.' The Empress was indeed an advance guard of that band of capable, public-spirited women who were to become relatively common in the latter part of the nineteenth century. Someone

114

115

has described her as a one-woman Ministry of Health, Education and Social Welfare. She set up schools, hospitals, foundling and maternity homes; she organized the inoculation of children against smallpox (begun by her mother-in-law, on her own young sons). She brought sick children from her hospital in Petersburg to convalesce in Pavlovsk, and she brought down older orphan children to learn botany, horticulture and farming. In 1806 she founded the first school in Russia for the deaf and dumb, and it proved very successful. Granville observed, after a visit in 1827, that she was activated by four main motives: a desire to promote and improve education among all classes of society; a wish to alleviate human sufferings; a disposition to support those without natural protectors; and great zeal in encouraging national industry and in patronizing science and the arts. He says that she founded appropriate institutions (or took over the direction of those existing), amounting to twenty-four in all – and this was no mere sinecure: she actually superintended the management and received sealed reports direct from the administrators.

Even that remarkable institution the 'Lombard' was placed under Maria Feodorovna's direction: it was a super-pawnshop in the same building as the Foundling Hospital, opposite the Marble Palace in 'Millionaires' Row'. The *Deux Français*, visiting Petersburg in 1791–92, wrote:

One first finds two rooms which look small for their purpose; in one are put the pawned effects, and sales are held there; in the other . . . are the valuers . . . and the cashiers who pay out the money . . . They get jewels brought to them, fabrics and skins of all sorts, no longer carriages as they have no room to put them in . . . They lend, against diamonds, a third or at least a quarter of their value . . . they are sometimes brought settings worth thirty to forty thousand rubles: one pays . . . 6% interest for land and houses; these last are pledged for one to five years. The funds of this establishment are sixteen million rubles and the turnover in a normal year is estimated at forty-five million.

Lyall, in 1816, quoting a passage in James's Journal, on the subject of the Russian nobility – 'Their expenditure also corresponds with their means, or not infrequently exceeds them' – comments, '*Generally* exceeds them: for almost all the nobility are in debt, and have their estates pledged to the Lombard.'

The Empress Mother continued to visit Pavlovsk until her death in 1828; but during the last years of her life she spent much of her time at Yelagin Palace, which her son Alexander I had commissioned Rossi to rebuild, to give her a quiet home in Petersburg (pages 89–90 and plates 57–59). After her death, Pavlovsk went to her youngest son, Grand Duke Mikhail Pavlovich, for whom Mikhaylovsky Palace had recently been built in Petersburg (see pages 90–91 and plates VIII, 60–65). He reduced all the expenditure at Pavlovsk, and the estate began to run down; but the coming of the railway from Petersburg, in the 1830s, brought new life. The charming railway station hall and gardens became the smart resort for social gatherings, and the concerts held there were famous. The railway also brought crowds of ordinary people, wanting a day out in the country. In 1842 Kohl wrote,

The gardens of Pavlovsk are less magnificent but more agreeable and charming than those of Zarskoje-Sselo . . . They are now decidedly the principal places of recreation of the middle classes of Petersburg, who resort hither daily in such numbers to enjoy the country, to dine, and to drink punch and champagne, that they are, in fact, almost the exclusive supporters of the railroad.

As Grand Duke Mikhail had no sons, his nephew, Grand Duke Konstantin Nikolayevich, inherited Pavlovsk; and in 1877 he published what is now a rare centenary volume on its history, which has been much drawn upon for this account.

117 The Theatre Gate, by Brenna

V Peterhof

THE HISTORY of Peterhof (now called by the Russian equivalent, Petrodvorets) is almost as old as Petersburg itself, since it dates from approximately 1707. At that time the Swedes, long the principal enemies of Russia, had been cleared away from the river Neva and the Gulf of Finland; and Peter the Great was determined to secure his position by constructing a powerful fortress on the island of Kronstadt, which lies a few miles off the coast from Petersburg. He constantly went to inspect the work, and finding it quicker to take a boat from a spot about thirteen miles to the west of the city, he ordered two wooden houses and a building for the workmen to be erected there. He always felt happiest near the sea; so he decided to make a permanent home on the empty coast, looking across to Kronstadt.

A little later, in 1710, Peter's prime minister, Menshikov, who already had in Petersburg a finer house than his Emperor (2), began to outdo him on this strip of coast also, by building a palace at Oranienbaum, a few miles further west. Peter was utterly uninterested in grandeur and formality. His Summer Palace in the city was a small family house (4, 5). His first permanent home at Peterhof was known as the Dutch House, and Peter himself is said to have chosen the name by which it has been known ever since: Monplaisir (**XXII, 134–136**). It never had more than seven rooms, and only one is of any size.

Peter quickly grasped the possibilities of his new site. He made a series of sketches to show his architects what he wanted. These are now in the Hermitage. Some cast doubts on their authorship: but they are exactly the kind of drawings which have always been made by those who cannot draw, but know what they want, and there is no one but Peter who meets this description at that date.

In the early eighteenth century, when planning to develop a thickly forested area, the only possible solution was drastically to fell and replant, to make straight avenues and geometric-figured paths: in short, to create a formal park out of wild nature – which had not yet begun to hold any charm for men. The first architect and landscape-gardener one hears of at Peterhof is J. F. Braunstein, who arrived in Russia in 1713. He began to give reality to Peter's sketches by planning the layout of the park and starting the building of Monplaisir. Three years later, while this work was in progress, there arrived from France the most considerable of the early authors of Peterhof: Jean Baptiste Alexandre Leblond. He was a pupil of Le Nôtre; Peter had met him in Paris, had been greatly impressed, and had promptly engaged him to be chief architect of Petersburg, replacing Schlüter, who had died only a year after he had taken over from Trezzini. Peter shrewdly made it a condition of Leblond's contract that he would teach his craft to Russian pupils 'without any secrets or deceptions'. Leblond had the disadvantage of reaching Petersburg before his patron,

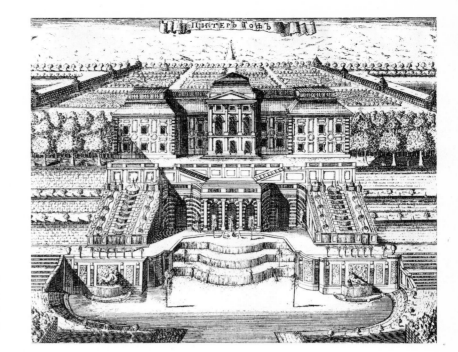

27, 28   Peterhof. Right, Zubov's view shows the north façade of Leblond's palace, exactly the width of the Grand Cascade. Above, the plan at first floor level: the original palace (the central section with projecting bays) has been enlarged by vast wings; *a* is the church, *b* the Throne Room

and falling foul of the powerful Menshikov – to whom Peter had particularly recommended him. But even though many of his plans for the city were frustrated, he was able to lay the foundations of Peterhof as we know it. The basic design of the park had been settled: Leblond made modifications and introduced the two large *étoiles*. Above all, he exploited the remarkable feature of this stretch of coast: the fact that the prevailing flatness is broken by a ridge some sixty feet high, running more or less parallel to the sea, about a quarter of a mile back. This was not only an ideal site for the larger building which Peter realized must be erected for the reception of foreign envoys and others, but it gave an opportunity for the cascade and fountains which he had wanted to create ever since he had seen Versailles. Perhaps it was the fact that Leblond was an even more brilliant landscape-gardener than architect which gave Peterhof the character it has always had, of being primarily a park, with a palace and pavilions to set it off – rather than primarily a palace, set off by a park. Leblond died tragically, of smallpox, aged thirty-six, only three years after his arrival in Petersburg; but he left his mark as the principal author of the whole complex of Peterhof, and his work was respected by his successors.

Looking into the beginnings of all the palaces one finds that the Russians never did one thing at a time, but had all manner of projects, large and small, going on together. This was because unlimited man-power was always available and, in the case of imperial building operations, the armed forces as well. Mrs Ward, in 1735, mentioning some tremendous construction project then under discussion, writes, 'You will say . . . "But how will it be put into execution?" Why, here, in time of peace, the troops are employed on such public works, and when they are begun, thirty thousand men are set to work at once.' For 'public works' read 'imperial works', and it becomes understandable at what speed whole complexes grew up. In those first years of the creation of Peterhof, Monplaisir was built; so was the first version of the Great Palace; so were the pavilions of Marly and the Hermitage; and so was the huge system of waterworks which supplied the Grand Cascade and the fountains, as well as many of the fountains themselves. At the same time, work was going ahead on the palace of Strelna, lying between Petersburg and Peterhof, where Peter liked to stay, as it, too, was on the coast opposite Kronstadt (it cannot now be visited, as it is occupied by a government organization).

Since Monplaisir was the earliest part of the conception of Peterhof, and since it still preserves most of its original appearance, it seems logical to begin there. It is regarded as being the joint work of Braunstein and Leblond, with decoration by Philippe Pillement and Nicolò Michetti. Michetti was an architect with special gifts as a decorator. His master in Italy was Giovanni Maria Fontana, who had long

Monplaisir
(figure 30, D)

203

preceded him to Petersburg, where he had worked with Schädel on some of its earliest buildings (the Menshikov Palaces in the city, 2, and at Oranienbaum, 138). After Leblond's death Michetti took over his post of architect general.

Monplaisir, originally the Dutch House, was just that: a single square shape with a heightened roof over the central hall (**134, 135**). From this central block straight galleries run out at each side to east and west, with a continuous row of round-headed windows on the south face, and ending in small pavilions. The house is so near the waterfront that the noise of the sea would never have been out of Peter's ears (figure 31); at times the galleries would have provided the only way of taking exercise, while protected from storms. The very simple plan consists of a Great Hall in the centre, which is the living room and dining room combined. Its high ceiling is marvellously decorated by Pillement, a pupil of Gillot, who came to Russia in 1717 (**XXII**). In the centre is Apollo with his lyre, and he is surrounded with comedy figures, garlanded heads, baskets of flowers and arabesques. At the four corners are pairs of sculptured heads representing the Seasons. They are probably the first work in Petersburg of Carlo Rastrelli, who had arrived in 1716.

Monplaisir: the Great Hall

Beneath all this colour and richness the hall is in the soberest Petrine style: oak-panelled walls, a chequered floor of light and dark marble, oak table and chairs. This was the first picture gallery in Russia, containing paintings which Peter himself bought on his visits abroad. They were mainly Dutch and Flemish, as they best met his tastes and he followed his tastes in all things. But he was genuinely interested in painting, as in all crafts and skills. Ker Porter, on a visit in 1805, reports,

I am told that it was in Holland and France that Peter the Great imbibed his taste for painting. He passed many hours in their academies, talking with the artists, and examining with all the attention of a scholar, their various works. His favourite painters were of the Flemish school; particularly those who excelled in naval subjects . . . Adam Silo, being not only an artist but an old seaman, delighted him much by the exactness with which he depicted the ocean and its war-like scenes.

The secretary's office

On each side of the Great Hall run three small rooms. On one side are Peter's bedroom, the Sea Cabinet (his office) and the secretary's office (**136**). All these rooms have handsome plasterwork by Michetti on the chimney-breasts and around the ceiling paintings. There are dados of Peter's much-loved Dutch tiles, but the furnishings are of great simplicity. On the other side of the hall are the room for serving food, the kitchen, with Dutch-tiled walls, like the kitchens of the Summer Palace (11); and the Lacquer Cabinet. This tiny room was its owner's only concession to pure decoration: it has scarlet lacquer-panelled walls depicting scenes of Chinese life, and ornamented with carved brackets holding precious porcelain. The ceilings of the side galleries are painted in much the same style as that of the Great Hall. Archdeacon Coxe, after a visit in 1784, writes of Monplaisir:

as the house and furniture has been preserved with a kind of religious veneration exactly in their original state, we can form some idea of the plain and frugal simplicity in which that monarch was accustomed to live . . . It is of brick, of one storey, and roofed with iron; the windows reach from the ground to the top; which, added to the length and lowness of the building, give it the appearance of a greenhouse. The habitable part consists of an hall and six small rooms, which are all furnished in the neatest and plainest manner. The mantel-pieces are ornamented with curious old porcelaine, which he greatly prized as being brought into Russia when the communication was first opened with China.

There is still 'a kind of religious veneration' of Peter the Great. Fresh flowers are always put on his tomb in Petropavlovsky Cathedral in Leningrad.

It was in this small simple house that Peter lived for some months each year, conducted government business and received his ministers and foreign envoys. But the Great Hall also saw drinking on a scale to match his stature. Uspensky quotes a contemporary account of a carousal:

The Tsar observed that, at the table where the Ministers were seated, not all drank the wines presented . . . His Majesty got very angry and ordered that everyone present had to drink as a punishment an enormous glass of Hungarian wine . . . I believe that vodka was added to the wine . . . The great Admiral Apraksin was so drunk that he fell dead. There were very few who were not completely drunk, and if I wished to describe all the stupid pranks which took place during all those long hours then I could write scores of pages.

Another hazard for visitors to Monplaisir was that of being roped in for hard work. An 1889 guide to Peterhof says, 'Certain alleys of trees were planted by Peter with his own hands as well as by his important guests. After a rich dinner and a rest, the Tsar and noblemen donned aprons and one would take a spade, the other a pickaxe or shears, and would work hard in the garden till the evening. Then came supper and plenty of drink and delicacies, with which Peter rewarded those who worked.' Andrew Swinton wrote in 1789,

Wherever I see a streight avenue, I know that Peter has been here, and has cut some of the trees formerly growing where I now walk . . . You may easily imagine that I feel myself a foot higher, in walking in a path which has been cleared for me by an Emperor! . . . Peter was never at ease in his robes: the hatchet and sword were always in his mind, and he sometimes forgot himself so far as to invite Ambassadors to assist him in cutting down trees for his Dock-Yards!

The investigation of the ridge behind the coast – in the hills of Ropsha, some thirteen miles from Peterhof – was undertaken as much in search of water for a system of fountains as to find a site for a palace. Indeed the plan for the water had to come first, because the palace had been designed to stand exactly above a Grand Cascade, and the cascade's position would be determined by the availability of water. Granville, after his tour of 1827, remarks that the idea of the waterworks 'belongs wholly to Peter, who returned from Paris full of it'. He describes how Peter was taking a walk with his ministers along the top of the hill when it occurred to him that, if he could find water there, he would have no difficulty in establishing a system such as he had seen at Versailles. He seized a hoe, and told his ministers to do the same. They soon came to a source. A reservoir and pipes were ordered, and connected to pumps.

Fedorova and Arkhipov tell us that the basic design of the Grand Cascade was made by Peter himself, but that Leblond, Michetti and Zemtsov took part in its construction, Leblond designing many of the sculptures. Carlo Rastrelli also designed numerous masks and reliefs for the Grand Cascade, and modelled the first statue of Samson forcing open the jaws of the lion for the central fountain. All these early statues were of lead.

While the Grand Cascade was under construction Leblond began to build a new palace, to exactly the same width. It was a relatively simple two-storeyed building, with a central pavilion and wings (figure 28). Already the canal was being dug to carry the waters of the cascade to the sea, a quarter of a mile away. Finally, in August 1721, the waterworks and fountains were ready. Peter went to Ropsha and dug away the earth which separated the water-pipes from the river Kovasha. The water rushed into the pipes, and before long the fountains began to play at Peterhof. The view from the roof of the palace (**126**) is still much the same as it was in Peter's time. Elsewhere, fountains are generally associated with inland sites, and it is the swift connection of the fountain-complex of Peterhof with the sea which gives it its special character.

Of course it was not long before the palace was clearly inadequate. Leblond had died in 1719, and Braunstein took over. The usual fire damaged much of the interior in 1721, and Michetti set to work to enlarge the rooms and to enrich the decoration. Among the great artistic creations of this period were the wood panels, designed by Nicolas Pineau and carved by Rolland, for the Tsar's study. Then, in 1723, Zemtsov was told to present a plan for enlarging the palace. He was assisted by Yeropkin, a most cultivated man and one of the first Russian architects to be sent to Italy on a

The early palace and Grand Cascade

scholarship. (He died on the scaffold, in 1740, through his friendship with the leader of a conspiracy.) In 1725 the work started; but in that same year Peter died. Zemtsov and Yeropkin continued with a certain amount of rebuilding and redecorating, but soon everything came to a stop and the palace remained in a state of suspended animation for about fifteen years. It came to life again when Peter's daughter, Yelizaveta Petrovna, became Empress Elizabeth. She had rather deserted Peterhof for Tsarskoye Selo; but all the same, immediately on her accession in 1741, she ordered alterations.

Rastrelli's enlargement of the palace

At first the work at Peterhof was a partial affair; but in some respects Elizabeth thought big, like her father, and by 1746 nothing but a complete reconstruction would satisfy her. Rastrelli was her chosen architect and between them it was agreed that Leblond's central building was to remain untouched. Rastrelli showed a very sympathetic restraint in not only observing this decision, but in designing his additions in such a way that the palace façade presents a remarkably unified appearance as you look up at it from the foot of the Grand Cascade (**XXIII**). Arkin tells us that Rastrelli raised Leblond's structure to three storeys, and added new three-storeyed wings. Whereas before the palace had been exactly the width of the Grand Cascade, it was now double that width. He further prolonged the palace with one-storeyed galleries, each ending in a pavilion: at one end a church, its cupola topped by a cross; at the other, what is called the Heraldic Pavilion, its cupola topped by a weathervane formed of three double eagles. The church pavilion was first finished with one dome; but the Orthodox establishment insisted on the traditional five-dome finish, which remained until the last war. When the restoration was made, Rastrelli's original one-dome scheme was used (**124**): the sad thing is that the church is now a post office – and it was once regarded as one of his supreme decorative achievements.

The church pavilion (figure 27, a)

But if Rastrelli was restrained in his exteriors, out of respect for Leblond, he let himself go in the interiors. Looking at pre-war photographs of the great *Salle des Marchands*, reached by the *Escalier des Marchands* (both so called from the great merchants and traders who had an honoured place at Peterhof's annual fête: of which more later), and of his exquisite ballroom and room for the ladies-in-waiting, one cannot wait for them to come to life again under the hands of the Soviet architects and craftsmen who execute so skillfully the original drawings which eighteenth-century architects made of every detail of their designs; though the ceiling and other decorative paintings by Valeriani and Tarsia have gone for ever.

The Rotari Room

Meanwhile the only glimpse we have of Rastrelli at full strength is in the Cabinet of Modes and Graces, sometimes called the Rotari Room (**120**). This has two pairs of superb doors that exemplify Louis Hautecoeur's remark that Rastrelli, like Meissonier, Boffrand and Pineau, loved white and gold *boiseries*, shells and foliage, curvilinear and irregular forms. Arkhipov and Raskin say that Vallin de la Mothe, the architect who built the Academy of Arts, was responsible for the décor of this room; but it is hardly possible that these great doors were his. He was a Neo-classicist, thirty years younger than Rastrelli, and the exuberant style of the doors, and the men who originally executed them – Nilsen the cabinetmaker and Rolland the sculptor – were before his time. The rest of the décor of this room could well have been de la Mothe's: it consists of two splendid fireplaces in pink marble, on which stand elaborate French clocks, and which are accompanied by particularly fine firedogs and fire-irons. The ceiling is a copy of the one originally painted by Tarsia.

The most noticeable decorations of the Rotari Room are the portraits, 368 of them, with which the walls are papered. They were painted by Count Pietro Rotari, who worked in Russia from 1757 until his death in 1762. Kohl alleges that 'Rotali' toured through the fifty governments of Russia to show the Empress how rich her great empire was in beauties; but the facts are less impressive. He used only eight girls for these portraits, and was the equivalent of a modern fashion photographer, with eight model girls, dressing up in different costumes, to be painted in different poses. Louis Réau says that they are 'little more than the heads of dolls, with hardly any individuality; but their smiling grace does something to compensate for their banal uniformity'. On the other hand, Granville, visiting the room in 1827, writes, 'The artist has acquitted himself admirably; but there is *poison* in most of these portraits; for, although designed and clad in the strictest sense of the word, and according to the most approved principles of decorum, they produce . . . a contrary effect on the beholder. This effect is due to the wanton attitude and sensual or voluptuous look given to the female figures.' The visitor of today is unlikely to find these portraits titillating, but will view them as a curious and effective piece of decoration.

War damage is not the only reason for the shortage of Rastrelli's decorative work at Peterhof. Veldten was commissioned to redecorate a number of rooms in the 1770s. In some cases he toned down Rastrelli's designs, in conformity with the taste of the time; sometimes he made a completely new decorative scheme. The latter is the case with a pair of rooms which Rastrelli originally decorated in the 1750s as one large rectangular State Bedroom, its length running from side to side of the palace. Twenty years later Veldten was commissioned to make radical changes. The room was partitioned, so that one half looks over the Upper Park and the other over the Lower Park. Each still keeps the name 'State Bedroom' as a subtitle to its new name. The first, on the Upper Park, is now called the Crown Room because, when the court was at Peterhof, the imperial crown was placed there. The second is called the Divan Room, from an immense Turkish divan shaped in a right angle and piled with embroidered white silk cushions. The rooms are divided very effectively by making two alcoves backing one another, each framed in elaborate gilded carving and intended to hold a bed. The Crown Room alcove (**122**) still holds an eighteenth-century gilded bed. The Divan Room alcove (**121**), decorated in markedly different style, is now empty. Parts of the walls of both rooms are panelled with the original painted Chinese silk which was removed in 1941 and brought back for the post-war restoration. Other furnishings saved and re-installed are Dutch marquetry commodes and Chinese vases.

The Crown Room
The Divan Room

Another room attributed to Rastrelli, but considerably altered by Veldten is the Partridge Room (**XXIV**), which takes its name from the silk which lines its walls, curtains its windows, and covers its gilded chairs – a silk which is patterned with partridges, cornstalks and flower garlands on a pale blue ground. This light, pretty room is touched with gold in the delicately gilded frieze and dado, the tall mirror in its Rococo gilded frame, the French clock in the form of a chariot drawn by lions, and the small table ornamented with gilded bronze.

The Partridge Room

The White Dining Room retains more of the Rastrelli character, but it also was somewhat altered by Veldten. The walls are decorated with white stucco reliefs of cupids, garlands, masks, birds and trumpets, outlined in palest green. The dinner service is cream and mauve Wedgwood (**123**); the tablecloth is looped up with mauve ribbons, and the five chandeliers are in crystal with a smoky mauve cast.

The White Dining Room

The Throne Room (**119**) seems far more Veldten than Rastrelli, though the double range of round-headed windows is typical of the earlier architect. Like the Cabinet of Modes and Graces it fills the whole width of the palace, so light streams in from both sides. Between the lower windows there are mirrors, and between the upper windows there are medallion portraits of the tsars and their families, some by Heinrich Buchholz. Archdeacon Coxe writes in 1784,

The Throne Room

The presence-chamber is ornamented with the portraits of the sovereigns of the house of Romanof, who have reigned over Russia since the year 1613. The most conspicuous amongst them was a whole length of the present empress [Catherine II, by the Danish painter Erichsen, **118**] as she made her triumphant entry into Peterburg the evening of the revolution which placed her upon the throne. She is represented dressed like a man in the uniform of the guards; with a branch of oak in her hat; a drawn sword in her hand; and mounted upon a white steed.

Portrait of
Catherine the Great

Her costume was historically correct: an officer of the Semyonovsky Regiment had

29 Alexander I and his brother, Grand Duke Konstantin Pavlovich – grandsons of Catherine the Great – at the foot of the Grand Cascade: an early nineteenth-century engraving after Shotoshnikov

given her his jacket. (For the circumstances of Catherine's coup, see pages 215–16.) Twelve superb crystal chandeliers and dozens of candelabra illuminate this great room. At the end facing the throne there are four huge paintings of the battle of Chesme, by the English painter, Joseph Wright: Swinton, seeing them in 1790, commented, 'The Turkish fleet, the town and fortress of Tschesme were totally destroyed, and here they appear still burning upon the canvas!'

The Neptune Fountain (figure 30, no. 1)

Before exploring the Lower Park, with all its fountains and pavilions, it is best to turn towards the back of the palace to see the comparatively small Upper Park, which is easily missed (**125**). The finest thing in it is the Neptune Fountain, which has an unexpected history. At the end of the Thirty Years' War two Nuremberg sculptors, Richter and Schneider, designed a fountain to be erected in Nuremberg marketplace. In 1660 the various parts were cast, and only then was it discovered that the amount of water available was insufficient. The pieces were left unassembled until 1799, when the Nuremberg Council offered them to Paul for sixty-six thousand goulden. He very wisely bought the fountain and erected it. The statue in the foreground is a copy of the eighteenth century's favourite antique sculpture, the Apollo Belvedere. Beyond the Neptune Fountain, one gets a view of the modest garden façade of the palace.

Going round to the front again, one walks along the broad terrace above the cascade, to look down the long line of the canal running into the Gulf of Finland (**126**).

Everywhere, among the trees, there is the glint of spray from fountains, and of gleaming gold from the sculptures of the cascade and the small cupolas of the pavilions at each side of the canal, built by Voronikhin in 1800–1809. At the end of the eighteenth century it was decided to replace with gilded bronze the original lead statues, and the leading Russian sculptors of the day were assembled. Mikhail Kozlovsky made the new Samson, whose dominion over the lion symbolizes Russia's victory over the Swedes at the battle of Poltava, fought on St Samson's Day. From the lion's jaws shoots up the seventy-foot plume of water blowing in the wind in plate **XXIII**. Martos, Shubin, Shchedrin, Prokofiev and Rachette (a Frenchman) were others who contributed sculptures. Some statues are casts of Renaissance and antique works. Voronikhin designed the huge vases and balustrade of the great grotto which tunnels under the palace terrace, and also the black and gold vases which stand at the side of the cascade, whose steps are decorated with reliefs.

The plan of the park (*30*) shows how to reach the three main pavilions. Monplaisir we have already explored; it is approached through its own small garden ornamented with four Bell Fountains (**135**) – so-called because when water flows over the vases supporting the statues it takes a bell shape.

Bell Fountains
(figure 30, no. 10)

Also on the edge of the sea is the Hermitage, that word which meant peace and privacy to the owners of the great palaces, who lived surrounded by courtiers and servants. This one is provided with a moat and drawbridge to emphasize its

The Hermitage
(figure 30, C)

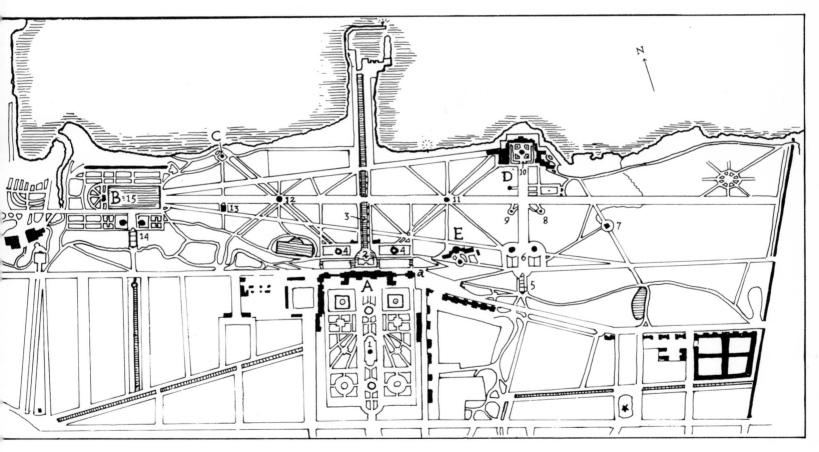

30	The grounds of Peterhof		Upper Park	4	Italian Fountains	10	Bell Fountains
A	Great Palace (*a*: church)	1	Neptune Fountain	5	Chessboard Cascade	11	Adam Fountain
B	Marly		Lower Park	6	Roman Fountains	12	Eve Fountain
C	Hermitage	2	Samson Fountain and	7	Pyramid Fountain	13	Lion Cascade
D	Monplaisir		Cascade	8	Parasol Trick Fountain	14	Marly Cascade, or
E	Orangery	3	Canal (ending in	9	Oak Sapling Trick		Golden Hill
			harbour)		Fountain	15	Marly Lake

inviolability (**132**). Its interior décor has been ascribed to Rastrelli, but the fact that it was all complete in 1725 (there is a record of Catherine I using it soon afterwards) would support Krasceninnicowa's attribution of the building to Leblond and its decoration to Michetti. The Hermitage is a charming little pavilion in white stucco, with bands of deep pink round the windows and in the grooves of the rustication. It has only one room on each storey, and originally there was no staircase to the dining room on the first floor (**131**): instead, there was a heavy machine (originally in the basement, but now in the entrance hall-kitchen) by which each guest was winched up in a special chair to the upper floor. Then the oval table, seating fourteen, was also winched up, ready laid with the first course. The great Delft soup plates are set in hollowed-out holders which can be raised or lowered together with the centre part of the table – an arrangement now hidden by the tablecloth. (An English visitor, Elizabeth Dimsdale, described a similar system in the Hermitage at Tsarskoye Selo: see page 161.) A bell would be rung to indicate that the next course should be served, and by each place was a menu on which the guest marked the dishes of his choice. The table glass is early eighteenth-century Russian. The walls are covered with a variety of paintings which Peter bought from abroad. Perhaps fortunately – in the light of the account of his carousals at Monplaisir – Peter did not live to see the Hermitage completed; for one cannot help wondering whether the glass and china and even the guests would have survived such scenes, if they had been played out in such precarious surroundings.

Walking in the Lower Park, you are hardly ever out of sight of a fountain. We show three here. The Italian Fountain (**127**), its slender column rising among the trees, appears in an engraving after an early nineteenth-century drawing by Shchedrin. The Roman Fountain is one of a pair first made in 1739, near the foot of the Chessboard Cascade. In 1799 they were completely rebuilt and decorated with coloured marble, and gilded bronze masks were set on the lower block of their pedestals, for the water to splash over (**129**). The fountain Eve (**128**) is naturally paired by an Adam, not far away: she was designed by the architect Usov at the end of the first quarter of the eighteenth century.

And so we come to Marly, seen in another engraving after Shchedrin (**133**). A pavilion with more rooms than Monplaisir, it started life in 1719–20 under the modest name of Small Seaside House. Arkhipov tells us that Peter gave orders to Michetti on its position, style and decoration. The walls of some of the rooms were to be panelled with oak and plane-wood, and the floors were to be of pine. Braunstein provided designs for the panels in the Oak Room. Peter was very proud of the house: he hung there part of his collection of paintings, and invited foreign envoys to admire it; but since it was only finished in 1724, and he died the following year, his enjoyment was brief. He gave the name Marly to the cascade nearby (**130**) after Louis XIV's Marly-le-Roi, which he had twice visited while he was in France – particularly to study the water-supply and the installation which provided the cascades. Later, the little house acquired the same name, though of course it was never intended to bear any resemblance to its namesake, that constellation of the sun and planets destroyed during the French Revolution.

In front of the pavilion of Marly there is an oblong lake on which water spectacles used to be held, with gondolas and firework displays. More practically, the lake contained a great supply of fish for the imperial table. Andrew Swinton, writing of a visit in 1790, says,

Upon the banks of a small lake, near the shore, is a house in which Peter . . . resided, and enjoyed himself in living without that pomp, which his residence in the larger mansion obliged him to assume. Here the servants show the fishing and hunting accoutrements of the Emperor, and the utensils of cookery with which this hero dressed his beef-stakes! I suggest that they are copies of the original . . . In the lake are a great variety of fish; perch, carp and other kinds. It is not permitted to any one to throw a hook, and the finny tribe are so familiar, from this good usage, that they will take a bit of bread almost out of your hand.

The Italian Fountain
(figure 30, no. 4)

The Roman and Eve Fountains
(figure 30, no. 7, 12)

Marly
(figure 30, B)

The Marly Cascade
(figure 30, no. 14)

PETERHOF
XXII Ceiling of the Great Hall in Monplaisir, by Philippe Pillement
XXIII The palace, by Leblond and Rastrelli, seen from the foot of the Grand Cascade. The tall plume of spray in the centre comes from the Samson Fountain

From the loud splashes one may chance to see in this lake, descendants of that same finny tribe still live there undisturbed. Another visitor to Marly, Granville, in 1827, examined a whole collection of Peter's clothes, including walking sticks, and gives the alarming information that one was 'a bar of iron of great weight, which Peter was in the habit of carrying about with him to give additional muscular strength to the arm, and as a means of personal defence.' Those same giant arms, carved for his Admiralty Chair at the Summer Palace (9) do not appear to have been in need of 'additional muscular strength'.

Privacy at Peterhof was jealously guarded in Peter's time. No one could visit it without his permission. In 1724 he himself issued a list of regulations for intending visitors: no one was to be allowed to stay at the palace without obtaining a card with the number of an allotted bed; he must sleep in that bed and no other; and before going to bed he must take off his boots or shoes. In later years Peterhof was still strictly guarded: even in the reign of Nicholas I Granville reported that it 'appeared to be in a state of substantial repair, watched by sentinels and livery footmen, as if their Imperial master were hourly expected.'

Yet the palace itself was never a favourite imperial residence. Catherine I stayed at Monplaisir; so did her daughter, Elizabeth – she enjoyed cooking, and often prepared the dinner in that delightful kitchen. Catherine II was staying in Monplaisir at the time of her accession coup, when history was made, both at Peterhof and at Oranienbaum. No one could tell the story more vividly than she does, in her *Memoirs*, and it brings to life the portrait in the Throne Room (**118**). Her husband Peter III had insulted her at table, had threatened to marry his mistress Yelizaveta Vorontsova, to divorce Catherine and put her in a convent. Not till then, she says, did she listen to the plot being laid by the Orlov brothers and the regiments of guards, to take the Emperor prisoner and proclaim her his successor. She writes,

Peter III lived and drank at Oranienbaum . . . I was almost alone at Peterhof, with my ladies, apparently forgotten by everyone . . . On the 28th of June at six in the morning, Aleksey Orlov came into my room, woke me, and said, very calmly, 'It is time for you to get up; everything is ready to proclaim you'. I did not hesitate . . . I dressed as quickly as possible, without making a *toilette*, and I got into the carriage he had brought . . . We got out [in Petersburg] at the barracks of the Ismaylovsky regiment . . . The soldiers arrived, kissed me, embraced my feet, my hands, my clothes . . . two carried up a priest with a cross, and they began to take the oath.

Regiment after regiment arrived, to the tune of fourteen thousand men,

in such a frenzy of joy as I never saw . . . I went to the Winter Palace to take the measures necessary for success. There we had a consultation and it was resolved that I should go at the head of the army to Peterhof, where Peter III would be dining.

Peter and his retinue were due to travel the few miles from Oranienbaum to Peterhof to dine with Catherine that night, when he would very probably have carried out his threat to divorce and imprison her. When he arrived at Peterhof and found Catherine gone, he knew that she had forestalled him. He was paralysed by indecision, and finally returned to Oranienbaum, from which he was fetched next day by Catherine's supporters. Her *Memoirs* continue,

After having despatched our couriers and taken all precautions, towards ten o'clock in the evening I dressed in guards' uniform . . . So we rode through the night towards Peterhof . . . Peter III renounced his empire, quite freely, surrounded by fifteen hundred Holsteiners. It was 29 June, St Peter's Day, at noon . . . Then the deposed emperor was taken twenty-seven versts from Peterhof, to Ropsha . . . After two days of great fatigue they [the army] gave the order to leave at ten o'clock at night: provided, they said, that she comes with us. So I left with them; and half way, I rested in the country house of Kourakin, where I threw myself fully dressed on a bed. An officer pulled off my boots. I slept two-and-a-half hours. I mounted my horse again.

PETERHOF
XXIV The Partridge Room, by Rastrelli, altered by Veldten

Catherine's second entry into Petersburg – this time on horseback – is the moment celebrated in Erichsen's portrait (**118**).

I went to mass; then they sang the Te Deum; then people came to congratulate me, me who since Friday at six in the morning had hardly drunk, eaten or slept. I was very glad to go to bed that Sunday night.

If Peterhof only had three days in the limelight of history, it had one day a year – a great summer fête – 'to which the 500,000 inhabitants of the capital have a general invitation', and which illuminated the memories of all who took part in it. Every visitor had something to write and, in the words of one of them, felt he must 'dip his pen in a sea of rainbow-coloured ink'. Bremner, in 1839, confines himself to the remark, 'At the great summer fête at Peterhof, where thousands of the people are assembled, [Nicholas I] dances and capers amongst them, as merry and free as any goat of them all.'

The Englishwoman in Russia wrote in 1855,

Every night during the festival the gardens of the palace were illuminated, Russians said that there were ten millions of lamps. Perhaps there were two or three millions at the most; but they always multiply every number . . . Walls of light were on each side of the walks and avenues, pyramids and obelisks from fifty to seventy feet in height . . . but the most beautiful sight of all [was] the fountains . . . rows of lamps were placed, over which the fluid rushed from the cascade like a shower of diamonds, whilst the flashing lights beneath had an indescribably brilliant effect; the fine bronze figures untarnished glittered like statues of gold in the rays of thousands of beaming stars . . . and the view was terminated by an enormous sun, sixty feet in diameter, that appeared to be hovering over the sea at a distance.

Martha Wilmot, one of the lively sisters whose *Russian Journals* cover the early years of Alexander I's reign, wrote home to describe the festival dress of 'a proper Merchant's wife':

She was array'd in a Jacket and petticoat of Damask brocaded richly with gold, stomacher distinct and chiefly composed of pearls, a plaited border of pearls as if it was muslin form'd the front of her cap, while a building scarcely half a yard high composed of pearls and diamonds completed the head dress. On her neck were twenty rows of Pearl, and on her Massy arms hung twelve rows (for I reckoned them) by way of bracelets.

Mrs Disbrowe, in 1825, writes as the wife of a diplomat: 'I hear that at the Peterhof fête, many people dress in their carriages, ladies as well as gentlemen, so I expect to learn lessons of contrivance in this country.' But she and her husband were in the privileged position of being given rooms in the 'Palais au Jardin Anglais', nearby – the English Palace, a most beautiful work by Quarenghi, which was irretrievably destroyed in the war. From there they went to Peterhof in

a carriage called a *ligne*, which holds eight, and is just like two sofas placed back to back on wheels; these are allowed to drive through all the gardens, the wheels being so broad they do not cut up the walks . . . We sat down fifty to dinner, at three, a most splendid repast. At seven the Emperor's carriages came to take us to the *bal masqué*. 130,000 people were said to be assembled. The Empress told Mr D. that upwards of four thousand carriages came to Peterhof that day, and the Emperor had four thousand horses of his own employed in the service of the Court. Of course lodgings for such a concourse was out of the question, and it was a most extraordinary sight to see the bivouacs, carriages of all sorts and descriptions converted into dressing and sleeping rooms . . . People of every class were admitted to the palace; and it was a striking spectacle to see courtly dames in gold and jewels, Emperor, Grand Dukes and Duchesses, Princes and Counts, whirling through crowds of rustics, men with long beards, women with russet gowns, who gazed with respectful astonishment, and though in close contact with these grandees, showed no symptoms of rudeness, and were as quiet and unpresuming as if they had been bred to palaces and balls. They stood close to the imperial party; there was no pushing or shoving or noise . . . I should think that such a fête could only be given in Russia, where the people are so docile and orderly. What a row English mobility would make in St James's, or a French canaille in the Tuileries . . . The gardens were open to all classes indiscriminately, no tickets or special permission necessary.

121

122

124

125

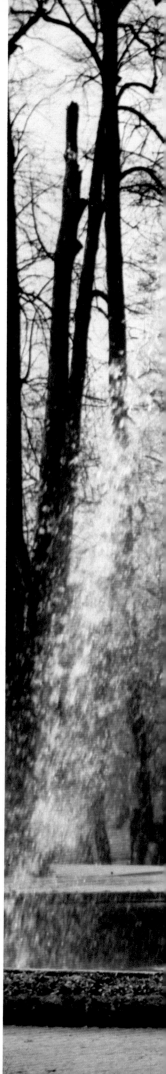

131

133

134

It was left to the Marquis de Custine, on his visit in 1839, to see below the surface of this fête to something more disturbing. He wrote,

I have never seen any thing more beautiful to contemplate, yet at the same time more saddening to reflect upon, than this pretended national reunion of courtiers and peasants, who mingle together in the same saloons without any interchange of real sympathy. From a social point of view the sight has displeased me, because it seems to me that the emperor, by this false display of popularity, abases the great without exalting the humble. All men are equal before God, and the Russians' God is the emperor . . . When he opens his palaces . . . he does not say to the labourer or the tradesman, 'You are a man like myself', but he says to the great lord, 'You are a slave like them, and I, your God, soar equally above you all' . . . As a spectator, I remarked that it pleased the sovereign and the serfs much more than the professed courtier.

The gardens of Peterhof were not congenial to the taste of Catherine the Great, as one might imagine from her letter to Voltaire: 'I hate fountains which torture the water and force it into a course contrary to its nature.' Yet happily, Archdeacon Coxe reported at the time, they were 'suffered to remain in their present state'. Now they are not only 'suffered to remain' but are devotedly restored and maintained. When the sun shines, and there is a touch of autumn colour in the park, you may think them one of the most beautiful sights in the world.

31 Monplaisir in the early nineteenth century. Shchedrin's view shows the pavilion, with its large windows, on the left. In the middle distance is the harbour at the mouth of the canal; beyond it, the Gulf of Finland

VI Oranienbaum

The Great Palace and the Palace of Peter III

ORANIENBAUM began its life at much the same time as Peterhof and about five miles further along the coast from Petersburg. While Peter the Great was building Monplaisir (134–136), the most powerful and audacious of his ministers, Prince Menshikov, decided that he also would like a summer palace on the Gulf of Finland. He had almost monopolized the services of Giovanni Maria Fontana in building his palace in Petersburg (see pages 26–28), but in the same year, 1710, Menshikov commissioned Fontana to design what became known as the Great Palace at Oranienbaum. Three years later, Gottfried Schädel arrived from Prussia and also entered Menshikov's service. His seems to have been the principal hand in the work on the Great Palace, which continued until 1725.

Oranienbaum means 'Orange Tree' – an unlikely name to find on a northern coast which is under snow for nearly half the year; but it refers to one of the great luxuries of the Russian nobility during two centuries, the orangery, which provided by artificial warmth fruits which could not otherwise be enjoyed in the north of the country. Now the whole area is called Lomonosov, after the great scientist and inventor of the mid-eighteenth century, who there set up his factory for the making of mosaics.

The Great Palace (figure 33, no. 1)

The Great Palace, like the palace of Peterhof, stands on a bank above the sea; not such a high bank, but sufficient to make effective terraces (**138**). The plan was the usual one of a central block, with wide galleries – here curving in a semi-circle and ending in large pavilions with domed roofs. The roofs of the galleries were promenades, decorated with a balustrade and vases. Even before the canal had been dug at Peterhof, to carry the waters of the Grand Cascade into the Gulf of Finland, a much wider canal had been dug at Oranienbaum, by which men of war could sail up to the palace quay.

Krasceninnicowa says of Schädel, 'He was able to draw upon very large sums of money; and his buildings were imposing, rich, stamped with a noble and flamboyant western Baroque'. Those 'large sums of money' were among the things that led to his patron's downfall in 1728, when an opposing faction of the nobility obtained his dismissal by the boy-emperor, Peter II. The interiors were still uncompleted when the blow fell. We are told that the architects had used various costly materials for the wall-coverings: leather painted with gold, silver and colours; silks, marbles and the Dutch tiles for which Menshikov shared Peter I's liking. But all this came to an end; and the palace, with its princely crowns set above the rooftops (figure 32), was taken over by the State. In 1737, together with its grounds, it was given to the Admiralty College as a naval hospital. They were not to occupy it for very long, for in 1743 the Empress Elizabeth brought from Holstein her nephew, Grand Duke Peter (who was

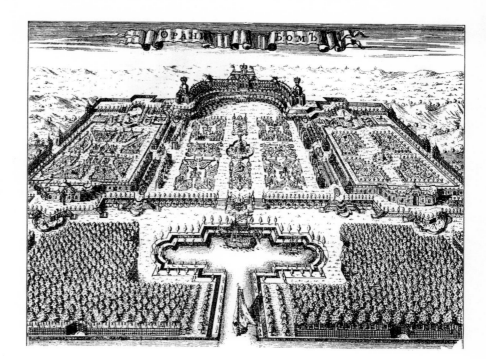

32 The Great Palace at Oranienbaum before *c.* 1740. Zubov's engraving shows the central and side pavilions decorated with Menshikov's giant crowns (compare page 27, figure *2*), the formal gardens, and the ornamental harbour with its canal

to marry the future Catherine the Great) to be her heir, and presented him with the estate of Oranienbaum as a summer home. The Great Palace was still the only building of note on the estate, and no doubt something was done to make it habitable for him; but he was only a boy of fifteen, and nothing worth recording happened during the next eleven years.

The great name at Oranienbaum is that of Antonio Rinaldi. Apart from the whole sections of Petersburg created by Rossi in the first quarter of the nineteenth century, no architect had such undisputed control over an entire area as Rinaldi had at Oranienbaum. Born in Italy in 1709, he was by no means unknown when he accepted an invitation, at the age of forty-three, to come to Russia to work for Count Kyril Razumovsky (younger brother of Aleksey Razumovsky, the lover and probably the morganatic husband of Elizabeth). Rinaldi built a small wooden palace for him at Baturin in 1752–53. Lo Gatto tells us that he then came to Petersburg to work for Vice-Chancellor Vorontsov, and in that way attracted the attention of the court – which caused him to be taken into the service of Grand Duke Peter. Perhaps he assisted Rastrelli in building the Vorontsov Palace; and he may even have become Rastrelli's son-in-law. In any case it would have been natural for Razumovsky to have passed him on to Peter, since they were always on good terms.

From 1756 Rinaldi worked at Oranienbaum. As far as one can tell, he worked nowhere else for ten years, until Catherine commissioned him in 1766 to build the palace of Gatchina, in the country south of Tsarskoye Selo (see page 167), and in 1768 to construct the Marble Palace in Petersburg (44–49), both of them for her lover Grigory Orlov. His first building at Oranienbaum was the small house for the Grand Duke, which is known as the Palace of Peter III (**142, 144, 145**). It is a very simple two-storeyed building, which would be perfectly square if there were not an indentation in one façade to form the entrance. It is painted pink and white and contains six rooms on the upper floor, which were Peter's private apartments. The ground floor originally contained plain service rooms; but after the restoration of 1952–53 an exhibition of Chinese decorative art was arranged there.

The Palace of Peter III (figure 33, no. 2)

The Grand Duke, rather surprisingly, collected paintings – Italian, German, Dutch, Flemish – and had a Picture Gallery to accommodate them in the approved manner: this consisted in setting them close together, completely covering the walls, only separated by narrow frames (**144**). The wall panels and doors of the Picture Gallery are painted in gold on lacquer by Feodor Vlasov. They are thought to be the only surviving example of work at which the Russians of the period were particularly adept. (The Lacquer Cabinet at Monplaisir, mentioned on page 204, was destroyed in the war and replaced in its original form by the craftsmen of Palekhovo,

Peter III's Picture Gallery

235

who have a tradition of lacquer-work going back at least two and a half centuries.) Deep green silk is hung on the walls of Peter's study (**145**), with silvery-grey lacquer panels in the window embrasures, echoing the colour of the small Chinese lacquer chest which stands on a lacquer table inlaid with mother of pearl. The console table, mirror and stools are Russian work, and so is the crystal chandelier.

During the nineteenth century the palace interiors suffered great changes. The silk coverings were removed from the walls, and replaced either with wood panels or poor quality decorative paintings. The doors survived better than the rest of the decoration. In 1952–53 a major restoration took place; the nineteenth-century alterations were removed and the original decorations were re-created.

While Rinaldi worked on Peter's small palace he also did extensive decoration at the Great Palace. Lespinasse's view (**138**) shows it in the third quarter of the eighteenth century, with large boats still sailing up the canal from the Finnish Bay. Archdeacon Coxe wrote in 1784 that when the Empress Elizabeth moved to Peterhof, Peter 'was permitted to reside at his favourite palace of Oranienbaum; where he indulged that taste for military pursuits, which became his sole amusement during the latter years of her reign.' One of the acts which made Peter particularly unpopular in Russia was that he brought soldiers from Holstein, and dressed them in German uniform, at a time when Russia was at war with Germany. (Frederick the Great was his hero, and on his accession he handed back to him, with fulsome apologies, all the land which Russia had gained during five years of war.)

Peter had a cantonment built – Peterstadt – as a kind of exercise in fortification. It was shaped like a twelve-pointed star, with turf-covered ramparts, and drawbridges over a moat surrounding it. Nothing now remains except a charming little gateway, with iron grilles in mock fortress style and a spire like a church (**137**). Peter also built wooden barracks capable of containing fifteen hundred soldiers. Coxe records that 'everything wore a martial appearance: the hours of morning and evening parade were marked by the firing of cannon; a regular guard was stationed; the troops were taught, under his inspection, the Prussian discipline. This house in the fortress was the principal scene of his convivial entertainments; there, when not employed in exercising his troops or in issuing his military orders, he amused himself in drinking and smoking with the officers, and he generally pushed the pleasures of the table to an excess of intoxication.'

Real soldiers, and play-acting in his fortress, were not enough. Peter played with toy soldiers by the hundred, setting them out on tables in such profusion that people could scarcely pass, and equipping each table with copper gratings which made a noise like rifle-fire when a cord was pulled. Catherine came into his room one day to find he had court-martialled and executed a rat which had been chewing his toy guardsmen; it was to be left hanging for three days as an example to the public. The wonder is not that Catherine finally agreed to make her *coup* against her husband in 1762, but that she had been able to steel herself to spend seventeen years as his wife in name only; to hide her ambition, even her brains, for the contrast with her husband could have been dangerous. But after he had been on the throne for a year and a half, her chance came. (Her coup is briefly described, in her own words, on pages 215–16.) All Peter asked, when he signed the act of abdication, was that his mistress Yelizaveta Vorontsova should go with him to Ropsha. Catherine refused. He then made the pathetic request to be allowed to take his poodle, Mopsy, his negro servant, Narcissus, and his violin. This was permitted. Within a week – after a visit from Aleksey Orlov, Feodor Bariatinsky and other officers, at which there was said to have been a scene, ending in a struggle – he was dead.

It is interesting to speculate whether Catherine's son Paul 'inherited' his passion for militarism from the man whom he believed – or made himself believe – was his father. There are certain marked resemblances between the two men and their careers. Both were deliberately excluded, by reigning empresses, from all affairs of state until their accession – Peter III at the age of thirty-three, Paul at forty-two. Both

plunged into an absorption with the trivialities of militarism. Both were admirers of the German military machine, and adopted German uniform. Both showed pent-up emotional reactions on their long-delayed accessions. Peter proceeded to undo all that his aunt's government had achieved in the five-year war against Germany, and scandalized everyone by his unconcealed joy at her death. Paul dismissed those his mother had employed; neglected or degraded the palaces she had built; and took the opposite course from hers in ways great and small. One of his first acts was to exclude the possibility of future empresses by establishing the succession on the principle of male primogeniture.

One has to piece together the palaces' subsequent history from travellers' tales. Again one turns to Coxe: writing during the reign of Catherine the Great, he says of the Great Palace (**138**), 'The middle part of the edifice remains the same as it was when erected by Mentchikof, and consists of two stories, containing a range of small apartments.' Of the Peter III Palace in the 'citadel' (**142, 144, 145**), he says, 'It remains in exactly the same state as during the life-time of the emperor, neither the furniture, nor the bed, in which he slept the night preceding his deposition, being removed. It had a white satin coverlet, and was on a large four-post bedstead, with curtains of a pink and silver brocade, and ornamented at the top with plumes of red and white feathers . . . Among several portraits of the unfortunate prince, one was pointed out to us as a striking resemblance: he is painted in his Holstein uniform; the complexion is fair, and the hair light; there is no expression in the features, and the countenance has a very effeminate look.'

Continuing to trace the history of Oranienbaum, one reads Storch, who lived in Petersburg in the late eighteenth century: 'The ground here rises and falls in little romantic hills and vallies . . . The late empress [Catherine II] towards the latter end of her reign, transferred the marine cadet corps from Cronstadt hither: this seminary is now removed to Vassily-Ostrov [in Petersburg] and the present emperor [Paul] has granted the palace of Oranienbaum to the grand duke Alexander.' Later, Oranienbaum was given by the Emperor Nicholas to his two imperial brothers, Grand Dukes Konstantin Pavlovich and Mikhail Pavlovich. In the nineteenth and early twentieth centuries the Great Palace was the home of the Grand Duke of Mecklenburg-Strelitz, who had a famous art collection. Now it is occupied by a government organization; and one can only see a cupola rising in the distance among the trees.

Grand Duchess Catherine used often to stay at Oranienbaum with her husband. The atmosphere would have been strained and unhappy, through Peter's uncongenial eccentricities, and his permanent association with Yelizaveta Vorontsova, whom he clearly wished to marry. The French Minister of the time, M. Breteuil, described Peter's passion as 'a strange taste. She has no mental gifts; as for her looks, they are the worst imaginable. She resembles in all respects a servant girl at a low-grade inn.' But Catherine must have had a fondness for Oranienbaum itself for, in 1762, shortly after her midsummer *coup*, she commissioned Rinaldi to build a house for her in the park.

This was a tribute both to Rinaldi's gifts and to Catherine's good judgment. If she had been ruled by emotional considerations, she might well also have dismissed the architect chosen by a husband she had despised and disliked. But she had had the opportunity to watch Rinaldi work at Oranienbaum, and she would have come to respect his talent and to feel in sympathy with his taste. Rinaldi flourished under her patronage, reaching far greater heights at the Chinese Palace and Katalnaya Gorka than he had reached before, and ultimately gaining the important commissions of Gatchina and the Marble Palace.

Rinaldi had already built a 'Chinese Cottage' at Oranienbaum. It was later demolished by Paul, and the term 'Chinese' was then applied to Catherine's small

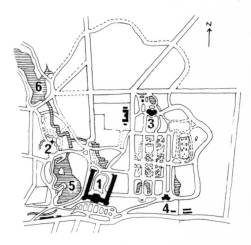

33 General plan of the grounds of Oranienbaum
1 Great Palace
2 Palace of Peter III
3 Chinese Palace
4 Katalnaya Gorka
5 Lower Lake
6 Red Lake

The Chinese Palace

CHINESE PALACE
XXVII Detail of the Glass Bead Room (see plate 147)

palace. As with Monplaisir at Peterhof (134), though with far less justification, Catherine's palace had begun life as the 'Dutch House', and was later referred to as 'the Empress's Own House' or 'the Solitude'. In Menshikov's time a formal garden had naturally been made at the Great Palace, and trees in the park nearby had been cut and replanted to a plan, according to current taste; but the rest of the large area – the Upper Park – had been left far more to chance, and consisted – as it still does – of woods and open spaces, with some artificial ponds: a landscape very much to Catherine's liking. An engraving after Rinaldi shows the Upper Park (141), with the line of the great slide of Katalnaya Gorka dividing formal beds on the left from picturesque, meandering paths and a fanciful serpentine lake on the right.

The Chinese Palace was built as far away as possible both from the Great Palace and from the Palace of Peter III (see the plan, figure 33). Catherine was passionately interested in building and liked personally to supervise the progress of work which she had commissioned. There is a record that in the summer of 1763 she went to inspect her new house, which as yet only consisted of walls and roof. In the same year, through her Chancellor, Count Bestuzhev-Ryumin, a Major Jacoby was instructed to buy wallpaper in China, for use in the 'Dutch House'. A rather desultory trade went on between the two countries, and he was going off to purchase such things as tea, spices, silks, porcelain and other art objects. The wallpaper caused a diplomatic incident, for the Chinese delayed delivery for a number of years, waiting for payment in advance. The paper was finally forwarded from Irkutsk in 1775 and installed in the palace; but ill-luck persisted: it had not been up long when it was ruined by faulty guttering which let in the rain.

The exterior   The Chinese Palace, as it appears in a contemporary engraving based on Rinaldi's project (139) and today (143), is far more modest in size and decoration than anything one associates with the period of Rastrelli. Lo Gatto, the great authority on the work of Italian architects abroad, describes Rinaldi as 'an architect of the transition' – the transition from Baroque to Neo-classicism. His exteriors at Oranienbaum have no hint of the classical, and his interiors are pure Rococo, but he brought something quite new to architecture and decoration in Russia: a lightness and delicacy, a subtle and exquisite taste, a fragile colour sense utterly removed from that of Rastrelli. He was like a woodwind instrument taking up a theme from the brass. Rinaldi, architect of the transition, later turned strongly towards Neo-classicism when he built the Marble Palace in Petersburg (44–49). It was a measure of his artistic sensitivity that at Oranienbaum he designed for a life of private pleasure, and at the Marble Palace he created something quite different for a life of public appearances.

The Chinese Palace is built on a stone terrace with its south front looking over a lake – originally dug in 1770 as a rectangular basin with stone surrounds, for a sense of formality in such things still persisted. The palace, of a single storey throughout, has a segmental pediment on the slightly raised centre section, offset, on the northern side, by a projecting main entrance topped now (though not in the engraved view from the north, 139) by three statues. The wall surfaces are lightly broken by pilasters ending in garlanded Ionic capitals. There is a sloping roof, and a balustrade decorated with vases. The original colour scheme has been reproduced since the war: the walls are painted pale pink, and the decorative details are picked out in cream rather than white.

The word 'Chinese' is by no means a dependable description of this palace, as the exterior has not a trace of chinoiserie, and only three or four rooms are decorated in a Chinese Rococo style. Krasceninnicowa points out that the mixture of oriental styles used in some of the decoration was known in Russia as the 'Chinese style'. Clearly, to the Russians, 'Chinese' stood for the mysterious East – which was indeed mysterious, as communications were comparatively recent and still extremely tenuous. It was the very remoteness and unknown quality of China which made it such a powerful attraction, and also made it possible to pin the label 'Chinese' on anything exotic.

The decorators who worked in Oranienbaum with Rinaldi were of particular importance, because they did not merely execute his designs, but were themselves creative artists. The painter-decorators were all Italians, and obviously worked in perfect artistic harmony with Rinaldi and with one another. They were Stefano Torelli and the brothers Giuseppe and Serafino Barozzi from Bologna. In this third quarter of the eighteenth century many decoration techniques were known both in Russia and in Western Europe, and Rinaldi drew upon them all. Plasterwork was an art and a craft in itself, which was exploited to the full at Oranienbaum, and which had many distinguished Russian exponents. Russian craftsmen, led by the masters Vlasov and Gianni, executed the white and gilded stucco which appears in most of the rooms in the Chinese Palace as mouldings, wall tracery and frames for paintings, with stylized plant motifs as the main theme. These lent themselves to the new delicacy in decoration: there are no Rastrellian Atlas figures, heads or busts. Other forms of decoration employed are imitation marble, mural painting, fine carving, wall coverings of hand-painted silk and paper, and beautifully intricate inlaid floors. Mosaic was used importantly: the Peterhof Stone-cutting works were near-by, and masters of mosaic assembled to ornament the palace. They made what was regarded as a superb mosaic floor for the Glass Bead Room, but this was unaccountably removed in the nineteenth century, perhaps for greater comfort, in a cold climate. They made fine table tops, and they were also enthusiastic about the idea of mosaic fireplaces – but Rinaldi refused to design these, saying that they would never stand the heat.

At that period it was customary to decorate the ceilings with large paintings on canvas, which were set in plaster frames. These paintings were sometimes specially commissioned, but sometimes simply bought as one would buy a picture to hang on the wall. The size and shape had to be right for the position, as well as the style and subject matter, but that was all. Rinaldi commissioned mainly rectangular and oval paintings, for the rooms of the palace are for the most part rectangular, with rounded corners. The most famous ceiling painting of the palace is the only one which is missing. Detailed measurements of the slightly domed ceiling sections of the Great Hall were sent to the famous Venetian artist Giovanni Battista Tiepolo, and he duly delivered paintings on the theme of 'Mars in Repose'. At the outbreak of war, when it was feared that Oranienbaum would be captured, the canvases were taken down and transferred to Pavlovsk for safety. Pavlovsk was captured and its remaining treasures removed; Oranienbaum escaped. The ceiling was sold to a wealthy man in a neutral country, who refuses to restore it to the position for which it was created.

The engraved bird's-eye view, even though the entrance is modified, gives an idea of the layout of the Chinese Palace and the simplicity of the conception (**139**). The *The plan* enfilade of state rooms runs from east to west (left to right), with the three great rooms – the Hall of the Muses (**XXV, 146**), the Great Hall (**148, 149**), and the Large Chinese Room (**XXVIII, 153**) – at the far left, centre, and far right. Between these fall the Blue Drawing Room and the Glass Bead Room (**XXVII, 147**), to the left; and the Lilac Drawing Room (**150**) and Small Chinese Room (**151, 152**), to the right. The two projecting sections pointing south towards the lake contain the four-roomed private suites of Catherine, to the left (**154–158**), and of her son Paul (**159–162**). Between these projections and behind the Great Hall are three rooms – the Vestibule (**XXVI**) and two small service rooms – making seventeen rooms in all. A house for the ladies-in-waiting stood nearby, and a kitchen pavilion was built on the road to Ropsha. The pavilions at each side of the lake in plate **139** have disappeared, and so has the colonnade at the end of the lake, and its stone-bordered edge. A small formal garden remains between the south façade of the *The garden* palace and the lake (**143**). It is fenced by a fine wrought-iron railing and dotted with superb Chinese pottery tea barrels, which are a reminder of the way tea was carried overland from China. (To this day the Russians claim their tea is superior to anything known is Western Europe, since it does not have to cross the sea.)

243

The Hall of the Muses

Inside, we may start at the east end with the Hall of the Muses (**XXV**, **146**). From the high windows along both sides light pours into this exquisite room, with murals of the Nine Muses painted by Stefano Torelli in light colours on a pale green ground. The hall is alive with graceful curving lines: rounded corners to the room, rounded coving above the cornice, rounded motifs above the doors, and a rounded central design to the inlaid floor. The ceiling painting, also by Torelli, is bordered by a multi-curving frame. Against the eastern wall are marble busts made in Italy in the eighteenth century: that in plate **146** is Lucretia. Great Chinese porcelain vases of the same period stand around the walls. Flanking the western door, which leads back through the enfilade, are Russian vases of carved marble on pedestals. This hall was once called the Picture Gallery: in the 1760s there were valuable Dutch, Flemish and Italian paintings in the palaces of Oranienbaum. Then it was called the Billiard Room, and used as such. Now it simply takes its name from the murals which dominate it.

The Glass Bead Room

Walking back through the enfilade one soon comes to a room of breathtaking beauty, whose decoration is unique: the Glass Bead Room (**XXVII**, **147**). Three of its walls are ornamented with panels in which marvellous birds stand and fly among fantastic trees and plants. The panels are separated by gilded palm trees, each carved from a single beam over eleven feet high, and with fronds curving inches from the wall. The bird-landscapes are embroidered in thick silk, and the birds' feathers are sometimes softly touched with paint, which can scarcely be detected, but which deepens and strengthens the shading. The background that gives these matchless compositions their dream-like, moonlit quality is entirely composed of small cylindrical beads of milky glass, sewn horizontally. They shimmer in the light, in the faintest possible tones of blue, mauve and pink. There are estimated to be two million beads in these twelve panels. The embroidery was done in France, by special order: the drawings are said to have been made by the decorative artist Jean Pillement, who had created a 'Chinese Room' for the king of Poland. There is a suggestion that the glass beads were made at Lomonosov's Ust-Ruditskaya factory, and that the background was stitched in Russia: but the facts are not established. The ceiling is one of six painted for the palace by Gasparo Diziani. With his sure taste Rinaldi kept the fourth wall, above the mantel, entirely in white on white: delicate flower motifs, moulded in stucco, break up the surface unobtrusively.

The Great Hall

With the next room we return to the centre of the palace and its largest room, the Great Hall (**148**, **149**). Through an excellent sense of contrast, this is impressive by its very simplicity, and its majestic proportions. At each side of the doors leading to the enfilade are columns with Corinthian capitals, and above each door is a large bas-relief medallion – one of Peter the Great (**149**), the other of his daughter, Elizabeth. Both were made in 1768 by Marie Anne Collot, a pupil of Falconet, who so successfully modelled the Tsar's head for his equestrian statue (**1**). Each medallion is mounted on a grey-blue and red glass composition, overlaid with gilded and enamelled copper, and framed in a bronze ring. The walls are lightly decorated with intricate mouldings of stylized leaves and branches, flowers and birds, with occasional groups of martial emblems treated in the same light spirit. During the post-war restorations it was found that this hall had originally been panelled with artificial marble in various colours, though it had been painted a uniform white during the nineteenth century; and that the same marble had been used for the columns. There is talk of restoring it to its former state. The artificial marble used in the Chinese Palace and, most effectively of all, for floors at Katalnaya Gorka (XXIX, XXX), was a secret process known only to the Italians at that time. They executed such work to Rinaldi's designs, and refused to impart their knowledge to the Russians. Peter I knew what he was doing when he made it a condition of Leblond's contract in Petersburg that he would teach his craft 'without any secrets or deceptions'.

Important dinners and receptions were given in the Great Hall, and the table is shown in plate **148** set with the palace's special Hunting Service, made in the 1760s at the Imperial Porcelain Factory. A few pieces of Meissen decorate the table setting. The glass is all from the Imperial Glass Factory. The glory of this room – and probably the main reason why the rest of the decoration was kept so simple – was the Tiepolo ceiling painting, whose fate was told on page 243.

Moving into the Lilac Drawing Room next door (**150**) there is again a most satisfying change of atmosphere. From stately grandeur we come into a room of tender colouring, with garlands and tendrils moulded and painted, and three large paintings of mythological love scenes (in our photograph, *Diana and Endymion* by Torelli). To complete the amorous setting, the ceiling painting represents a Hymn to Venus.

The Lilac Drawing Room

The next room, the Small Chinese Room (**151, 152**) brings us to our first example of the style called 'Chinese' but actually compounded of various Eastern motifs. The fire screen is certainly Rococo and hardly Chinese, but the mantel carries a splendid orientalizing piece of decoration which makes fanciful use of geometric motifs. The walls are a beautiful re-creation of the original painted Chinese silk with which the room was hung. Chinese dragons spread their convulsive wings in the corners of the ceiling, which is also geometrically patterned – and in the centre of which sits, rather incongruously, the usual placid allegorical figure (**152**).

The Small Chinese Room

In the next and last room of the enfilade, the Large Chinese Room created by the brothers Barozzi, we find the palace's strongest expression of the Chinese style (**XXVIII, 153**). This room, balancing the Hall of the Muses at the far end of the palace (**XXV**), is in the greatest possible contrast, being richly sombre as against the other's light sweet mood. Its walls are decorated with panels of inlaid wood depicting Chinese landscapes with figures, and fantastic birds. The woods used as veneer are Karelian birch, rosewood, Persian oak, amaranth and boxwood. The prevailing deep yellows and browns are relieved by occasional touches of green-painted foliage, and painted ivory inlay for the faces. From the scalloped cornice, a coving elaborately decorated with every form of geometric and stylized leaf pattern, with writhing dragons thrown in (plate **153** shows a corner), curves towards its central feature, a highly-coloured painting of a Chinese wedding. Chinese and Japanese porcelain, and a very fine Chinese wood sculpture of the Goddess of Spring, stand on the floor. Finally there is a richly carved billiard table in mid-eighteenth century style by an English cabinetmaker, Clark.

The Large Chinese Room

The Vestibule (**XXVI**), formerly a dining room, is a room to linger in rather than simply to pass through. It is entered from the south, opposite the lake, rather than from the main northern entrance. (In this country palace, arrangements were less formal: it would house only invited guests, who were free to roam as they wished.) The ornamental designs on doors and walls are by Serafino Barozzi, but the rather conventional landscapes, in their curvilinear frames, are nineteenth-century substitutes for what are described as 'frescoes on somewhat licentious subjects'. The ceiling is ornamented with fine white and gold mouldings and, in the centre, Torelli introduced visitors to Catherine II's cultivated company by a painting of Apollo and three females representing Architecture, Painting and Sculpture. The handsome candelabra are nineteenth-century Meissen.

The Vestibule

In the suite of the Empress's private apartments, in the projecting south-eastern wing, her Chinese Bedroom is outstanding (**154, 155**). The typical arched alcove for her bed can just be glimpsed at the left of plate **155**. Plate **154** shows the alcove itself: the fine Rococo mirror marks the position of the bed. Large mirrors were very exciting to decorators of the period: some in the Chinese Palace were ordered from France, but many were made at the Imperial Glass Factory (unfortunately using a primitive method of blending mercury and lead as a backing, which produced vapours lethal to the workmen). By multiplying the intricate patterns of the carving, of the ornamental door and mirror frames, and of the cornices, they make this white and gold room glitter seductively. The walls, hung with white satin, still

Catherine II's Chinese Bedroom

have fragments of the Chinese-style drawings in gouache by Feodor Vlasov and Feodor Danilov. Small pieces of Chinese and Japanese porcelain are shown on an extraordinary multi-curving stand (at the right, in plate **154**), while large vases stand on the floor.

Catherine's dressing room

Next comes Catherine's dressing room (**157**), panelled in soft-toned carved wood, on which are hung eleven pastel portraits by Jean de Sampsoy of Catherine's ladies-in-waiting. They are shown dressed in masquerade, and are somehow meant to symbolize the Seasons, the Elements, and other abstractions of Natural History. Both floor and ceiling feature ancient geographical symbols, reportedly a reflection of the interest taken by the intelligentsia in the progress of geographical research in Russia at the time.

The Portrait Room

The Portrait Room, beyond (**158**), features the work of that same Pietro Rotari whose portraits cover the walls of the Cabinet of Modes and Graces at Peterhof (120). Here there are only twenty-two, all young girls and boys of different nationalities, set into moulded frames and linked with garlands and leaf sprays.

Catherine's study

The last room in Catherine's suite is her private study, otherwise known as the Golden Cabinet, from the profusion of gilded ornaments and designs. Serafino Barozzi executed the delicate paintings on the walls. On the Empress's French writing table (**156**), ornamented with gilded bronze, is a bust of Voltaire, with whom she corresponded devotedly, but never met. The small library she once kept here was moved to the Hermitage in 1792. One may speculate whether it was a piece of flattery, or at her own request, that Diziani made Philosophy the subject of his allegorical ceiling painting. Catherine liked to appear in the role of the philosopher on the throne, though Pushkin savagely punctured her pretensions, writing that 'she was brought to the throne by a conspiracy of mutineers, whom she enriched at the expense of the people.'

Her son Paul, aged only eight when his mother started building this palace, and who may hardly even have visited it, was provided with a suite consisting of drawing room, bedroom, study and dressing room. The study, an alcove off the bedroom, has walls decorated by Barozzi, inset with panels of marble and plaques of wood and soapstone: plate **159** shows some of these plaques, as well as the fireplace which is set in a corner. The boy's education was to be influenced by allegorical paintings, including one of Geometry on the ceiling. Paul's bedroom – sometimes called the Silken Bedroom on account of its original wall hangings – has a remarkably pretty trellis-patterned bed alcove, just visible in plate **160**, and garlanded designs spring from the corners of the ceiling to the central painting by the Venetian, Domenico Maggiotto (**162**). It was no accident that in this room, destined for the heir to the throne, the ceiling features the Muse of Astronomy, Urania, shown teaching youth to be victorious, while holding in one hand a golden statuette of Niké, goddess of Victory. The floor of the bedroom (**161**) is an example of the magnificent inlaid floors which appear in almost every room of the palace – their complex coloured designs sometimes made by using as many as fifteen different kinds of wood.

Paul's study

Paul's bedroom

After seeing this singularly beautiful palace – so rich in artistic impulse and in superlative craftsmanship – it is a shock to learn that Catherine never actually lived in it; never, it is said, even stayed in it. In all, she is reported to have spent forty-eight days there during a reign of thirty-four years. She is, however, on record as inviting diplomats and other important guests to dine there: in 1769 foreign ministers were taken to see the newly finished decorations; and in 1774, after the peace which concluded the war against the Turks, the palace received the whole diplomatic corps. But as Oranienbaum is so close to Peterhof and these festivities would only have taken place in the White Nights of summer; and as they dined early at that period, even in Petersburg, it is very possible that the whole party would have returned to Peterhof for the night. Certainly, the Chinese Palace is a pleasure pavilion on the grand scale – presenting a series of rooms through which guests would wish to

CHINESE PALACE
XXVIII The Large Chinese Room. The English billiard table is a later addition

KATALNAYA GORKA by Rinaldi
XXIX The Meissen or Monkey Room
XXX The Circular Hall, looking towards the staircase

wander, during a day's invitation, but could not expect to sleep. But it is hard to imagine that Catherine would not sometimes have escaped from the official round to stay there privately with Grigory Orlov, her lover for twelve years. It is a setting made for love. The strange truth seems to be that after a time the palace ceased to be well cared for. It was not properly heated, and its treasures suffered from neglect and damp. After the war, though it escaped serious damage, it needed restoration. This it got in full measure. It has been restored to its first perfection, and is a distillation of the finest decorative achievement of its period.

Katalnaya Gorka

The small palaces of Oranienbaum are pleasure pavilions on a habitable plan; but Katalnaya Gorka (**XXIX–XXXI**) had no other purpose than to make a setting for a day's amusement. A drawing of Rastrelli's similar building at Tsarskoye Selo (no longer existing) shows that Rinaldi approached the problem in much the same way, but kept his ornamentation much simpler. A double staircase climbs the height of a semi-basement – for the service rooms – to the terrace which surrounds the ground floor. This is set back behind a whole range of columns spaced in an interestingly varied way and supporting a wide balcony that runs all round the first floor. Here pilasters are the main decoration. Above the three projecting sections of the building are flat roofs, and above all a further balcony encircling the conical cupola. All these balconies and roof tops are bordered with balustrades, ornamented with vases. The whole structure rises lightly into the air, tier upon tier like a wedding cake, and itself looks like a piece of sky and cloud, in its clear light blue colouring, touched with white.

Inside, a fine staircase with wrought-iron balustrade leads to the first floor, where one enters the immense Circular Hall that occupies almost the whole area of the building. Plate **XXX** shows part of this room, with the staircase beyond. The exquisite decoration was painted by Giuseppe and Serafino Barozzi, who also worked on the Chinese Palace. The motifs twist and spring as if they were alive, and deer leap in a circle round the low, trellis-patterned dome. The floor is of artificial marble in flowing arabesque designs: like the walls and the beautifully decorated doors, it is in pale melting shades of fawn, green, pink, yellow and blue. The few items of furnishing are mantelpieces and small console tables, mirrors with curving frames and delicate ornaments, all set along the walls, with nothing to disturb the lovely space. From every window in the great curve of wall light pours in, and one looks out on the sea and the park.

This is the major miracle of the pavilion, but there is a minor miracle on the same floor: the Porcelain, Meissen or Monkey Room. It answers to all these names, as you can see from plate **XXIX**, for the decoration is composed of brackets, several in the form of monkeys, holding pieces of eighteenth-century Meissen. Arabesque designs and garlands link the brackets. The ceiling echoes the arabesque motifs and so does the artificial marble floor. Again the colours are faint sweet tones of pink, green, yellow and blue, with the stucco brackets white, partly gilded. Serafino Barozzi was the master executant of all this painting, and also of the decorative doors. This is a triumphant example of unity of theme, faultless grouping and dazzling technique. A few pieces of simple furniture are the only other elements in this room, which leaves the walls to make the whole impact.

It was said earlier that Katalnaya Gorka had no other purpose than to make a setting for a day's amusement. All those terraces, balconies and flat roof-tops seem to be made for spectators: but of what? One cannot now guess from seeing the building; but plate **140** gives the clue. The amusement was a highly sophisticated version of the most popular of Russian sports, the 'Russian mountains', as they were called in the rest of Europe, with the name 'ice hills' for the winter version. Lo Gatto and Réau both tell us that, since they lacked natural hills near Petersburg, the Russians had the custom of constructing artificial slopes on which they would let themselves

The Circular Hall

The Meissen Room

The switchback

KATALNAYA GORKA
XXXI The pavilion from the south-east

251

slide; in the summer, in specially built carriages, and in winter on little sleighs, both raised by a special mechanism to the highest point, where a terrace had been made. At this point of departure, a pavilion would be built, where one could take refreshment and rest between slides. Such a pavilion was Katalnaya Gorka. Plate **141** shows, in plan, the triangular pavilion (at the bottom) attached to the long straight slide and its encircling colonnade – described by Archdeacon Coxe, below.

This sport, in various forms, was enjoyed by everyone from emperor to peasant, outdoors and in, winter and summer; though the peasant could only afford the winter version, outdoors. An early description by Mrs Ward, wife of a diplomat, in 1735, seems to refer to a slide arranged in the courtyard of the Winter Palace, in the reign of Anna Ioannovna. She speaks of

a new diversion we have had at court this winter. There is a machine made of boards, that goes from the upper story down to the yard; it is broad enough for a coach, with a little ledge on each side. This had water flung upon it, which soon froze, and then more was flung, till it was covered with ice of a considerable thickness. The ladies and gentlemen of the court sit on sledges, and they are set going at the top, and fly down to the bottom; for the motion is so swift, that nothing but flying is a proper term. Sometimes, if these sledges meet with any resistance, the person in them tumbles head over heels; that, I suppose, is the joke ... I was terrified out of my wits for fear of being obliged to go down this shocking place, for I had not only the dread of breaking my neck, but of being exposed to indecency too frightful to think on without horror.

The young man who wrote *Letters from the Continent* in 1790 says of 'ice hills', 'the Ambassador had one made in his *room*, for the amusement of his company; understand that it was built with boards, and rendered slippery by means of soap and water. We all climbed to the top, then sat in little sledges, and slided down with great velocity.' Archdeacon Coxe, writing in 1784, brings us right to Katalnaya Gorka:

In the gardens of Oranienbaum is a very extraordinary building, denominated the Mountain for Sledges ... It stands in the middle of an oblong area, enclosed by an open colonnade with a flat roof, which is railed for the convenience of holding spectators. The circumference of this colonnade is at least half a mile. In the middle of the area stands the flying mountain, stretching nearly from one end to the other. It is a wooden building, supported upon high brick walls, representing ... a mountain composed of three principal ascents, gradually diminishing in height, with an intermediate space to resemble vallies: from top to bottom is a floored way, in which three parallel grooves are formed. It is thus used: a small carriage containing one person, being placed in the center groove upon the highest point, goes with great rapidity down one hill; the velocity which it acquires in its descent carries it up a second; and it continues to move in a similar manner until it arrives at the bottom of the area, where it rolls for a considerable way ... It is then placed in one of the side grooves, and drawn up by means of a cord fixed to a windlass ... At the top of the mountain are several handsome apartments for the accommodation of the court and principal nobility; and there is also room for many thousand spectators within the colonnade and upon its roof.

So, summer and winter, the court of Catherine the Great would amuse themselves for a few hours, return to the pavilion, take their refreshment and rest in its lovely rooms, and watch their friends from the terraces and balconies. But when the court no longer went to Oranienbaum, the 'flying mountain' fell into disrepair, was pronounced dangerous, and dismantled in the mid-nineteenth century. With it went the summer houses, the formal gardens, the elaborate maze. Only the pavilion remains – but that is enough.

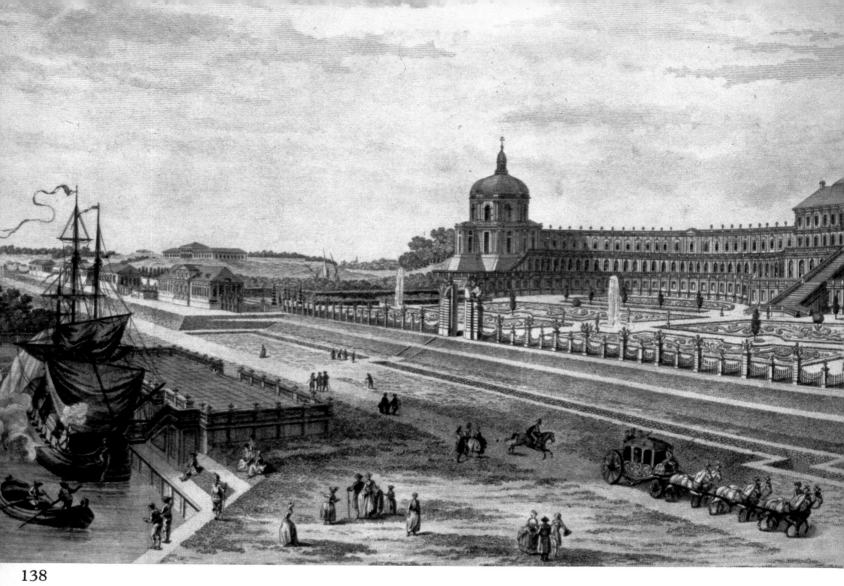

138

139

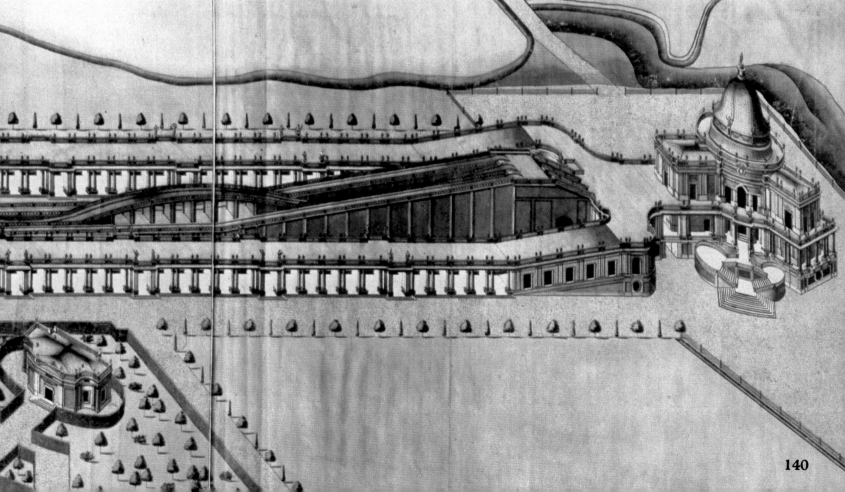

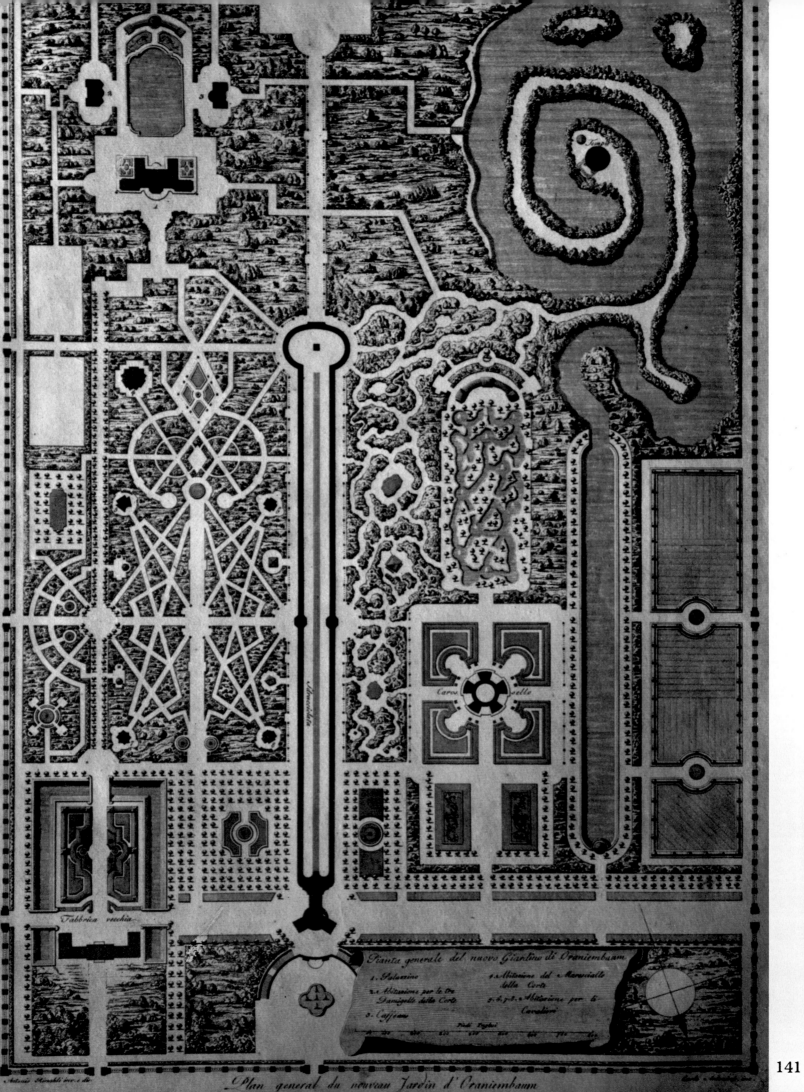

Pianta generale del nuovo Giardino di Oraniembaum.

1. Palazzino
2. Abitazione per le tre Damigelle della Corte
3. Caffeaus

4. Abitazione del Marescialo della Corte
5.6.7.8. Abitazione per li Cavalieri

Piedi Inglesi

Plan general du nouveau Jardin d'Oraniembaum

141

142

143

144

153

160

161

163

164

165

166

167

168

169

170

171

172

173

174

The Architects

163 BARTOLOMEO RASTRELLI, born 1700, in the Veneto or Bergamo. Arrived in Petersburg in 1716 with his sculptor-father, Carlo Rastrelli. Studied in France and Italy. Returned to Russia; became the favourite architect of Empress Elizabeth and the leading exponent of Russian Baroque. Designed most of the great buildings of the period: Winter Palace (various versions, 1732–68); Peterhof, extensive additions; Smolny Cathedral and Convent; Vorontsov and Stroganov Palaces; Yekaterininsky Palace, Tsarskoye Selo. Catherine II dismissed him; he left in anger for Warsaw. Died in 1771 in the palace he had built for Anna Ioannovna's lover, Biron, in Courland.

164 ANTONIO RINALDI, born in Italy in 1709. Invited to Russia by Count Kyril Razumovsky in 1752; worked for him at Baturin. In 1756 entered the service of the future Peter III at Oranienbaum; altered the Great Palace and built him a small new palace. An architect of the transition from Baroque to Neo-classicism. Catherine II commissioned from him in 1762 the Chinese Palace and Katalnaya Gorka, Oranienbaum; in 1766, the palace of Gatchina; in 1768, the Marble Palace: both these last, gifts to her lover, Orlov. He built an early version of St Isaac's Cathedral. Died around 1794.

165 SAVVA IVANOVICH CHEVAKINSKY, born 1713. A distinguished exponent of the Baroque style in the mid-eighteenth century. Worked on the Yekaterininsky Palace at Tsarskoye Selo in the late 1740s, building the church with five golden domes. When Rastrelli became chief architect of the palace, Chevakinsky built the 'circumference', the single-storeyed range enclosing the court-yard. He designed Sheremetev Palace, built 1745–50. His masterpiece is Nikolsky Cathedral, with its separate tall belfry – one of the few 'active' churches in Leningrad. Last mentioned in 1783.

166 YURI M. VELDTEN, born in Petersburg in 1730. Studied in Germany, then worked in Russia until his death in 1801. He was an architect and decorator of great versatility. In 1764–65 he built the Little Hermitage, adjoining the Winter Palace. He was director of the newly-created Academy of Arts. He built Kamennostrovsky Palace (probably from Bazhenov's designs) and Chesme Palace and Church, and redecorated state rooms at Peterhof. His most enduring monument is the system of granite quays which control the Neva, and make it the city's main artery. His most admired design is the railing of the Summer Garden.

167 VASILY IVANOVICH BAZHENOV, born 1737, of humble parents. Studied under Ukhtomsky in Moscow and at the Academy of Arts, Petersburg. Sent on a scholarship to Paris and Italy. Catherine II favoured foreign architects and though she gave him commissions, few were realized. He submitted a design for Smolny Institute, but Quarenghi got the commission. His Kremlin Palace was not executed. Tsaritsino Palace, near Moscow, was not completed. The House of Pashkov, Moscow ('Old' Lenin Public Library) shows him as a fine Neo-classicist. He probably designed Kamennostrovsky Palace; almost certainly, Mikhaylovsky Castle: both were executed by other architects. Died 1799.

168 IVAN YEGOROVICH STAROV, born around 1743. Studied at the Academy of Arts in Petersburg, under Vallin de la Mothe; and was sent on a scholarship to France and Italy, where he became a passionate admirer of Palladio. On his return to Russia he was made an academician and professor. He built the Bobrinsky and Gagarin villas in Baroque style–then became one of the first Russian Neo-classicists in his rebuilding of the Troitsky Cathedral of Alexander Nevsky Lavra, and as architect of Tavrichesky Palace. Died 1808.

169 CHARLES CAMERON was a London Scot, born in 1743. He went to Rome, worked under Clérisseau, made a study of antique buildings. In 1779 he went to Petersburg to work for Catherine II at the Yekaterininsky Palace, Tsarskoye Selo. He delighted her with his decoration of three suites of apartments (only one has been restored) and by his construction of the Agate Pavilion and Cameron Gallery in 1783–85. He designed the palace of Pavlovsk in 1782, but considerable modifications were made to his plan, and the Italian and Grecian Halls represent his chief decorative work remaining there. Died in Russia in 1812.

170 GIACOMO QUARENGHI, born near Bergamo in 1744. Studied painting in Rome, then studied architecture. Knew Palladio's designs well. Went to Russia in 1799 and became one of Catherine II's favourite architects. Held the post of architect to the court under Paul and Alexander I. His principal works were: the English Palace at Peterhof (destroyed in the last war); Hermitage Theatre; Academy of Sciences; Assignation Bank; Aleksandrovsky Palace, Tsarskoye Selo; Chapel of Knights of Malta and Orthodox Chapel, both at Vorontsov Palace; Anichkov Palace Colonnade; Manège; Smolny Institute; decoration at Winter Palace and Pavlovsk. Died in Petersburg in 1817.

171 VINCENZO BRENNA, born in Italy in 1745; went to Russia in 1780. At first worked as assistant to Cameron at Pavlovsk; but in 1786 he supplanted him, made considerable additions to the palace and designed a large part of the interior decoration. He was first architect to the court under Paul I, for whom he did some rebuilding and much redecoration at Gatchina, and built Mikhaylovsky

Castle (1796–1800) to a design by Bazhenov, which he modified. Worked on Rinaldi's unfinished plan for an earlier St Isaac's Cathedral. In 1802 left Russia for Dresden, where he died in 1820.

172 ANDREY NIKIFOROVICH VORONIKHIN, born 1760 to a serf on the Stroganov estate. He was almost certainly the illegitimate son of Count A. S. Stroganov, who educated him as an architect. He studied under Bazhenov, then travelled widely in Europe. On his return to Petersburg in 1790, Count Stroganov gave him important interior decorating commissions in his palace. He worked with Brenna at Pavlovsk, where he designed a number of rooms – the Lantern Room being the most famous. His finest building is the Neo-classical Kazan Cathedral on Nevsky Prospekt. His death in 1814 was rumoured to be suicide.

173 VASILI PETROVICH STASOV, born 1769. Studied in Moscow under Bazhenov and Kazakov, then travelled in Europe. On his return, he was made a member of the council set up by Alexander I to control building in Petersburg. Carried out alterations at Oranienbaum and Peterhof; put in charge of Yekaterininsky Palace, where redecoration was needed after the fire of 1820. After the Winter Palace fire in 1837, he directed the whole reconstruction, assisted by A. P. Bryullov. Other works in Leningrad include the Imperial Barracks and the Narva Gate, a structure by Quarenghi which he rebuilt in brick faced with ornamented copper sheets. Died 1848.

174 CARLO ROSSI, born in Naples in 1775; his mother, an Italian ballerina; his father, possibly from the Ticino, possibly Paul I. Pupil of Brenna; assisted in building Mikhaylovsky Castle. Travelled abroad 1801–03. Entered service of court at Petersburg, 1816. Last great exponent of Russian Neo-classicism. Distinguished town-planner, who created Leningrad's finest ensembles. Designed every detail of his interiors. Built library and did decoration at Pavlovsk. Decorated Military Gallery at Winter Palace. Principal works: Yelagin Palace; Mikhaylovsky Palace; Arch and General Staff Building on Palace Square; Aleksandrinsky Theatre, with street and square; Public Library; Senate and Synod. Died 1849.

Bibliography

ART AND ARCHITECTURE
GENERAL

BENOIS, A. (ed.), *Les Trésors d'Art en Russie*, 6 vols., St Petersburg 1901–06

BILLINGTON, JAMES H., *The Icon and the Axe: an interpretative history of Russian culture*, London 1966

FALCONET, ETIENNE MAURICE, *Correspondance de Falconet avec Catherine II 1767–1778* (ed. L. Réau), Paris 1921

FOELKERSAM, BARON A. E., *Inventaire de l'argenterie conservée dans les garde-meubles des Palais Impériaux*, St Petersburg 1907

GOLLERBAKH, ERIC, *La Porcelaine de la Manufacture d'Etat*, Moscow 1925

GRABAR, IGOR, *Istoriya Russkovo Iskusstva*, vol. III: *Petersburgskaya Arkhitektura XVIII u XIX vekov*, Moscow 1912
Russkaya Arkhitektura pervoi poloviny XVIII veka, Moscow 1954

GRIMM, BARON FRIEDRICH MELCHIOR VON, *Correspondance artistique avec Catherine II* (ed. L. Réau), Paris 1932

HAMILTON, GEORGE HEARD, *The Art and Architecture of Russia*, Harmondsworth 1954

HAUTECOEUR, LOUIS, *L'Architecture classique à Saint-Pétersbourg à la fin du XVIIIe siècle*, St Petersburg 1912

Istoriya Russkoi Arkhitektury, Moscow 1951

JONES, E. A., *Old English Plate of the Emperors of Russia*, London 1909

KAGANOVITCH, A. L., *Arts of Russia, 17th and 18th centuries*, Geneva, Paris and Munich 1968

KRASCENINNICOWA, MARIA GIBELLINO, *L'Architettura Russa nel passato e nel presente*, Rome 1963

LO GATTO, ETTORE, *L'Opera del genio italiano all'estero*, vols. II, III: *Gli Artisti Italiani in Russia*, Rome 1935, 1943

LOUKOMSKI, G. K., *Mobilier et décoration des anciens palais impériaux russes*, Paris 1928

MARSDEN, CHRISTOPHER, *Palmyra of the North. First days of St Petersburg*, London 1942

Pamyatniki Arkhitektury Leningrada, 1st and 2nd ed., Leningrad 1958, 1969

PILYAVSKY, V. I., *Arkhitektura Leningrada*, Leningrad and Moscow 1953

RÉAU, LOUIS, *L'Art russe de Pierre le Grand à nos jours*, Paris 1922
Etienne-Maurice Falconet, Paris 1922
St Pétersbourg, Paris 1913

Russkoye Zodchestvo, Pervaya polovina 18vo veka, Vtoraya polovina 18vo veka, Pervaya polovina 19vo veka, Vtoraya polovina 19vo veka, Moscow 1953

SCHWARTZ, V., *Khudozhedsvennye Pamyatniki*, Moscow 1956

TALBOT RICE, TAMARA, *A Concise History of Russian Art*, London 1963

USPENSKY, A. I., *Imperatorskie Dvortsy: Oranienbaum, Pavlovsk, Peterhof, etc.*, Moscow 1913
sundry essays in *Les Trésors d'Art en Russie*: see Benois, A.

ON INDIVIDUAL ARCHITECTS
Bazhenov

BELETSKAYA, E. A., *Arkhitektor Bazhenov*, Moscow 1949

GRIMM, G. G., *V. I. Bazhenov*, Moscow 1940

MIKHAYLOV, A. *Bazhenov*, Moscow 1951

Cameron

LOUKOMSKI, G. K., *Charles Cameron*, London 1943

RAE, ISOBEL, *Charles Cameron*, London 1971

TALEPOROVSKI, V. N., *Charles Cameron*, Moscow 1939

Quarenghi

QUARENGHI, GIACOMO, *Edifices construits à Saint-Pétersbourg*, St Petersburg 1810

QUARENGHI, GIULIO, *Fabbriche e Disegni di Giacomo Quarenghi*, Milan 1821

TALEPOROVSKY, V. N., *Quarenghi*, 1954

Rastrelli

ARKIN, D., *Rastrelli*, Moscow 1954

DENISOV, YU. M. D., *Zodchy Rastrelli*, Leningrad 1963

Rossi

GRIMM, G. G., *Rossi Ensembles*, Leningrad and Moscow 1946

PILYAVSKY, V. I., *Zodchy Rossi*, Moscow 1951

Stasov

PILYAVSKY, V. I., *V. P. Stasov*, Leningrad 1970

Voronikhin

ARKIN, D., *Voronikhin*, Moscow 1953

GRIMM, G. G., *A. N. Voronikhin*, Leningrad and Moscow 1952

ON INDIVIDUAL BUILDINGS

Oranienbaum

SOLOSINA, G. I., *Gorod Lomonosov*, Moscow 1954

Pavlovsk

KUCHUMOV, A. M., *Pavlovsk*, Leningrad 1970

KURBATOV, V., *Pavlovsk,* St Petersburg 1911

Pavlovsk 1777–1877 Centenary Volume. History and Description compiled by the order of His Imperial Highness Grand Duke Konstantin Nikolayevich, St Petersburg 1877

Peterhof

ARKHIPOV, N. I. and RASKIN, A. G., *Petrodvorets*, Moscow 1961

FEDOROVA, N., *Petrodvorets*, Leningrad 1954

SHURYGIN, YU. I., *Petrodvorets*, Moscow 1952

Tsarskoye Selo

BENOIS, A., *Tsarskoye Selo v Tsarstvovanie Imperatritsy Yelizavety Petrovny*, St Petersburg 1910

BRONSHTEIN, S. S., *Arkhitektura goroda Pushkina*, Moscow 1940

PETROV, A. N., *Pushkin – Dvortsy u Parki*, Leningrad and Moscow 1964

Winter Palace

SOKOLOVA, T. M., *Zimny Dvorets*, Moscow 1956

Yelagin

Le Palais Yélaguine, publ. by Société Impériale des Architectes, St Petersburg 1912

SOCIAL AND HISTORICAL BACKGROUND

Primary sources

BREMNER, ROBERT, *Excursions in the Interior of Russia*, London 1839

CATHERINE II, *Mémoires* (ed. D. Maroger), Paris 1953, English trans. London 1955

CLARKE, E. D., *Travels: Part I, Russia, Tartary and Turkey*, London 1810

COXE, WILLIAM, *Travels into Poland, Russia, Sweden and Denmark*, London 1784

CUSTINE, MARQUIS DE, *La Russie en 1839*, Paris 1843

'Deux Français': see Fortia de Piles

DISBROWE, C. A. A., *Original Letters from Russia 1825–28*, London 1878

The Englishwoman in Russia, London 1855

GRANVILLE, A. B., *St Petersburg, A Journal of Travels to and from that Capital*, London 1828

JAMES, *Journal of a Tour in Germany, Sweden and Russia*, London 1816

KER PORTER, ROBERT, *Travelling Sketches in Russia and Sweden during the years 1805–8*, London 1809

KOHL, J. G., *Russia and the Russians*, English trans. from German, London 1842

LA MESSELIÈRE, COUNT, *Voyage à Petersbourg* (1757), Paris 1803

Letters from the Continent describing the manners and customs of Germany, Poland, Russia and Switzerland in the years 1790–92, London 1812

LIGNE, PRINCE DE, *Mémoires*, Paris 1827–29, English trans. London 1899

LYALL, R., *Journal of a Tour in Germany, Sweden and Russia*, London 1816

MASSON, C. F. P., *Secret Memoirs of the Court of Petersburg*, English trans. from French, London 1800

FORTIA DE PILES, A. DE, *Voyage de deux Français dans le Nord de l'Europe 1790–92*, Paris 1796

RITCHIE, LEITCH, *A Journey to St Petersburg and Moscow: Heath's Picturesque Annual for 1836*, London 1836

Scenes in Russia: describing the Manners, Customs, Diversions of the Inhabitants of that Country, printed by J. Wallis, London and Sidmouth 1814

SÉGUR, COMTE DE, *Mémoires 1780–1790*, Paris 1824–26, English trans. London 1825–27

SMYTH, C. PIAZZI, *Three Cities in Russia*, London 1862

STORCH, H. F. VON, *Picture of Petersburg* (1792), English trans. from German, London 1801

SWINTON, ANDREW, *Travels into Norway, Denmark and Russia in the years 1788–1791*, London 1792

TURGENEV, A. I., *La Cour de la Russie . . . 1725–1783, Extraits des dépêches des ambassadeurs anglais et français*, Berlin, Paris and London 1858

WARD, MRS, *Letters from a Lady who resided some years in Russia* (written in 1729–39), London 1775

WILMOT, MARTHA and CATHERINE, *Russian Journals 1803–08* (ed. Londonderry and Hyde), London 1934

General History

ANTONOVA, L. V., *The Sheremetev Household*, Leningrad 1964

HINGLEY, RONALD, *The Tsars*, London 1968

LOUKOMSKI, G. K., *La Vie et les moeurs en Russie de Pierre le Grand à Lénine*, Paris 1928

OLDENBOURG, ZOÉ, *Catherine de Russie*, Paris 1965, English trans. London 1965

PARES, BERNARD, *A History of Russia*, London 1955

SCHUYLER, EUGENE, *Peter the Great*, London 1884

A Note on transliteration and pronunciation

We have adopted the system devised by Professor W. K. Matthews, which is used by the *Slavonic and East European Review*. We make one deviation from this system, however, by omitting the apostrophe which indicates a soft sign in the Russian original. This is clearly important for linguistic studies; but, in a book like this, for the general public, written in a language which associates an apostrophe only with the possessive, it seemed to us unnecessary. A far more difficult problem for non-Russian speakers is that of laying stress on the correct syllable: yet usually it is only in lesson books for students that such stresses are indicated. In regard to palaces featured in this book, the reader may like to know that the stresses fall as follows – and that, in Russian, every letter is pronounced: Aleksándrovsky, Aníchkov, Belosélsky-Belozérsky, Chésmensky, Kamennostróvsky, Kíkina, Katálnaya Górka, Ménshikov, Mikhaýlovsky, Pávlovsk, Púshkin, Sheremétev, Shuválov, Stróganov, Tavríchesky, Tsárskoye Seló, Yekateríninsky, Yelágin, Yusúpov.

Genealogical table of the Romanovs

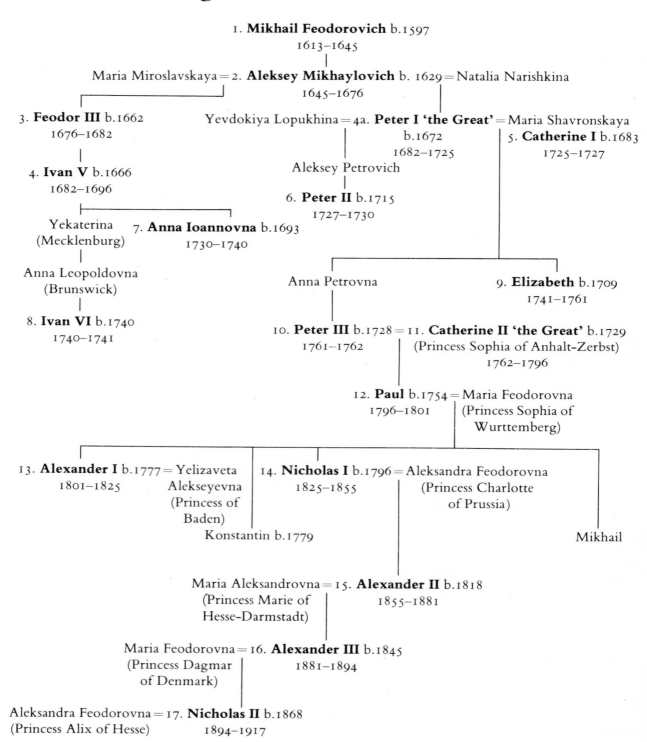

1. **Mikhail Feodorovich** b.1597
1613–1645

Maria Miroslavskaya = 2. **Aleksey Mikhaylovich** b. 1629 = Natalia Narishkina
1645–1676

3. **Feodor III** b.1662
1676–1682

Yevdokiya Lopukhina = 4a. **Peter I 'the Great'** = Maria Shavronskaya
b.1672

5. **Catherine I** b.1683
1725–1727

1682–1725

4. **Ivan V** b.1666
1682–1696

Aleksey Petrovich

6. **Peter II** b.1715
1727–1730

Yekaterina
(Mecklenburg)

7. **Anna Ioannovna** b.1693
1730–1740

Anna Leopoldovna
(Brunswick)

Anna Petrovna

9. **Elizabeth** b.1709
1741–1761

8. **Ivan VI** b.1740
1740–1741

10. **Peter III** b.1728 = 11. **Catherine II 'the Great'** b.1729
1761–1762　(Princess Sophia of Anhalt-Zerbst)
1762–1796

12. **Paul** b.1754 = Maria Feodorovna
1796–1801　(Princess Sophia of
Wurttemberg)

13. **Alexander I** b.1777 = Yelizaveta
1801–1825　Alekseyevna
(Princess of
Baden)

14. **Nicholas I** b.1796 = Aleksandra Feodorovna
1825–1855　(Princess Charlotte
of Prussia)

Mikhail

Konstantin b.1779

Maria Aleksandrovna = 15. **Alexander II** b.1818
(Princess Marie of　　　1855–1881
Hesse-Darmstadt)

Maria Feodorovna = 16. **Alexander III** b.1845
(Princess Dagmar　　　1881–1894
of Denmark)

Aleksandra Feodorovna = 17. **Nicholas II** b.1868
(Princess Alix of Hesse)　　1894–1917

Index